GOVERNING BABEL

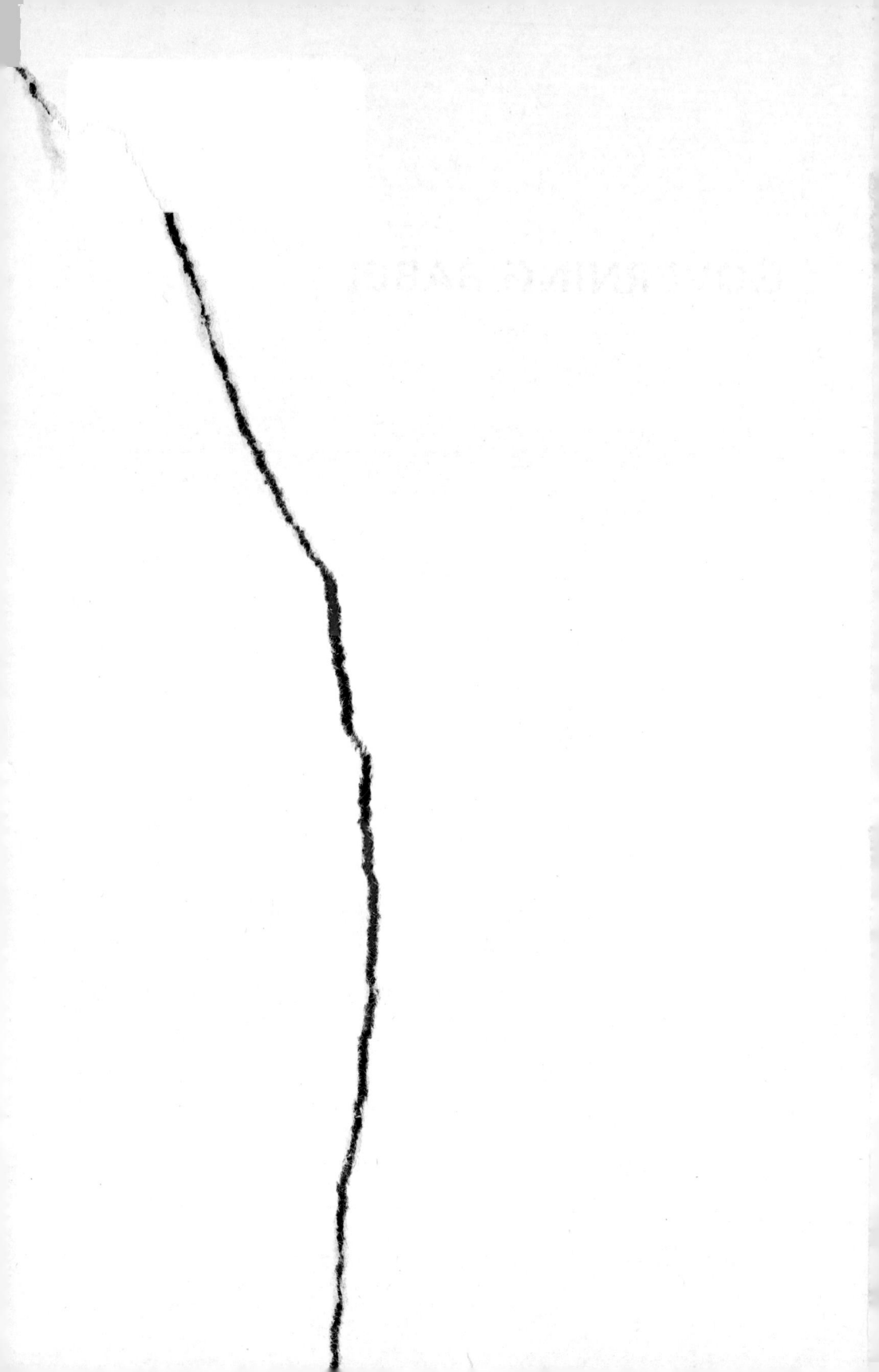

GOVERNING BABEL

THE DEBATE OVER SOCIAL MEDIA PLATFORMS AND FREE SPEECH—AND WHAT COMES NEXT

JOHN P. WIHBEY

THE MIT PRESS   CAMBRIDGE, MASSACHUSETTS   LONDON, ENGLAND

The MIT Press
Massachusetts Institute of Technology
77 Massachusetts Avenue, Cambridge, MA 02139
mitpress.mit.edu

The MIT Press would like to thank the anonymous peer reviewers who provided comments on drafts of this book. The generous work of academic experts is essential for establishing the authority and quality of our publications. We acknowledge with gratitude the contributions of these otherwise uncredited readers.

This book was set in ITC Stone and Avenir by New Best-set Typesetters Ltd. Printed and bound in the United States of America.

Library of Congress Cataloging-in-Publication Data

Names: Wihbey, John P., author
Title: Governing Babel : the debate over social media platforms and free speech—and what comes next / John P. Wihbey.
Description: Cambridge, Massachusetts : The MIT Press, [2025] | Includes bibliographical references and index.
Identifiers: LCCN 2025002144 (print) | LCCN 2025002145 (ebook) | ISBN 9780262049917 paperback | ISBN 9780262384322 pdf | ISBN 9780262384339 epub
Subjects: LCSH: Social media—Government policy | Internet governance | Freedom of speech
Classification: LCC HM742 .W545 2025 (print) | LCC HM742 (ebook) | DDC 302.23/1—dc23/eng/20250625
LC record available at https://lccn.loc.gov/2025002144
LC ebook record available at https://lccn.loc.gov/2025002145

10 9 8 7 6 5 4 3 2 1

EU Authorised Representative: Easy Access System Europe, Mustamäe tee 50, 10621 Tallinn, Estonia | Email: gpsr.requests@easproject.com

CONTENTS

INTRODUCTION
OUR MEDIATED MOMENT

So the Lord scattered them abroad from thence upon the face of all the earth: and they left off to build the city. Therefore is the name of it called Babel; because the Lord did there confound the language of all the earth.
—Genesis 11:8–9

Every medium of information has made names—and meanwhile, values. New media have meant new values. Since the dawn of history, each new medium has tended to undermine an old monopoly, shift the definitions of goodness and greatness, and alter the climate of men's lives.[1]
—Erik Barnouw, *A Tower in Babel* (1966)

POSTCARDS FROM JANUARY 2021

Social media platforms are in serious need of an intervention. Hate speech is coursing through networks around the world, uniting dangerous, and previously disparate, actors.[2] Disinformation campaigns seek to disrupt societies and their institutions and electoral processes. Across various flashpoints worldwide, online mobs incite individuals and groups to perpetrate real-world violence. Further, generative AI could, exploited by bad actors, accelerate the destabilization of knowledge about what is true in the world, sowing doubt and skepticism about even well-grounded facts.

Everywhere now, voices, messages, clicks, and signals become electrons that travel together as groups, gathered as packets, switched and routed through vast communications systems of fiber optic cables, traveling undersea and over the air, sometimes pinging off low Earth orbit satellites, then reconstituted as web pages through browsers, or as data inputs to other connected applications. A vast field of communications signals tries to pass along freely, with no "friction"—filtering, moderation, censorship, enforcement—at the application or website level. Governments may try to alter this model, and sometimes they win; but sometimes the open platforms model prevails. And in the middle are the social media managers, pulled by competing incentives—profit and growth, political power and conformity, and the relentless creative energies of human users, with all manner of motives and needs.

Around the world, there has been a growing contest between platforms and government power, often resulting in damage to human rights and free speech. Nearly every society is facing a common set of questions about who sets the rules and where the lines are. Consider the global scene during, say, January 2021. It is surely a month that will go down in history for the storming of the U.S. Capitol, as a mob tried to stop the certification of the presidential election. Perhaps it will turn out to be an irreversible breaking of the dam, a historical pivot point for democratic backsliding and norm-breaking. But in any case, as we raced into the third decade of the twenty-first century, many other perilous events also took place. Warning signals from around the world had a similar cast. These events were all connected in some deep sense by social media—and the underlying logic of hands-off communications rules.

On the sixth day of January 2021, a large, unruly crowd assembled on the steps of the U.S. Capitol before bursting into the building and, eventually, into the legislative chambers, ransacking offices and perpetrating violence against law enforcement. Members of the mob threatened to assassinate political leaders in the opposition (and even in-group conservative leaders like Vice President Mike Pence, who declined to help disrupt the peaceful transfer of power.) All these actions were powerfully aided and fueled by an out-of-control online communications environment.[3]

About a week later, on January 14, 2021, election disinformation revved into high gear in Uganda, primarily advanced by the ruling regime. The Ugandan Communications Commission issued an order banning numerous social media platforms, including Facebook, Twitter, and WhatsApp. The reason? The incumbent president, Yoweri Museveni, claimed to have concerns about election security and blocked platforms that enforced restrictions on disinformation and inauthentic accounts. He singled out Facebook. "That social channel you are talking about, if it is going to operate in Uganda, it should be used equitably by everybody who has to use it," Museveni said in a live televised address. "We cannot tolerate this arrogance of anybody coming to decide for us who is good and who is bad."[4]

The next week in January saw yet another important controversy, this time in Russia, as the Kremlin critic Alexei Navalny (who subsequently died in prison) was arrested and citizens took to the streets—and to social media—to protest. On YouTube, TikTok, and Instagram, millions of messages proliferated with the hashtags #FreeNavalny and #23January—the day of the mass protest.[5] Censors in Russia tried to quell the online rebellion, while the authorities meanwhile rounded up protestors and arrested them in the streets. From the far eastern city of Vladivostok and parts of Siberia all the way to Moscow, the authorities struggled to contain the protestors. Law enforcement agencies began using social media as policing tools to help them reverse-engineer the social communities sponsoring the protests and identify suspects.[6]

Meanwhile, thousands of farmers in India flooded the streets of New Delhi to protest a series of new laws relating to the sale prices of goods and crops. Indian Twitter boiled over with messages urging the people to revolt against the government's new laws. The authorities swung into action, censoring the online environment. They justified their actions by citing the country's information technology rules, which empower regulators to crack down on platforms that they claim facilitate the violation of laws. Regulators within Prime Minister Narendra Modi's government ordered Twitter to suspend accounts using the hashtag #modiplanningfarmersgenocide, on the Orwellian pretext that those accounts were themselves promoting genocide. One of the suspended accounts is the official account of a magazine, followed by nearly three hundred thousand other accounts, which was merely reporting on the protests.[7] Authorities arrested activists who circulated an online "toolkit" or playbook for the protest.[8]

These scenes are just a handful of postcards from a few weeks in a given January. While each of the events has its own unique history and context, they share basic themes and questions about networked communication. Who gets to do the gatekeeping—the global social platforms or national governments? To what degree do platforms respect higher principles, such as international human rights law, that transcend nation states? What if the regimes in the nation states are objectively corrupt or authoritarian? And quietly, behind the scenes, there are enormous, and ominous, questions about privacy, as dissidents and protestors become the targets of police inquiries. The police then, naturally, knock on the door of companies to get more information about their targets. The companies are compelled to make foreign-policy level decisions on how much, and with what degree of supplication, to comply with local law.

This book attempts to make an intervention where the public debate has become confused and, often, hopelessly cynical and skeptical. What I hope is to add much needed contextualization to a hot-button topic—what to do about the ills of social media—that people often talk about devoid of any meaningful sense of wider perspective or history. We all have hard opinions about social media's shortcomings, and we all have assumptions about what we think will make social media better. We also all have some varying degrees of cynicism when it comes to whether anything can happen to motivate these platforms to improve things.

It would be absurd not to acknowledge that such cynicism and skepticism are, to some extent, well justified. We have seen a global trend toward authoritarian populism, bouncing from country to country, that undoubtedly feeds on and is fueled by the unbridled communications tools provided by social platforms. We have also seen a steady and grinding decline in freedom on the internet and digital rights for nearly two decades now.[9] Some large portion of the globe seems in no mood for rational compromise and carefully crafted new rules that might balance the competing concerns of free speech and social order.

The 2024 election of Donald J. Trump for a second term portends a period of profound policy uncertainty in the communications realm. Given that Trump is an owner of a platform, Truth Social, and his erstwhile allies such as industrial mogul Elon Musk own others (X, formerly Twitter), new policy solutions that would constrain them in any way seem wholly unlikely in the short term. Musk's moves to throw out most rules for X, in particular, spurred a "race to the bottom" through the 2024 election cycle, in terms of governing social media platforms.[10] Bowing to new political pressures, Meta CEO Mark Zuckerberg rolled back his company's content moderation rules as President Trump's second term began. Passing any government rules for social media in the United States, of any kind, seems a dim prospect—except when it might involve displaying an assertive posture toward China, such as banning TikTok. Even conservative legislative attempts at new rules—that would *limit* content moderation—have failed in the courts. The nonregulation status quo for social media seems destined to be sustained, at least in the short run, in the United States.

Yet around the world, many new things are happening in this policy space, and if we look carefully both globally and within American history, we can discern the beginnings of another story emerging—and perhaps anticipate new chapters in that story. As will be discussed, some countries are formulating the outlines of new rules for social media, even as there does not seem a great appetite currently for sensible reform and modest regulation in the libertarian hothouse of the United States. This book attempts to take the long view, which, if history provides any lesson, is necessary in the realm of communications technologies. Such technologies take a long time to percolate in the system, norms around them evolve as technologies mature, and regulation often takes decades, even generations, as we shall see.

THE HUNDRED-YEAR JOURNEY

Today we worry a great deal about information—who generates it, where it goes, and how it gets there. We worry about who controls it, who filters it, who governs its spread. Information is understood, in this sense, to be a kind of agent, a substance or force present in the world. Scientists, meanwhile, have made information a central concept in communications and computing, a mathematical and engineering discipline focused on the processing of electrical signals and the movement of bits, of ones and zeros.[11] But "information" also retains traces of an older meaning. Stretching back centuries, the term often referred to the process of molding and shaping the mind—hence, a "formation" taking place. The mind is, so to speak, like clay, with information molding the brain with an impression and potentially changing a person's character.[12] So Chaucer could write in *The Canterbury Tales* of "dame Prudence," with "hire wise informacions and techynges" (teachings), while Thomas Jefferson would remark in a letter on "The book I have read with extreme satisfaction and information."[13] And Ralph Waldo Emerson could proclaim in his essay "The American Scholar" that great historical heroes have existed despite "almost no other information than by the printed page."[14]

This more archaic idea of forming and molding of consciousness and character persists below the surface of contemporary use. We remain very much concerned about information planting and growing seeds in the mind—of doubt and certainty, hatred and love, war and revolution, and action of every kind. We worry about information warping minds. We worry about it twisting societies, forming new antisocial, antidemocratic values. And so we worry a great deal, in this era of radical connectivity, about the control of information.[15] As we should.

The central entities that now control most of the information—who "mediate" our moment—are large, corporate global communications platforms that network the world's publics. It is urgent that we address the accountability, responsibility, and transparency of these platforms, particularly social media.[16] This book is intended as a guide for general readers interested in understanding communication platform dynamics and challenges, especially with an eye toward their sensible regulation. The narrative may also be useful to research specialists whose domains are more technical but who may be interested in a consolidated guide to some relevant ideas. I also hope to contribute to the broader policy debate.

Governing Babel brings in perspectives using various cultural, intellectual, historical, and global lenses. The challenge the book addresses is vast—creating new rules to deal with the ills of our communications and media systems—but the central argument it develops is relatively simple. The idea is that those who create and manage systems that host user-generated content have both a responsibility to look after their platforms and a duty to respond to problems. And they should be judged, and subject to sanction, according to the good faith and persistence of their efforts.

Even as the book provides a global tour, its policy recommendations in the end focus on the United States, which has a moral obligation—and leadership opportunity—to help find solutions to many of the problems it has set in motion. The next set of technological innovations and regulatory moves taking place within the United States, where the likes of Google, Meta, X, Apple, Microsoft, and OpenAI are headquartered, matter enormously. The issues at play are inherently global in scope and implication. Still, any new American innovations in governance and rules provide perhaps the best chance at scaling and helping the world grapple with deep challenges unleashed by contemporary communications technology platforms.

In the narrative here, I build toward a central "response principle," that is, a duty for all those running networked online platforms to take reasonable action when potential harms present themselves. I believe our collective experiments in media and communications, and the wisdom earned over the past century through them, point us in a definite direction at this historic moment of confusion, which is being driven in some part by social media, internet-connected devices, and advanced machine-learning technologies such as generative AI. In the social media era, there are often no right answers in terms of content moderation. We have entered what this book refers to in subsequent chapters as the "era of probability," where automated systems make consequential decisions that are no more than estimates. Humans must tune those probabilistic, estimating systems with an eye on the public interest. I advocate that we set up systems that are flexible, emphasizing transparency and iteration of rules and judgments. Ultimately, this is an "effects-based" approach, where regulation does not specify how social platforms attend to online harms but rather focuses on what the outcomes are in terms of mitigating or reducing harms.[17] In the final chapter, I outline a potential new regulatory body that could help bring social media companies into line with public interest values and impose more responsibility, even while respecting the First Amendment.

In every other walk of life, in every industry, stewardship rules—a "duty of care," as ancient common law has long known it—are expected and unremarkable.[18] Not so, so far, with new media, including social media platforms and related communications applications. Yet we should remember that, in many other cases in other industries, such rules took a while to develop. It took from roughly 1912 to the 1960s to formulate rules around mass media in the United States. Analogously, it is as if we are somewhere in the early 1930s, when the Federal Communications Commission was first being set up (1934). We likely still have decades to go before we fully get our arms around social platforms and the new world of networked expression.

Understanding the history of ideas that informs "content moderation"—the governance of public speech and ideas, frequently applied in the context of social media and digital communications technologies[19]— can be very useful.[20] History can suggest solutions, ethical resources, and important lenses for scoping the many seemingly novel problems that the United States and global societies face regarding media platforms and communications technologies. Much of the discourse about social media and online platforms emphasizes novelty, particularly around dimensions of speed, scale, and personalization. Certainly, aspects of digital communications media are radically novel. But it is simply ahistorical to think that nothing from the past, no public interest values, can be usefully extended here. The largely pessimistic public conversation about regulating social media, and the handwringing over online ills and harms, often neglects the long experiences human beings have had in negotiating crises in the communications sphere.

In the United States, the central law that governs the internet is Section 230 of the Communications Decency Act of 1996. That law has protected platforms from ruinous legal battles (given them "safe harbor") as they have taken down dangerous or harmful user-generated content but also allowed companies to ignore deep problems. Congress may choose to "sunset" Section 230, but this book contends that any new rules for the decades ahead should involve both safe harbor and more legal responsibility to address foreseeable risks.

Solving the problem of contemporary networked communication is not a matter of a "just right" policy tweak. Rather, it should be a matter of ongoing translation based on a tradition of values, as well as growing global norms. Such reform is best framed as part of what I call here the hundred-year journey. This book is about the stories of humans struggling to adapt to new media and communication circumstances, both in the past and present. It goes back in history to understand the country's own experiments with propaganda and disinformation, the earliest major First Amendment decisions by the Supreme Court, and the simultaneous creation of broadcast regulation. It also explores international human rights law and the formation of new global norms and laws through the United Nations and other international bodies, many of which were conceived and based on American values. This book reexamines the pioneering work of Eleanor Roosevelt relating to human rights and speech, and the resonance of this work today.

In the present day, I flesh out discussions of policy with stories from the people who design, run, and participate in the information and knowledge machinery of the world, from managers at Facebook (Meta) and Twitter (X) to those running Africa Check, part of the global fact-checking movement, which is now very much under siege. I share the story of Nobel Laureate and media justice advocate Maria Ressa, of the Philippines, as well as that of Saudi Arabian writer and dissident Jamal Khashoggi. A wide variety of policymakers, from China to Europe to the United States, as well as leading academics, are featured in these pages. I resurface the founding ideas of earlier thinkers, including the social science savant Harold Lasswell, who proposed an "instant label plan" in the 1940s to grapple with Nazi disinformation, and Walter Lippmann, whose powerful ideas continue to frame many of the great puzzles for media and communications governance and regulation.

The story here also goes further behind the scenes of the January 6, 2021 storming of the U.S. Capitol to examine the chaos and clear instances of incitement to violence that unfolded in digital space—and how the social media platforms involved missed opportunities to stop it. The analysis here attempts to understand how we got to our current media and communications moment and what kinds of general ideas it will be important to carry forward and translate into future rules, especially as AI technologies begin to mediate much of the information environment.

In this narrative, I consider the dawn of modern mass communications and the early world of propaganda and propaganda studies as a kind of "founding period," a touchstone that provides vitally important perspective. In the late 1910s and 1920s, jurists and public intellectuals framed the communications and media problems for democracies, outlining the central traditions for addressing harmful speech while not undermining democratic life in the process. From the 1940s through to the late 1960s, prominent thinkers set out the idea of social responsibility for those managing the public's communications space. For a long period, thoughtful regulation evolved such that content on radio and television was not micromanaged; rather, rules functioned more as the "spirit of responsible broadcasting."[21] In the late 1990s, Section 230 drew on these earlier traditions to allow and encourage websites to be active stewards of their information spaces.

We cannot understand our moment without understanding this earlier thinking. This is because contained in prior regulatory regimes were deep principles that are now obscure to us. We need to rediscover these principles and apply them to our new communications technology paradigm. Revisiting founding periods seems especially appropriate at this moment, when the United States is approaching its semiquincentennial, the 250-year anniversary of its independence, on July 4, 2026. It does not appear that it will be a moment of great stability. Part of the peril of the moment emerges from our profound failure to renew traditions and extend core principles to address a new set of technology-driven information challenges. So in the latter stages of the story here, I explore emerging ideas from the international context as well as new technological approaches compatible with deep democratic principles. The only way forward is to root new technology and communications rules squarely in democratic traditions, grounded in history and continuous with the deep structures of open societies.

MODERN BABEL

The eternal curse of human civilization is, according to the Book of Genesis, the curse of many tongues. Our linguistic diversity stands not as a blessing or testament to human creativity, but as a way of dividing us. This division was God's punishment for humans' prideful lifting of the Tower of Babel toward heaven, something humanity could only attempt because those original builders shared a single language. The capacity for collective action, a seeming virtue, gave rise to hubris. The ancient author who conjured the witty and enigmatic tale of Babel's overreach ("babel" is derived from the Hebrew word "to confuse") might be astonished, some three thousand years later, at our present condition: nearly two hundred nations, seven thousand languages, and a single, new technology, the internet, that reinjects God's original concern about communicative unity.[22]

Seven major social medial platforms—YouTube, Facebook, WhatsApp, Messenger, Instagram, WeChat, and TikTok—have more than one billion active users.[23] We are, so to speak, building technological towers. But the condition of Modern Babel is one of permanent unruliness, a multiplication of voices and views. Proper governance across such scale, I will argue, requires a firm but flexible management approach that prevents systemic harms from accruing in Babel. Social media platforms may have God-like powers in some respects, but they do not have omniscience or any monopoly on wisdom, and therefore we must leave room for human diversity to flourish and tolerate some amount of risk.

The amount of content and data shared across the large platforms is nearly incomprehensible. More than a decade ago, when platform user bases were much smaller, longtime Google CEO Eric Schmidt noted that the volume of content generated on digital platforms in twenty-four to forty-eight hours likely exceeds the total sum of all information ever recorded in human history, prior to the advent of the social web.[24] Much of this content is benign and prosocial, to be sure. But there has also been an explosion of mis- and disinformation, hate speech, incitement to violence, exploitation, technology addiction, and war and genocidal propaganda, as well as various new kinds of "deep fakes" and AI-generated false content. This content has proliferated virally and washed over many societies, contributing to changes in their fundamental character. We can argue about the precise contribution of social media to society's ills, but few now doubt that these technologies have remade how governments and citizens understand, relate to, and function in the world.

Governing Babel focuses on four categories in particular: mis- and disinformation; hate speech; incitement to violence; and the emerging challenges associated with generative AI, particularly what I call the problems of "epistemic risk." To the extent that we have attempted to respond to many of these problems, the response frequently takes the form of "content moderation." Companies and institutions of many kinds are beginning to commit themselves to ethical principles that attempt to ensure fairness and access for users who engage with their brand, products, and platforms. Debates surrounding social media content moderation impact activism, journalism, and media and communications industries. Indeed, the question of "content moderation" has become an area of public debate globally, not only about the rights and responsibilities of online platform or forum hosts, but also about the design of all social information systems, the behavioral science that can guide such design, and the obligations companies owe to both individual users and the societies in which their communications technologies are embedded. It is a debate, ultimately, about what rights and obligations human beings are afforded in public, what harms they can legitimately ask to be guarded against, and which kinds of messages must be tolerated.

A new field, "trust and safety," is emerging as roles related to keeping digital platforms open, viable, profitable, and not dangerous are professionalizing.[25] Heated policy conversations around the world are changing norms and expectations across a variety of related domains: corporate social responsibility; governance and rights of citizens; public informational health; cybersecurity; data privacy; algorithmic fairness and justice; transparency of corporations and government; and independent oversight of technology products. Corporate and institutional commitments often come in the form of terms of service policies that govern standards for individuals and communities of users. These terms and standards, now being formulated in the pressure cooker of our current debates, are likely to evolve and pervade many areas of public and private life through the twenty-first century. This grand, global debate is also transforming the boundaries between private corporations and governments, redrawing the lines of the field on which public and private actors play and contend.

Social media, or networked, peer-to-peer communications technologies, are a young set of applications, most hardly more than twenty years old. Beginning exactly two decades ago, in a period of roughly forty months, society saw a kind of Cambrian explosion of technologies—from microblogging to video sharing to handheld internet connectivity—whose initial effects are still reverberating: Facebook (2004), YouTube (2005), Twitter (2006), and the launch of the iPhone (2007). These are early days still. Throughout communications history, it has taken a long time for rules to be put in place.

NEW MAGNA CARTA?

In key spots around the world, we are beginning to have an inkling of what it might mean to govern the tongues of modern Babel. Although uneven in its distribution, a new set of principles is beginning to take shape that might bring a little more unity, and sanity, to the current state of our disordered and frankly dangerous communications media moment. A new chapter in the internet's history is here.[26]

The European Union (EU), by some measures the largest market in the world, has already put in place new rules in the form of its Digital Services Act (DSA). The DSA mandates that large technology platforms both behave as responsible stewards of the information environment and disclose their practices regularly to the public. This follows Germany's earlier Network Enforcement Act (NetzDG), which in 2017 began holding social media platforms liable for not taking down content that is illegal under German law. NetzDG became a new kind of standard around the world, as many countries began considering similar rules.[27] Further regulations around market behavior and emerging technologies, such as artificial intelligence, are being rapidly developed in the EU. For its part, the Indian government has put forward its Information Technology Rules, which restrict certain kinds of content on social platforms. The United Kingdom has its Online Safety Act, which establishes obligations for online platforms, particularly in relation to youth. Meanwhile, China and Russia, among others such as Iran, have made the affirmative decision to wall off their people from the open web and give strong censorship power to state technology and communications ministries.

Amid all of this, the critical—and critically indecisive—actor has been the United States. For a time, American leaders were content to wave the banner of "internet freedom," a kind of ideological belief in the technologically deterministic principle that the possibility of open communication meant the enduring certainty of open, and healthy, democracies.[28] Silicon Valley's leaders were content to spout reinforcing platitudes that to wire the world was to save the world. But the world has had other plans, and at home there has been more than a little trouble. As Tom Wheeler, the former chair of the Federal Communications Commission (FCC), has noted, "Compared with the EU, UK, and China, the United States is on the sidelines watching [while] the race is on to develop national policies that will be spread internationally by the same network that created the need for the regulation in the first place."[29] We hear talk of America's old Section 230 rules—the "Magna Carta" of the internet[30]—being replaced by Europe's "New Constitution" of digital space, while countries such as India, Australia, Thailand, and Brazil chart a third way, sometimes particular and idiosyncratic, and the likes of China, Iran, and Russia increasingly lock down and vigilantly police their cyber borders with a kind of neo-feudal zeal.

Citizens across the world are waiting. And their leaders know there needs to be a change. Nearly everyone recognizes that new rules, of some kind, are necessary to bring accountability to social media and communications platforms. Yet we all see that our information environment is surrounded by a mist of distrust. Part of the puzzle is that the United States has very deep free-speech traditions, which adds to the inherent difficulty of governing media and communications. Equally, though, the problem is a lack of deep thinking and creativity to address the new era.

The solution is to expand and deepen the way we see the problem. We need to consider new approaches to regulating internet platforms as continuous with traditions and the past. To many, that might sound counterintuitive, perhaps impossible. Internet platforms seem to present novel problems, requiring novel regulatory frameworks and rules.[31] While this is true, what I argue here is that the past can nevertheless suggest some possible solutions. For the past one hundred years, at various intervals, American society has found free speech-preserving solutions on matters of communications. Today, we can create a similar system of regulation that does not regulate specific instances of speech but rather monitors and guides platform governance on patterns of harm and risk. As will be discussed, the landmark U.S. Supreme Court decision *Moody v. NetChoice, LLC* (2024), contains hints that even a conservative court majority might support new possible forms of regulation that do not directly curb social media platforms' "expressive," or free speech, rights, but rather relate to more infrastructural, technological design, and various forms of algorithmic (including AI-mediated) functions within the platform companies.[32] From a historical perspective, perhaps the most important fact relating to this area is that the traditional "laissez-faire free speech consensus"— the free speech maximalism from both left-oriented civil libertarians and limited-government conservatives—has broken down as it relates to communications platforms; the political right and left are both rethinking the principles that define boundaries and limits in this domain.[33] This intellectual rupture is something genuinely new and novel in American policy and politics.

To conservatives who would decry an apparent Big Brother regime in any attempt to regulate speech, one need only point to the prior communications regime in the twentieth century—a very successful "American century," as some would have it—when the country was governed by a set of rules that embodied what some have called the "spirit of responsible broadcasting." Translating this "spirit" into the era of internet platforms is tricky but not impossible. To liberals who would point out the extraordinary harms wrought by social platforms—from doxxing (maliciously releasing individuals' identifying information) to the spread of child sexual abuse material (CSAM), election interference to hate speech—and the need for much heavier regulation, two things must be said: One, there is an obvious First Amendment constraint in ordering information communications companies to suppress speech. Two, these platforms reflect what goes on across all walks of public life. Algorithms and anonymity may make things worse in some cases, but we can't expect to thoroughly expunge human depravity. We can, however, open up more data to legal scrutiny, and make sure the platforms have the resources in place and the will to respond to patterns of harms.

As broadcast media and all other regulated industries from finance to health care, education to energy have done in prior generations, internet platforms should comply with a system of periodic, perhaps quarterly, reporting about areas of harm. Independent watchdog agencies and researchers should be able to audit and check their claims. A group of commissioners should judge them on their general pattern of compliance, perhaps pausing user or advertising growth if platforms are not responsive to problems. The way platforms might address patterns of harm might be diverse, and they will certainly evolve as generative AI and other technologies iteratively create new problems. All of this will be discussed in this book.

Governing Babel seeks to build toward policy solutions and general regulatory approaches that are, I believe, consistent with deep democratic traditions and that might help chart a course for the future. Numerous bills before the U.S. Congress—including, to take just two examples, the Digital Services Oversight and Safety Act (DSOSA) and the Platform

Accountability and Transparency Act (PATA)—have tried to move the needle in this direction, creating regular auditing and data transparency requirements.[34] Some bills have gone further and tried to circumscribe or even scrap Section 230 protections for online platforms. Apart from child safety-related legislation, nearly all such internet policy reform efforts have consistently stalled in Congress.

America needs an answer to Europe's DSA and China's surveillance-state, "cyber-sovereignty" model. Having unleashed a great deal of risk and harm in the world, all the while reaping vast economic benefit, the country has both an obligation and an opportunity to formulate a kind of minimum viable policy solution. Rather than spelling out exactly what kinds of nitty-gritty policies should be enacted in the United States, this book seeks centrally to provide the wider cultural and historical justification for an American alternative to the European DSA.

Given the vastness of the task of organizing the world's speech and information, it is obviously worth questioning whether any single perspective should prevail; perhaps there are many valid ideas, all competing in a pluralistic universe. I have no doubt that pluralism is essential, given the diversity of global histories and human experiences. Yet it is worth thinking about aspirations and our collective direction of travel, about the rules and norms that might, if adopted by many communities, stand the best chance of contributing to the endurance of free, flourishing, and relatively stable societies. The needs of democracies in our increasingly topsy-turvy world of whiplash global communications are not exactly clear at this moment. Here I try to surface stories, knowledge, and wisdom that can help to provide some vital context and, perhaps, to chart a path forward.

1

FOUNDATIONAL RULES AND MODELS

Truth and understanding are not such wares to be monopolized and traded in by tickets and statutes and standards. We must not think to make a staple commodity of all the knowledge in the land, to mark and licence it like our broadcloth and our woolpacks.[1]
—John Milton, *Areopagitica* (1644)

The peculiar character of the problem of a rational economic order is determined precisely by the fact that the knowledge of the circumstances of which we must make use never exists in concentrated or integrated form, but solely as the dispersed bits of incomplete and frequently contradictory knowledge which all the separate individuals possess.[2]
—Friedrich von Hayek, "The Use of Knowledge in Society," *American Economic Review* (1945)

We are now at a historical moment that demands new rules for the media and communications industries. History will likely look back at the mid-2020s as a period when, having lived through the heady early days of the social web and internet—beginning, let's say, with Facebook's founding in 2004—entities like the EU began implementing stringent regulations designed to reign in some of the most challenging aspects of networked communication, including misinformation and hate speech. As yet, however, the United States has contributed remarkably little to communications governance besides instituting the laissez-faire, hands-off approach of Section 230 of the 1996 Communications Decency Act.

As a result of this inaction, the United States is now on its heels, with no real answers or ways to reassert leadership on the way forward in digital space. The vacuum created has fostered chaos, invited authoritarians to jump in, and generally left an ad-hoc system to deteriorate in terms of fostering democratic systems, protecting human rights, and facilitating high-quality knowledge and understanding of events. Any real change in the U.S. regulatory environment starts with revising that crucial law, Section 230, which allows digital platforms to host user-generated content without themselves being liable for what is published.[3] The provision was obscure upon its passage, as most of the discussion surrounding the Communications Decency Act centered on a kind of moral panic over how the emerging internet might hurt children and degrade society by allowing obscene materials to proliferate. The congressional vote on the all-encompassing Telecommunications Act of 1996 was lopsided (414–16 in the House, 91–5 in the Senate), and the ideas behind what would become Section 230 were a footnote for most lawmakers. Most of the CDA, signed by President Bill Clinton, was subsequently rejected by the courts, but Section 230 survived. Reflecting a growing mood of internet utopianism, Clinton and Vice President Al Gore exuded a giddy enthusiasm at the bill's signing ceremony in 1996, as they accelerated the new information "superhighway."

Thirty years on, the limitations of Section 230 for governing networked communication have become abundantly clear. But while we need new rules, we need not start from scratch. A century ago, the American public was struggling with strikingly similar issues related to the dawn of modern mass communications technologies. As the First Amendment scholar Lee Bollinger, former president of Columbia University, has noted, "We have been through this before. In fact, this is more or less exactly the situation we found ourselves in with broadcasting beginning in the first half of the last century, with similar concerns."[4] At that time, the public and policymakers responded by setting up the Federal Communications Commission, which provided a structure for overseeing broadcast media for decades to come. It was not, however, an easy, predictable, or linear path, as the FCC's rulemaking constantly evolved in response to new challenges and innovations. Rules must be continuously updated, and they must be agile enough to adapt to each new stage of technical evolution.

For our purposes, the most salient point about the creation of the FCC is that the public attempted to solve an emerging media problem, starting with some big principles and getting more specific over time. What we need, then, is to identify the general principles that we can use to begin

Figure 1.1 President Bill Clinton, with Vice President Al Gore, signs the Telecommunications Act of 1996 at the Library of Congress. Included in this legislation was the basis for what would become Section 230 of the Communications Decency Act (part of the general act), which would go on to power and structure the internet's development over the coming decades. Courtesy, William J. Clinton Presidential Library.

the process of iterative rulemaking regarding digital communications platforms. Private social media companies are currently largely unregulated, and the traditional understanding of the law is that the FCC has no real authority to regulate them.[5] New principles must be deeply grounded in democratic and humanistic values if they are to be durable and serve the purposes that would justify any government intervention in public discourse. It is here that our best guide may, in part, be the past.

In the United States, any discussion of speech starts with the First Amendment. Many readers may be surprised to learn that the First Amendment had essentially no real, uniform meaning until roughly a century ago (1919), when the U.S. Supreme Court began to decide cases on issues of free speech and the press at the end of World War I. Although communications laws had existed in the nineteenth century, most issues involving the press were governed locally, and there was no existing body of jurisprudence to govern the explosion of radio and television in early days. In other words, the founding concepts of media and communications law are only a century old. It took a long period of argument, regulation, and legal interpretation to get to a set of relatively successful and stable rules. The advent of cable television, satellite broadcast, and the internet then upended those rules. Today, it is imperative that we renew the original traditions.

What traditions might we draw on? The original founding period of media governance—from roughly the 1920s to the 2020s—is rich with principles that, despite flaws and trade-offs, in some deep sense *worked*—at least until they failed to be reinvented to keep up with new technologies. They worked because they spoke, for many decades, to the needs of humans and societies. They also worked because they accompanied a period of relative peace, growth, and expansions in civil and political rights through the 1990s and early 2000s. It is not guaranteed that such expansions will continue.

At the level of law, whether in the United States or around the world, media regulation has depended on the continual development of free speech and free press principles. American constitutional law and its interpretation—including in such landmark cases as *Times v. Sullivan*, which protected the press from libel suits and enshrined the ability to criticize public officials—have globalized, influencing numerous societies as a model and standard starting point.[6] The development of international human rights law and principles—at their origin, a deeply American effort—was equally important for extending related rights of expression around the world. Within the more technical area of communications law, ideas such as the Fairness Doctrine and the right of reply—all enshrined in various ways, with different twists in many nations—have also been powerful.

In this chapter, I explore how both historical rules (laws and jurisprudence) and models (frameworks and metaphors for understanding) apply to the social media age. The rules of the last century may not appear, on their face, to be relevant given the differences in media type, but in fact they draw to the surface key democratic principles that can inform our current moment. Conversely, certain historical models (e.g., the "marketplace of ideas"), appear useful on their face and continue to be widely used in the social media age, but in fact they obfuscate key dynamics and risk wrongly framing the problem.

THE FAIRNESS DOCTRINE

People often lament that there is such polarization in American public discourse, and fewer and fewer people hear "both sides" of issues. This lament invariably leads to discussions of the merits of the older U.S. media system. Both liberals and conservatives have critiques of past rules, too, but there is a sense that the older media order was more stable. In broadcasting, the most prominent manifestation of these rules was the so-called Fairness Doctrine. The United States has traditionally had a two-track system for regulating media: For print, government has not been allowed to have virtually any regulatory role; for broadcast, however, a number of unique features of the medium and its circumstance, specifically the scarcity of the airwaves, justified regulation. In the popular perception, the Fairness Doctrine was a rule that required news outlets to give voice to both sides of any issue. But the Fairness Doctrine's origins, history, and actual application are much more complicated.

It is worth beginning with the intellectual foundations of the doctrine. A sprawling, messy, and very specific regulatory debate had begun unfolding in the United States, beginning as early as the 1910s, about what to do with the fast-growing technology of radio. The debate would ultimately crystallize into what has become the central organizing idea on which turns almost all argument about media governance then and now: the Fairness Doctrine.

In the hours after the sinking of the R.M.S. *Titanic* in 1912, early radio operators broadcast various rumors and misinformation, triggering a U.S. policy debate about who should have a license and who should be allowed to inform the public. Just months later, that national debate resulted in the U.S. Radio Act of 1912, the first in a long series of rules that attempted to tame the airwaves by structuring licensure and establishing conditions for holding licenses. The frequencies on which radio operators and early stations could broadcast were necessarily scarce, meaning that the early airwaves were full of conflicting signals and, in dense urban markets, some amount of chaos. The need to decide how to allocate frequencies became an increasingly powerful rationale for government regulation, culminating in the landmark Radio Act of 1927 (when the Federal Radio Commission, or FRC, began, with a mandate for license holders to hew to a public interest standard) and 1934, when the Federal Communications Commission was finally set up under the landmark Communications Act of that year. In a broad mandate, the FCC was charged with overseeing and governing access to broadcast frequencies according to "public interest, convenience and necessity."[7] This "public interest standard," as it became known, governed the broadcast age in America and structured regulation of content.

The FCC's mandate was to make sure that broadcasters fulfilled public interest obligations as a condition of granting licenses (held by hundreds of local stations across the country.) Yet defining the public interest and putting in place stable and predictable policies that ensured it often proved vexing in the context of a democracy where contending sides are constantly jockeying for power over regulatory agencies like the FCC, and where a commercial sector is assiduously trying to find every possible financial advantage over rivals. Political conservatives and commercial lobbies such as the National Association of Broadcasters (NAB) worked tirelessly to undo new 1941 rules—called the Mayflower Doctrine—set out by the FCC to restrict editorializing by radio station owners, and attempts by the FCC to spell out the public service obligations in the so-called 1946 Blue Book proved controversial. The first fifteen years of FCC regulation with respect to news and public information was "erratic" at best, in terms of formulating licensee responsibilities and obligations.[8]

The influential Hutchins Commission, officially known as the Commission on Freedom of the Press, was established in 1942. The commission, comprised of luminaries in the press, academia, and intellectual life, spent several years meeting and doing fact-finding before publishing its final report in 1947. The commission was a civic and nongovernmental affair, but it was well timed, as this was the exact period of ferment when federal policymakers in the Federal Communications Commission (FCC) were coming up with the Blue Book, the basis for FCC regulation of broadcast media, defining what authorities the FCC would have. As with our time in the twenty-first century, the news business in the 1940s had come under withering public scrutiny, and newspapers were held in increasingly low regard. This public perception helped motivate the formation of the Hutchins Commission.

The Blue Book, drafted and published during the period 1945–1946, sought to make licenses conditional on broadcasters exercising social responsibility and encouraged broadcasters to be more responsive and accountable to the needs of their local communities. When the Blue Book was issued, the Hutchins Commission called it "the most significant milestone in the entire history of radio regulation."[9] Yet the Blue Book immediately made enemies among commercial broadcasters, as it aggressively called out broadcasters for violating the spirit of existing FCC regulations. The Blue Book called for hearings, which after wide pushback from industry never happened. Nevertheless, it inspired the work of the Hutchins commissioners,[10] and it led to a new push to get sensible and enforceable rules on the books.

In its 1947 report titled *A Free and Responsible Press*, the Hutchins Commission issued findings and recommendations that reflected many ideas that centered on the emerging media system as a whole (both print and broadcast) and its owners having a sense of responsibility. There were also concrete ideas that never quite caught on, including a "right of reply," theoretically allowing persons or groups who felt they had received unfair treatment in the media to present their perspective and provide an alternative view. Overall, the idea of right of reply was to give persons the

chance to offer additional context, correct falsehoods, or generally present their side of the story. All of this would be in the service of making
news media more responsible to society and potentially more balanced in
the views it presents, consistent with key policy recommendations of the
overall Hutchins report for greater "social responsibility."

Despite the triumph of earlier progressive policies by the FCC, culminating in the Blue Book, more conservative and reactionary voices
increasingly dominated the airwaves by the late 1940s, a result of fears
over the rise of communism and the investigation and purging of many
liberal on-air national radio commentators.[11] Early progressive dreams for
a less commercial radio industry had been lost, as advertising and corporate interests grew more dominant. In that milieu came the ideas that
would be enshrined as the Fairness Doctrine, a central communications
policy idea that anchored the American media system for four decades
and that has come to define, for many nostalgic liberals and political
moderates, a lost era of fact-based, reasonably balanced news and public
information—even as libertarians and conservatives continue to bid good
riddance to that regulatory doctrine.

What, exactly, was the original Fairness Doctrine? The FCC's articulation of it, set out in the 1949 report on *Editorializing by Broadcast Licensees*, included two basic principles: (1) devoting time to matters of public
importance and (2) providing room for contrasting viewpoints on those
matters. The original language had a certain amount of flexibility built
in. In creating the FCC, Congress had originally mandated that radio be
maintained as a "medium of free speech for the general public as a whole
rather than as an outlet for the purely personal or private interests of the
licensee." Therefore, broadcasters had certain general obligations: "This
requires that licensees devote a reasonable percentage of their broadcasting time to the discussion of public issues of interest in the community
served by their stations and that such programs be designed so that the
public has a reasonable opportunity to hear different opposing positions
on the public issues of interest and importance in the community. The
particular format best suited for the presentation of such programs in a
manner consistent with the public interest must be determined by the
licensee in the light of the facts of each individual situation."[12] The big
news from the 1949 FCC report was that stations were now allowed to

editorialize. But they had to devote time to exploring contrasting perspectives, and they needed to set aside some time to community issues. Importantly, these rules were not meant to be rigid, where an "honest mistake or error in judgment on the part of the licensee will be or should be condemned where his overall record demonstrates a reasonable effort to provide a balanced presentation of comment and opinion on such issues."[13] Although there were some investigations and cases involving obscure local broadcast stations in subsequent years, between 1949 and 1968 no national networks were found in violation of the Fairness Doctrine. During that nearly two-decade period, the Fairness Doctrine "began to function more as the spirit of responsible broadcasting than as the letter of the law," as former CBS President Fred Friendly noted in a history he wrote in the 1970s about the doctrine.[14]

The constitutionality of the Fairness Doctrine was unanimously upheld by the Supreme Court in 1969, in the case of *Red Lion v. FCC*.[15] That case involved a particular application of the Fairness Doctrine to situations where an individual is attacked in a broadcast and the rights of reply of that individual. (A separate and distinct FCC rule also related to giving political candidates "equal time" in the context of elections.) Many subsequent legal battles proved that the controversial regulations were difficult to uniformly enforce in their particulars. Critics complained that the doctrine had a "chilling effect" on certain kinds of information formats, a point that some scholars believe was validated by the dramatic changes in formats that radio in particular saw post-1987, when the doctrine was repealed amid the deregulatory ethos of the Reagan era.[16] Certainly, most observers agree that the rise of right-wing talk radio in the 1980s and 1990s was fueled in part by such deregulation, although that same period also saw the rise of major technological changes, such as satellite delivery of content, cable television, and the internet.

The Fairness Doctrine no longer applies to media outlets and companies across the United States. It became too politically controversial to be sustained, ultimately, but it is worth remembering that from 1949 to 1968 it operated as a kind of North Star—media operators generally accepted it as a norm, but government was not wildly and intrusively handing out citations for violating it. The rule had a shaping function, a force that came from societal expectation, gathered around a general idea of fairness. This history is in some sense forgotten. But the important lesson is that it is possible to achieve some public interest goals without necessarily turning a society into Big Brother and resorting to censorship and micromanagement. There was a principles-based approach within American communications history that saw real success, at least until there wasn't.

RECOVERING RULEMAKING

The Fairness Doctrine remains deeply controversial, with some liberal commentators nostalgic for it, seeing it as a net good, and conservatives maintaining that it was a major affront to the First Amendment. Yet these were just American debates. And as media technologies grew across the world, other societies were coming to their own conclusions about how to think about, and perhaps regulate, the new broadcast technologies. The American debates helped ignite, and were parallel to, a series of national debates around the world about how speech and expression over mass media might be structured and regulated.

As mentioned, many promising ideas were also lost or cast aside during the original era of mass communications, one of which is beginning to resurface. A recurring theme throughout media and policy communications history has been the concept of counterspeech, which is a diverse concept that is generally defined as "communication that seeks to counteract potential harm that is brought about by other speech."[17] This can mean a variety of things, including counterspeech voiced directly by targets and victims, or by bystanders, interest groups, or any number of other kinds of actors; they may use different strategies and tactics to counteract harms—from direct disagreement to contextual information to asking questions or using deflective humor. Harms that counterspeech seeks to mitigate are likewise potentially quite diverse, as they might be "physical harms (e.g., borne of false information about vaccine safety), status-related harms (e.g., stigma, loss of dignity, or other social inequalities resulting from expressions of negative affect or hatred), as well as diffuse harms to social and political institutions (e.g., the erosion of democratic norms)."[18]

The power and importance of counterspeech as a cure-all communications tool is a kind of article of faith in the more libertarian environment of the United States. The mantra in an American context, where a wide-open First Amendment dominates, is that the way to treat problematic expression is for people to talk back, to argue against it. The theory, at least in basic form, found its most eloquent early articulation by Supreme Court Justice Louis D. Brandeis in *Whitney v. California* (1927). The case was a complex one involving communist anti-war activism during World War I and the role of Charlotte Anita Whitney, a wealthy suffragette who had ended up supporting a communist labor group that espoused violence. Although Whitney's conviction (for aiding organized crime) was unanimously upheld by the Supreme Court, Brandeis famously outlined limits to government attempts to curb free speech:

Those who won our independence by revolution were not cowards. They did not fear political change. They did not exalt order at the cost of liberty. To courageous, self-reliant men, with confidence in the power of free and fearless reasoning applied through the processes of popular government, no danger flowing from speech can be deemed clear and present unless the incidence of the evil apprehended is so imminent that it may befall before there is opportunity for full discussion. If there be time to expose through discussion the falsehood and fallacies, to avert the evil by the processes of education, the remedy to be applied is more speech, not enforced silence. Only an emergency can justify repression. Such must be the rule if authority is to be reconciled with freedom.[19]

The passage that has echoed down through the ages is that the "remedy to be applied is more speech, not enforced silence," a ringing, pithy summation of the rationale underlying counterspeech.

In our contemporary digital context, groups such as the Dangerous Speech Project (DSP) have been assessing new dynamics in the networked environment and creatively exploring new ways for counterspeech to play a role in helping to mitigate online expressions of hate and abuse that can lead to violence.[20] One central issue is that, as a field, counterspeech in digital space has not yet been a systematic area of study, a dynamic that DSP has been trying to change; a whole new field is forming that is using observation and experiments to test out strategies and to see how social norms can be shifted and hate-filled speakers might either change their behavior or be opposed by prosocial messages. Best practices that can truly work are still being studied and validated.[21] Violence may be prevented in various ways, the Dangerous Speech Project has noted, such as by "inhibiting the speech, limiting its dissemination, undermining the credibility of the speaker, or 'inoculating' the audience against the speech so that they are less easily influenced by it."[22] Founded and led by the human rights lawyer Susan Benesch, DSP has also examined crucial issues such as how activist, ethical bystanders can speak up—what they call "counterspeakers"—and under what conditions this type of prosocial behavior can be both incentivized and made effective.[23]

While there continues to be global disagreement on how exactly to treat hate speech and incitement or "fighting words," most of the world's democracies often agree that counterspeech is generally the right direction to go in when people or groups have been insulted, critiqued, or possibly libeled—where personal or group reputation and rights seem affronted. There are deep traditions relating to counterspeech, often articulated in law, that span the globe. Counterspeech-related laws sometimes include what is known as the formal right of reply, mentioned earlier, which typically spells out rules for how news organizations must provide space or time for accusations to be answered. One scholar has called the requirement of reply "elementary fair play."[24]

The Hutchins Commission in 1947 endorsed the right-of-reply approach in its report. Also in 1947, the commission's vice chairman, Zechariah Chafee, the preeminent First Amendment scholar of mid-century America, made a push on a United Nations subcommittee to enshrine the right of reply, feeding into larger efforts, led by Eleanor Roosevelt (as will be discussed), around free expression as the Universal Declaration of Human Rights was being formulated.[25] Chafee's scholarship was a major influence on the leading legal minds in the space, Supreme Court Justices Oliver Wendell Holmes and Louis D. Brandeis. It is now largely forgotten in the American context, but the right of reply was originally part of the mainstream mix of ideas in terms of how to protect and buttress free speech and free press—part of the founding period of modern First Amendment jurisprudence following World War I, where the ideas of free speech and free press were brought into the modern era.

Yet the United States never quite embraced the right, and it died what some see as a premature death in a case decided by the Supreme Court in 1974, *Miami Herald Publishing Company v. Tornillo*.[26] The facts of the case involved a candidate for the Florida legislature, Pat Tornillo, trying to force the *Miami Herald* to carry a rebuttal to editorials it had run against him and his candidacy. Tornillo was taking advantage of state law requiring a right of reply; in a unanimous decision, the Supreme Court struck down the state law as in violation of the First Amendment's protections for freedom of the press.

Notably, *Tornillo* was decided in the pre-digital era, and although the case is still held up as part of the canon of domestic cases that protect free press in a narrow sense—preventing outside interference in the editorial business of news—there has been little subsequent discussion in the United States about how this might apply to digital platforms and the kinds of distinctive "interactive computer services" that Section 230 specifically identified as unique in the publishing ecosystem.[27] What scholars continue to note is that the position of the United States on the right of reply is out of synch on the international stage. "The U.S. backpedaling on the right of reply stands out from other mostly civil-law countries in that the right of reply is increasingly recognized in foreign and international law," Kyu Ho Youm, a media law scholar at the University of Oregon, noted in a comprehensive global review of the right of reply.[28] Diverse countries around the world have enshrined the right either in their constitutions or in statutes, and scholars examining the effects of such rights have generally found no chilling effect on the press.[29]

Many decades of creative and powerful thinking about this right ended in the United States in the 1970s with a narrow dispute over whether a politician could print a rebuttal in a commercial newspaper. Most legal scholars agree that *Tornillo* was likely decided properly given that fact pattern, at that time in media-technology history. But given the vastly expanded publishing and speech environment we have now in digital space, it is unclear how far the precedent should extend, or whether there is room to revive the rich history of the right of reply, in new guises, to deal with current problems.

FROM *TORNILLO* TO *NETCHOICE*—AND BEYOND

The right of reply and the importance of counterspeech can be debated on their own merits. But one essential facet of the right-of-reply issue is that it drove the *Tornillo* case and finding—it prompted the Supreme Court to prohibit interference of any kind in the editorial decision-making of the traditional press. However, there are finally signs of potential rupture with regard to this legal status quo, as our new era of media and communications technologies raises new questions and possibilities. Beginning in the 2010s, American society began debating the right of the social media platforms to moderate content and take down speech, on private platforms, that violates terms of service or community guidelines. A conservative legal movement has recently driven the debate, resulting in state laws in places such as Texas and Florida that prohibit forms of content moderation. This debate over a broader "right to post" is substantively different than the right of reply tradition, which relates more narrowly to the ability of individuals and groups who have been challenged directly by claims, not to the status of all speech of any kind and the right to express it.[30]

Suddenly, after decades of relative acceptance, the precedent in *Tornillo* has come sailing back into the center of public debate. A prominent new case, in which controversial state laws tried to force social platforms to serve as "common carriers" of all speech, with no moderation, directly challenged the principles articulated in *Tornillo*. In 2022, the U.S. 11th Circuit Court of Appeals struck down the Florida law (Texas passed a similar but distinctive one), pushed by political conservatives who opposed social media "censorship." The appeals court cited *Tornillo*, which protected publishers' rights to choose what they publish—and rejected a right of reply.

In 2024, the U.S. Supreme Court, pulling together two similar cases addressing laws passed in Texas and Florida (together *Moody v. NetChoice* and *NetChoice v. Paxton*), ruled that government interference with social media company operations, at least as propounded by the Texas and Florida laws, was not allowable, and they sent the cases back to the lower courts.[31] While the majority of justices came down in favor of the social media companies and their right to noninterference—analogizing them to newspaper publishers, as in *Tornillo*—there were strong hints that some of the key swing justices might be open to other types of government rules. Justice Amy Coney Barrett, who was in the majority and sided with the social media companies, noted in her concurrence some vital possible exceptions. She acknowledged that the government cannot interfere in the companies' "expressive" speech rights—the platforms have the right to use algorithms, for example, to pick and choose the types of political content they want to moderate according to the wishes of the human beings running them. But, she notes, not all algorithms should be treated the same:

But what if a platform's algorithm just presents automatically to each user whatever the algorithm thinks the user will like—e.g., content similar to posts with which the user previously engaged? . . . The First Amendment implications of the Florida and Texas laws might be different for that kind of algorithm. And what about AI, which is rapidly evolving? What if a platform's owners hand the reins to an AI tool and ask it simply to remove "hateful" content? If the AI relies on large language models to determine what is "hateful" and should be removed, has a human being with First Amendment rights made an inherently expressive "choice . . . not to propound a particular point of view"?[32]

Barrett opened the door to seeing certain computationally driven actions by the social platforms as less "expressive" and protected; the implication is that perhaps algorithms that have a kind of broad, infrastructural function might be regulated lawfully. A general axiom in American law is that the government can regulate conduct but not speech. Perhaps some layers of social platform activity may ultimately be judged conduct in subsequent cases? It is difficult to say.

Under the current Supreme Court configuration, Barrett is often a crucial swing vote, and her opinion makes clear that the Court may have a lot more thinking to do if government rules and regulations are more clearly focused on less "expressive" functions and more on regulating infrastructure, design, and automated tools—machinery that does not involve or is distant from human choices. As Barrett also says in her *NetChoice* opinion: "Technology may attenuate the connection between content-moderation actions (e.g., removing posts) and human beings' constitutionally protected right to 'decide for [themselves] the ideas and beliefs deserving of expression, consideration, and adherence.' . . . So the way platforms use this sort of technology might have constitutional significance."[33] Indeed, Barrett strongly suggests that there is likely no blanket First Amendment protection for social platforms, as the newspaper publishers enjoyed under *Tornillo*, but rather that the law will need to consider which function or activity is being targeted by the government. As many legal scholars have noted, the *NetChoice* cases involved some poorly written laws in Texas and Florida; a more careful and thoughtful attempt at social media regulation may well get more sympathetic attention from the likes of Barrett and other justices.

In any case, social media companies themselves might conceive of more ways to enshrine the right of reply in their platform's governance and functionality. Where individuals and groups are insulted and criticized, even when they encounter hate speech, the right of reply stands as a rule of elementary fair play. Communications systems could more frequently allow persons and groups to stand up for themselves and talk back, to not allow accusations and slurs to go unopposed, and for algorithms to ensure proportionate publicity for multiple sides. Mandating another fairness doctrine may not be workable. But a spirit of responsible platform behavior could be promoted through an ongoing, audit-based process of review. Further, there must be ways for citizens to get access to these rights, to even the playing field more between media and communications owners and the average-citizen voices and users of those platforms. Any new regulatory regime in the United States could validate such techniques and approaches that offer the right of reply, counting such measures as part of platforms' responsible stewardship. Even *Tornillo* does not preclude platforms from proactively choosing to establish a version of their right of reply on their platforms as part of their duty of care, and for government to see such platform policies as a valid tool in their exercise of responsible management in the public interest.

MARKETPLACE FAILURE

The policy and enforcement questions for content moderators on social platforms directly echo wider debates that have recurred through the ages for democratic societies and potential regulations relating to speech and communication. How far can ideas go before they are too dangerous for public consumption? How hateful can they be before they are considered incitements to violence or threats? At what point does tolerance of subversive ideas go too far, threatening democratic life and the survival of a community? These are pressing questions in the age of social media and the era of "digital democracy," a whole new field of research that is just coming into being.[34] Such questions seem increasingly pressing with each passing day, with each new threat, conflict, and global controversy.

And yet the questions raised often seem so novel, and highly context-dependent, as to induce paralysis. Attempts to create any kind of general rules, to referee or to "moderate," can seem almost naive during a time when a deluge of viral ideas appears to seep through every crack in the communications landscape, like them or not.

The chief reality we must acknowledge—and live with—is that there is no single, linear progression of thought, action, or case law that can help us build some idealized speech situation that is both First Amendment–preserving and protective against every conceivable harm or offense. There has never been a time of perfect balancing between expression and safety, speech and harms, selling and exploiting, protesting and subverting. The messy situation we now see being played out on social media, both domestically and around the world, is mirrored by a very messy past and evolving set of historical frameworks and rules prior to the digital era. Progress in communications rulemaking, such as it has ever come about, has often come in fits and starts, with contingency and ambiguity haunting policies at every step.

Entering the 2020s, the United States, and many other democracies, had hit a maximum point of policy inertia in the digital communications realm. Free market-inspired ideas solidified this inertia in recent decades, making public policy seemingly impossible with respect to the new communications technologies. Scholars characterize this free market-propelled movement as being defined by "consumer sovereignty."[35] The basic theory is that everyone should have full choice over anything that the private marketplace can and wants to provide, and public policy should be limited and modest. Following a deregulatory trend in the United States beginning in the 1970s and 1980s of the communications (and many other) industries,[36] we have reached a logical conclusion: Many people now seem unable to imagine regulation of almost any aspect of public discourse, except that of traditional television and radio (both of which can now be streamed digitally, making even that regulation largely moot).

For a century, the central idea that has structured thinking and rules around the speech and communication environment has been the metaphor of a "marketplace," where things can be bought and sold, traded and exchanged. However, this seemingly simple concept, or metaphor, has its own set of complexities, as there are questions about, figuratively speaking, the design of the speech market, who owns the space, and who decides who the sellers are and what the prices may be. The marketplace metaphor, or its variants, has infused policy thinking across the generations. Today, social media platform companies' own internal policies draw on the metaphor, and it influences their decision frameworks as they remove content, reduce its reach, or label it. The metaphor's long history demands unpacking.

As the Hutchins Commission swung into full gear in the mid-1940s, one of the chief academics involved, Harold Lasswell, decided to make sure that his fellow commissioners were fully informed about the debate over universal principles relating to expression, speech, knowledge, and democracy. To do this, he looked not to recent Supreme Court cases but to the years approximately 399 BCE, and 1644 and 1859 AD—to the works of Plato (*Apology*), John Milton (*Areopagitica*), and John Stuart Mill (*On Liberty*), respectively.[37] Lasswell apparently distributed copies of these works. Plato gave voice to the character of Socrates, who at his trial and death in the *Apology* argued that he had a moral duty to pursue the higher cause of truth relentlessly, rather than submit to the civil authorities who made false accusations against him. Milton argued against the state suppression of printed materials, asserting that free expression is most likely to lead to truth. And famously, Mill articulated the "harm principle," whereby the "sole end for which mankind are warranted, individually or collectively in interfering with the liberty of action of any of their number, is self-protection. That the only purpose for which power can be rightfully exercised over any member of a civilized community, against his will, is to prevent harm to others."[38] These concepts provide some of the classic conceptual frameworks that are used to justify the wide-open circulation of ideas in a society—or how wide open the marketplace should be, and why.

Such classical arguments put on the table fundamental big ideas, but there is another dimension of the free speech question that also deserves to be raised. This dimension relates to the question of social norms and social validation. What if many ideas are just ignored because they are considered too radical? Perhaps the death of such ideas will not come from the censor's hand, but rather from silence, indifference, even mockery and laughter. The free-market libertarian Joseph Overton put forth the thesis that there is a window of discourse that is acceptable on any given policy issue, and the way to change what is mainstream is to widen the window by powerfully advocating for unpopular ideas.[39] The "Overton window" is a way of thinking about where the boundaries are on the spectrum of any issue.

Yet perhaps the most enduring modern metaphor in this domain remains not that of building architecture and "windows," but that of commerce and commercial life. The concept of the "marketplace of ideas" is a central framing concept and metaphor that has guided much of the public's (and policymakers') thinking in the United States—and ultimately, in the twenty-first century, has scaled in peculiar ways to the world. To understand this central concept, we must return to a point in time a century ago, in the aftermath of World War I, when this key concept would come to dominate Americans' thinking about free speech and censorship was born. The "marketplace of ideas," coined in a dissenting opinion in the Supreme Court case *Abrams v. United States*, decided on November 10, 1919, carried with it a ring of common-sense pragmatism and a nod to commerce and capitalism.[40] The concept seemed apt for a diverse and bustling new industrial superpower that had just arrived on the global stage. The theory it contained was simple. Bad words, weird words, upsetting words, perhaps dangerous words—these would face equal competition in the metaphorical marketplace with other kinds of words and ideas. And in theory, the better words would win.[41]

Yet it was never that simple, and the metaphor has always been deceptive. Notably, Supreme Court Justice Oliver Wendell Holmes never actually wrote those precise words, instead noting that the "best test of truth is the power of the thought to get itself accepted in the competition of the market."[42] The idea itself was not even decisive in the case. Holmes coined the idea in dissent of a strong 7–2 majority opinion, in which his colleagues reaffirmed the sentencing of a group of people to prison (most of whose lives eventually ended in sickness, exile, and misery).[43] Issues of cultural clash and increasing diversity in the country provided important context in this situation. Over the three decades prior to the marketplace coinage in the 1919 case, the United States had taken in masses of people from many corners of the globe, millions through Ellis Island alone, and many came with new ideas. Among these were people of Russian origin who retained moral ties to the homeland—and to some of the ideas, such as anti-government anarchism, that had just helped birth the new workers' revolution in Russia. A half-dozen such persons in New York City—all Russian-born Jews—held the idea that the U.S. government was not legitimate. Jacob Abrams, Mollie Steimer, Hyman Lachowsky, Jacob Schwartz, Gabriel Prober, and Samuel Lipman were self-declared rebel "revolutionists" and anarchists. None had bothered to apply for naturalization, but for five or ten years had simply lived in the United States among the masses of other new immigrants. Now, as the United States was finishing up prosecuting a war on the European continent in aid of its allies, it had made moves to aid the old regime in Russia against the Bolshevik Revolution led by Lenin. Begun in 1917, that revolution had heightened fears across the United States about leftist movements; related domestic terrorism and bombings had shaken the U.S. domestic political landscape.

In 1918, the group of Russian emigres decided to protest. They did so by throwing leaflets out of a Manhattan building in English and Yiddish that aimed to change the course of U.S. military aims. "Know you lovers of freedom that, in order to save the Russian revolution, we must keep the armies of the allied countries busy at home," one leaflet stated. The revolutionists stated that they intended to create so "great a disturbance that the autocrats of America shall be compelled to keep their armies at home, and not be able to spare any for Russia."[44] Following the leafleting, all six immigrants were indicted and charged with violating the Espionage Act of 1917 and related subsequent amendments, which restricted interference with military operations or recruitment and government conduct of the war effort, among other things.

It was in this context that Holmes objected. He had supported other government actions to stop persons from interfering with the war efforts and upheld the wartime limits on subversive actions and expression. But in this case, *Abrams v. United States*, the authorities had gone too far, Holmes believed: "It is only the present danger of immediate evil or an intent to bring it about that warrants Congress in setting a limit to the expression of opinion where private rights are not concerned. Congress certainly cannot forbid all effort to change the mind of the country. Now nobody can suppose that the surreptitious publishing of a silly leaflet by an unknown man, without more, would present any immediate danger that its opinions would hinder the success of the government arms or have any appreciable tendency to do so."[45] These words were, in fact, some of the first to come from the high court to support limits on government's right to infringe on the free speech of individuals—even largely preventing punishments after the fact. It was part of a series of early free speech cases, decided a century ago now, that came to define both law and public norms. What gave Holmes's dissent particular power in this case was in part the stirring words he used to build toward the market metaphor, in what has become a widely quoted passage over the decades:

To allow opposition by speech seems to indicate that you think the speech impotent, as when a man says that he has squared the circle, or that you do not care wholeheartedly for the result, or that you doubt either your power or your premises. But when men have realized that time has upset many fighting faiths, they may come to believe even more than they believe the very foundations of their own conduct that the ultimate good desired is better reached by free trade in ideas—that the best test of truth is the power of the thought to get itself accepted in the competition of the market, and that truth is the only ground upon which their wishes safely can be carried out. That, at any rate, is the theory of our Constitution. It is an experiment, as all life is an experiment.[46]

We may believe we know the truth and have a "fighting faith" in such belief. But because some further "experiment"—some new event or revelation—may determine something new about the world, a "free trade in ideas" is the only sure path to ultimate truth.

For much of early U.S. history, such principles relating to protections for speech and expression had remained weak and often dormant, overridden by local laws and community norms. Earlier in his career, Holmes himself had endorsed the view that the First Amendment only prevented prior restraints on publication, not punishment for words after the fact. But in a series of cases following World War I that included *Abrams*, Holmes's words provided fresh justification for a new kind of constitutional—and societal—interpretation and an invigorated First Amendment.

METAPHORICAL STRUGGLES

On June 8, 1789, James Madison had proposed the embryonic ideas that would ultimately become, after some workshopping in congressional committee, the First Amendment and its protections for speech and the press: "The people shall not be deprived or abridged of their right to speak, to write, or to publish their sentiments; and the freedom of the press, as one of the great bulwarks of liberty, shall be inviolable."[47] But for 130 years in the country's history, free expression in its full form—largely protected not just from prior restraint but even from post-publication, after-the-fact punishment—was not a right generally enforced by the courts for individuals, and much discretion had been left to state and local governments.

Scholars have noted that, while freedom of expression rights and ideals have a rich history in Enlightenment thought,[48] there was no legally effective, actively implemented protection of the freedom of speech in the United States for much of the country's first century and a half.[49] The First Amendment of the United States Constitution reads, with the addition of freedoms of religion and assembly, "Congress shall make no law . . . abridging the freedom of speech, or of the press." Behind these words of the First Amendment is a fraught and contentious history of ideas. In the minds of the Founders were precursors: coauthors John Trenchard and Thomas Gordon's *Cato's Letters* (1720–1723), written under the pseudonym Cato (95–46 BC), in which the two British pamphleteers articulate the importance of free speech to free government.[50] Beyond Trenchard and Gordon, an intellectual genealogy stretches back to Milton's *Areopagitica* (1644),[51] which uses marketplace-type concepts to emphasize the importance of free expression.[52] Yet there is no linear path from these ideas. Despite George Washington's and Alexander Hamilton's warnings, the Founders descended into factionalism; ideals relating to free expression diverged as different party leaders contended for power in America's early decades.[53]

The First Amendment was not always a virtually absolute protection of freedom of speech—the prevailing view of today. The Founders had no such view. The John Adams administration signed the Sedition Act in 1798, severely restricting certain forms of political speech. That law sent the likes of James Thomson Callender to prison for writing violating speech and disseminating it through political pamphlets.[54] Further, Adams and the Federalists were not the only ones to question free speech. Thomas Jefferson, Adams's political opponent, thought the press should be liable for "false facts" and defamation.[55] Through a process of hindsight bias[56] and ideological backfilling,[57] we have, scholars believe, traced a historical line from Milton, through Trenchard and Gordon to John Stuart Mill,[58] and up through *Abrams*. But that provides a false sense of First Amendment jurisprudence, hiding the historical contingency and relative recency of today's prevailing principles.

Legal scholar Stanley Ingber has called the marketplace of ideas a "legitimizing myth," a deceptively pliable system of thought that maintains the status quo and does not give power to the voiceless.[59] The modern presentation of the marketplace metaphor has twisted the historical record of free speech thinking: It was originally a tool to check abuses of power or emphasize the value of free thinking (as emphasized by, for example, John Stuart Mill), but it has become a weird method of achieving some kind of market equilibrium.[60] Of course, free speech metaphors have often proved both resilient and slippery. For instance, "shouting fire in a crowded theatre" from *Schenck v. United States* (1919), a case that is a kind of closely related companion to *Abrams*, is still used as an example of a situation where speech may be banned.[61] The marketplace metaphor continues to be used in all manner of public and expert discourse.

References to a "marketplace of ideas" were actually rare in Supreme Court cases from the 1920s through the 1950s and only began to become rhetorically prominent starting in the 1970s, about a half-century after Holmes's dissent first codified the metaphor.[62] Then, as it picked up speed in public usage, it was employed by justices in favor of both communication regulation *and* deregulation.[63] The marketplace of ideas was used, for example, to buttress the validity of the Fairness Doctrine in *Red Lion Broadcasting Co. v. FCC* (1969).[64] But then the metaphor's meaning morphed. During the Reagan era, the metaphor was used to promote neoliberal deregulation in communication as well as other areas of life.[65] Here the deregulatory ideology also was influenced by economic thinking that emphasized the efficiency of open markets to aggregate important signals, ideas propounded by the likes of Friedrich A. Hayek and Milton Friedman.[66] Ultimately, the regulatory battles suggest that the marketplace metaphor can be leveraged by nearly anyone, with any position. The resilience and impact of the metaphor has less to do with its ability to frame speech situations clearly, but rather because the metaphor can legitimize conflicting views.

POST-MARKETPLACE ERA?

All of this brings us back to the marketplace of ideas metaphor and its relationship to content moderation and platforms. Simply put, the metaphor is failing. We need something new.

In recent years, the marketplace metaphor has been central to how social media platforms thought about themselves, their role in modern communication, and their approach to content moderation.[67] Historical marketplaces took the shape of the town square, newspapers, pamphlets, or broadcasting, but today's modern "public square," as Supreme Court Justice Anthony Kennedy in *Packingham v. North Carolina* (2017) suggested, is social media.[68] However, the history, structure, moderation practices, technological affordances, and business of social media have twisted the marketplace beyond traditional recognition. As early as the 1990s, commentators began to warn of the inadequacies of the metaphor for the internet, and many of their concerns have become only more valid since the advent of the social web.[69]

If internet platforms are the modern locale for the marketplace of ideas, then there are several problems with the market's function, including these three: One, social media provides for multiple sharing and expressive functions, and thus there are participants who engage in activities on the platforms that do not involve ideas at all, nor do the participants necessarily have an interest in ideas in the first place. The problem is that the non-idea activities take place in the same arena as idea-based exchange. Some participants deliberately purvey noise, rather than ideas; some commentators have analogized their presence as "pollution."[70] Two, when purveyors and buyers of ideas are engaged in idea-based activities on social media, ideas rarely compete, and the participatory role of social media blurs the line between buyer and seller. And three, a true free marketplace of ideas requires free entry into, and exit from, that market. Freedom of access, if it has ever been true about the marketplace of ideas, certainly cannot be applied to today's digital public square in which social media platforms are regulated by private corporations with evolving moderation regimes.

The metaphor simply does not apply to our current dynamic environment of information exchange, distributed as it is across the internet and applications, and guided by algorithms.[71] Technological affordances, network structure, and human behavior affect social conditions online, and in turn, limit the usefulness of treating the interactions as a marketplace. Furthermore, the unsuitability of the marketplace metaphor poorly frames society's discussion of how freedom of expression, and by extension content moderation, should be conducted online.

Simply put: the marketplace of ideas is the wrong model to regulate platformed communication. Fortunately, it is not the only historical model we have available to us. It may be difficult to justify a full-on public interest standard for social media platforms, the likes of which long governed how broadcasters used the scarce airwave frequencies. However, a policy requiring socially responsible management of communications platforms, with regular auditing and disclosure to reinforce broad norms and expectations as well as constant court oversight, remains promising. Whatever is implemented, it must seek to avoid micromanagement and speech-infringing overregulation, lest the whole effort run into profound First Amendment difficulties. The key is to define responsibility around bedrock democratic principles such as providing counterspeech—and attending more broadly to a need to be responsive as a management obligation. Of course, there will need to be some limits defined, and these will include controversial categories of behavior, content, and expression. It is here that the concept of responsible and responsive governance must be applied to our new communications technologies' capacity for producing new varieties of social or systemic harms and risk. We need to define better what these risks are. The following chapters unpack the areas of disinformation, hate speech, incitement, and AI-generated misinformation, and for these categories of harm, they consider what socially responsible management might look like.

2

DISINFORMATION: DEEPER HISTORY

To illuminate the mechanisms of propaganda is to reveal the secret springs of social action, and to expose to the most searching criticism our prevailing dogmas of sovereignty, of democracy, of honesty, and of the sanctity of individual opinion.[1]

—Harold Lasswell, *Propaganda Technique in the World War* (1927)

Political warfare. *Dezinformacija*. Active measures. Propaganda. *Désinformation*. Computational propaganda. Networked propaganda. Influence operations. Fake news. Lies. Damned lies . . .[2]

Both the past and present are littered with terms like these that attempt to capture the idea that some messages are not what they appear to be. Our "disinformation age" abounds with definitional controversies and arcane arguments over what exactly we are talking about when we say "disinformation," a term thought to be originally borrowed from the Russian *dezinformacija*.[3] Some people now think that the study of disinformation is itself some kind of partisan disinformation campaign. It brings to mind an ancient logical paradox: "Epimenides the Cretan says, 'All the Cretans are liars.'"

Beyond dispute are two facts that represent both a quantitative and qualitative change in how information travels in global societies: First, digital technologies have enabled a global onslaught of something we might loosely call "disinformation," with generative artificial intelligence systems poised to accelerate this trend; second, the demand for disinformation appears to have grown, both because more people are susceptible to it given personalized, digitally enabled targeting strategies (thus inviting more actors to take advantage) and because authoritative institutions (the press, government, universities) have lost trust and their ability to ground people in facts.[4] Trends in politics, the business model of social media, and underlying sociocultural trends around identity and polarization fuel heightened risks of pervasive corrupted information.[5]

Still, there is always the possibility that the threat is being overhyped, but the resulting atmosphere of panic and skepticism itself leads to damaging distortions in the public sphere, as people begin to doubt everything. Scholars often find that those engaging with false information constitute small, highly motivated groups of individuals who actively seek it out, engage with it, and spread it.[6] The degree of public exposure to false information depends on the event and the context, but the average phenomenon primarily involves small slices of social media users.

The capaciousness of "disinformation" seems to group together disparate communication acts that have little in common. Should a shady advertising campaign touting an unproven health supplement be treated analytically the same as a set of fake news stories intended to swing an election? When a person says on Twitter (X) that she accepts the possibility of human-induced climate change, but does not think the problem is that bad currently, is that statement a form of "disinformation"? What about a political candidate who says he will balance the budget within a single term, when it is financially impossible to do so? Or a kid falsifying a parent's signature on a report card? Scale and degree of harm must be considered in what counts as "disinformation."

The types of disinformation that have attracted the most attention from researchers are those threatening core democratic/government functions, such as ensuring free and fair elections and public health, but disinformation affects many other domains, from perceptions of immigrants and collective political will to address climate change to such perpetually vexing areas as public understanding of historical events (the Holocaust, the JFK assassination, the Moon landing, the 9/11 attacks) and the lives of celebrities.[7] The World Wide Web has proven to be the greatest knowledge tool in history, as well as a kind of open invitation to treasure hunt—a gamified playing field for skeptics[8]—based on random-seeming conspiracy theories. As the conspiracy groups like to say, "Do your own research."

Clearly, disinformation is dangerous. It can lead to mob violence, discredit democratic processes, and prompt people to make poor decisions about their health, finances, and life choices. For the most part, however, disinformation—and its cousin, misinformation—are not subject to regulation in the United States. The country's legal traditions understand disinformation and misinformation to be (mostly) constitutionally protected forms of speech. Private companies that run communications platforms have broad discretion over how they choose to moderate content. Over the past decade, new platforms have begun to address mis- and disinformation on their own by labeling misleading information (providing warning labels and contextual information, for example) and providing fact-checking at greater scale. Companies have also used their algorithmic ranking tools to attempt to limit the spread of disinformation.

All of these tools—labeling, fact-checking, and downranking—are imperfect, but they hold great promise if done correctly, and with sufficient energy and resources behind them. New AI tools also make it more likely that these approaches can be scaled. U.S. regulatory efforts could validate these approaches as tools for addressing systemic risks and patterns of harm, without endorsing censorship. But to understand why this approach might be workable—and how it fits into past traditions and thinking—we need to understand what mis- and disinformation are.

WHAT IS DISINFORMATION?

In distinguishing disinformation from misinformation, or even mere confusion, scholars and observers tend to focus on a central issue: intention.[9] If a social media user shares a manipulated image unknowingly or even carelessly—"Look at this shark swimming through a flooded road!"—that person is being misinformed and is misinforming others. There was no intention, *per se*. The person who doctored the photo by inserting a shark, and then shared it, is plausibly creating disinformation (in this case perhaps just for attention, or for clicks and money.) For something to be considered disinformation, it needs to be calculated and part of a strategy to deceive a person or group, without them knowing.[10] Disinformation also frequently involves true information reframed or taken out of context, or true information that is interspersed with minor falsehoods. It might be fabricated, manipulated, misleading, or suggestive in a way that falsely connects things. There nevertheless remains debate about where, exactly, the line between disinformation and misinformation falls.

The terms "propaganda" and "disinformation" have considerable overlap in meaning, and experts parse them in slightly different ways. "Propaganda" has been used since the seventeenth century (originally with a more benign meaning, as in promoting religious ideas),[11] while "disinformation" is a mid-twentieth-century coinage of Soviet-Stalinist origin. In a defining work for the contemporary research field, *Network Propaganda: Manipulation, Disinformation, and Radicalization in American Politics* (2018), Yochai Benkler, Robert Faris, and Hal Roberts at Harvard's Berkman Klein Center suggest that the distinction between the two concepts is increasingly blurred: What we often think of as the social media-driven problem of mis- and disinformation is, in fact, a deeper political and structural problem of the information environment.[12] Social media voices then amplify such corrupted information. In this context, these scholars have updated the definitions of the terms. They define "propaganda" as "communication designed to manipulate a target population by affecting its beliefs, attitudes, or preferences in order to obtain behavior compliant with political goals of the propagandist."[13] By contrast, they define "disinformation" as "dissemination of explicitly false or misleading information," which stands as a "subset of propaganda."[14] Under this set of definitions, then, the lower-level category of disinformation always sits logically underneath the broader umbrella of propaganda, which is itself a higher-level category that relates to population-targeting with political purpose.

Scholars in national security, social science, and more humanities-oriented fields frequently disagree on exactly where the lines are among these and related terms, with some contesting the coherence of disinformation as a field of study.[15] Those who do study it find that it can be analyzed at three levels: content, reception, and production.[16] In practice, this means examining three different aspects of potential disinformation: the messages themselves (the content); how they do or don't get in people's heads (reception), and the structures and incentives that motivate people to create disinformation (production).

We can also think about the problem historically. Even as disinformation campaigns consistently have as their goal an attempt to erode a population's faith in "factual authority," their specific objectives have changed over time.[17] Over the past century, disinformation has transformed from careful, hand-crafted interventions designed to trick journalists to industrial-level troll farms directly targeting voters. If early-twentieth-century propaganda focused on public opinion management, contemporary propaganda seeks to erode faith in democratic institutions.

The tactics—the practical ways of carrying out disinformation campaigns—are also diverse. In our current moment, digital technologies have transformed the art and the science of disinformation into something that easily scales across the globe. Contemporary techniques include cultivating fake online personas, accounts, and websites; using bots and computational tools to amplify messages using networks of accounts (what technology companies sometimes call "coordinated inauthentic behavior"); generating fake and synthetic images and videos; and amplifying existing conspiracy theories or devising fresh ones. Disinformation practitioners might also set up alternative platforms to help form group solidarity and activate allies. To further the reach of their campaign, they might get unsuspecting groups to repeat messages, target vulnerable groups who might already have sympathies toward a particular alternative belief, or generally exploit what are called "data voids," in which a Google search, for example, does not produce much credible information because the topic is novel or the event/issue is partially fabricated.[18] As Kate Starbird of the University of Washington has noted, some mass phenomena online are best characterized as "participatory disinformation" campaigns, enlisting both elites and influencers as well as average citizens in building and constructing false narratives.[19]

How did we get to this crisis point? How might society defend, inoculate, and prepare itself? And how does the history of disinformation relate to our present? The modern tale, at least, of disinformation begins almost exactly a century ago. Many aspects of the story continue to haunt us today—but they also provide keys to unlocking potential solutions.[20] At the modern origin point of the disinformation story, competing approaches and ways of understanding the possibilities and perils began to evolve. For simplicity's sake, let's consider the views of three "types"— the sales rep, the skeptic, and the scientist.

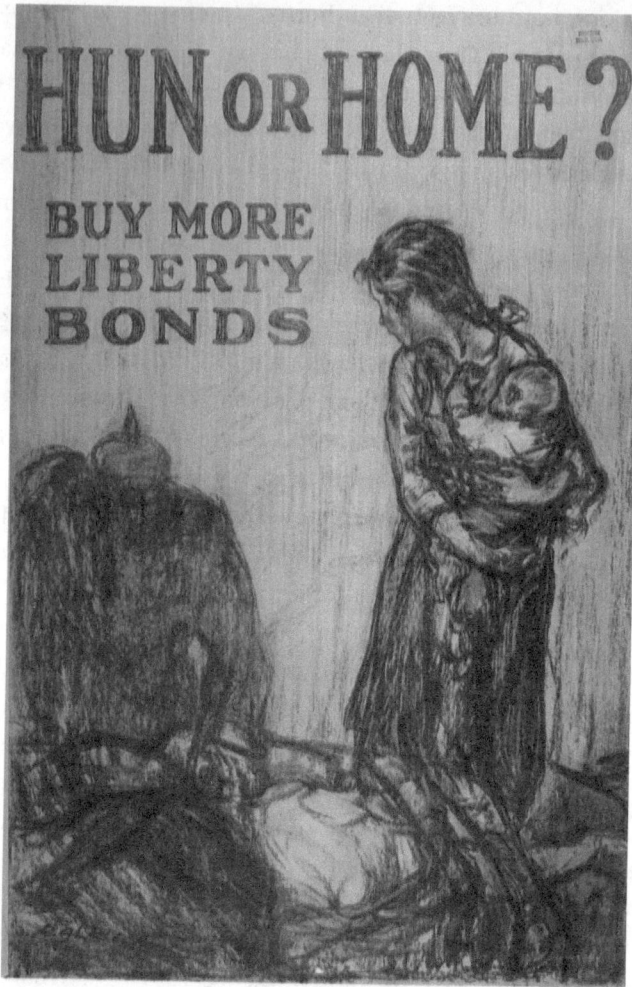

Figure 2.1 A U.S. poster from World War I, featuring a menacing German soldier ("Hun"). The war saw a massive proliferation of propaganda efforts on all sides. Library of Congress, Prints & Photographs Division, LC-USZC4-10331.

THE SALES REP AND THE FOURTH OF JULY FAKE

On the night of June 22, 1917, a convoy of American boats was plowing through whitecaps in the mid-Atlantic, racing to get the first batch of U.S. soldiers to Europe, where World War I had already been underway for three years. According to the admiral in charge, Albert Gleaves, an unusually brilliant phosphorescence speckled the ocean. The night was overcast and moonless, and a fresh breeze from the northwest whipped the waves.[21]

The first sign of trouble came at 10:13 p.m.: a perceptible white streak in the water off the bow of a ship, running starboard to port. The torpedo launched by an unseen, presumed U-Boat was followed by more, and U.S. gunners fired back into the night, their spotlights circling over the waves. The outcome was murky to all sailors involved. Perhaps a U-Boat was sunk; signs were that the gunners might have got it.[22]

The incident passed, and the ships sailed on. The skirmish ended with no casualties on the American side, and no ships damaged. By July 3, the last of this first batch of American soldiers would disembark in the French port of Saint-Nazaire, unscathed, to join the Allied fight. Across the United States, political and military leaders had been nervous, as General John J. Pershing's expeditionary force had faced real peril as it crossed through an ocean filled with U-Boats. The press had been under orders to print nothing until they landed. When Secretary of the Navy Josephus Daniels was originally told of the safe passage, tears came to his eyes. "What a Fourth of July present for the people!" he said to an aide.[23]

With the soldiers safely on French soil, every newspaper in the country printed the details of their ordeal. Headlines and front pages trumpeted the narrow escape and the happy ending. The public went wild with patriotic exultation and "joyful enthusiasm."[24]

Then came the backlash.

Correspondents in Europe were puzzled. They were hearing from their sources that the expeditionary force had faced no such submarine attacks. It was a fabrication, they believed.[25] An Associated Press reporter aboard on the voyage also reported that it had been smooth sailing. Suddenly, the press was inflamed with news of differing accounts of the passage; this ballooned into a scandal, and political rancor broke out. Republican

Senator Boies Penrose of Pennsylvania demanded an investigation not only of the "Fourth of July Fake," but also of the new wartime machinery of public information that had been built by the Democratic administration of President Woodrow Wilson.

Eventually, when some of the underlying documents were released to the press, it turned out that the sailors running the operation on the high seas had, in fact, believed they had been attacked multiple times by U-Boats and had fired shots accordingly. Given that the Navy had divided the operation into four different groups of boats, it was entirely possible that some boats had witnessed something that they believed to be an attack, while others had not. The whole incident, and cries of embellishment and propagandistic fakery, turned on a misunderstanding. Wilson provided evidence and demanded corrections, but, as corrections are wont to do, they received little prominence or public notice.

In the middle of all the commotion was a former journalist named George Edward Creel, who was leading a newly created government body called the Committee on Public Information. Creel had become, to put it simply, America's original propagandist—the war's chief salesman. And in this "Fourth of July Fake" incident, he got a first taste of how the business of persuasive messaging and managing public opinion is a complicated game. Years later, after the war, Creel would lament that portions of the public still believed they had been deceived and that the U.S. Navy flotilla had had an uneventful voyage. And the press would long remember the incident as the first of many perceived embellishments and deceptions.[26]

Born December 1, 1876, in the town of Blackburn, Missouri (population 214 in the 1880 Census), George Creel had by the age of eighteen begun his writing career at the Kansas City *World*. Like many journalists of that era, his work was a mix of reporting and partisan political crusading. Often sporting a three-piece suit, his dark hair slicked back and intense brown eyes suggesting a kind of pugnacity, Creel was a type—albeit a particularly talented version—of the early partisan "pressman." Having written newspaper columns on behalf of the Democratic National Committee and a 1916 campaign book titled *Wilson and the Issues*, Creel leveraged his connections to power, his campaign work, and his talents to become part of the inner circle of advisors to President Wilson.[27]

Propaganda and press-based deceptions—the use of fake stories, slanders, and general attempts to manipulate public understanding of events—had played a role in political affairs since the American Revolution, with the likes of Benjamin Franklin and Paul Revere stirring patriotism and organizing rebellion against the King's soldiers through slanted stories, slogans, and symbols. Later, the administration of President Abraham Lincoln had used propaganda techniques, censored journalists, and flooded the public with wartime messages to try to keep the Union united against the seceding states. But Creel's Committee on Public Information in World War I was like nothing the country had ever seen before.

Creel's committee, operating at the dawn of the broadcast age, ventured into all manner of propaganda and public opinion. It produced endless forms of persuasive media across every conceivable genre of communication; enlisted artists and writers by the thousands to produce reams of propaganda; issued strict oversight and censorship requirements across all manner of commercial news, entertainment, and opinion media; and co-opted thousands of advertisers, civic and religious groups, post offices, draft boards, and many newspapers. The Committee on Public Information recruited some seventy-five thousand people to roam the country giving brief, patriotic speeches. These speakers, dubbed the "Four Minute Men" for the duration of their sermons, fanned out across the country like an army of religious proselytizers fanatically pursuing new souls to save.[28] The committee's iconic posters, including Uncle Sam's "I want YOU for the U.S. Army," and "Boys and Girls, You can help Uncle Sam win the war. Save Your Quarters. Buy War Savings Stamps," are indelibly written into popular history and culture.

The committee additionally created ten foreign language bureaus within the United States that coerced communities to participate in patriotic exercises and rituals of devotion to the country. Creel wrote later that he wanted "no mere surface unity, but a passionate belief in the justice of America's cause that [could] weld the people of the United States into one white-hot mass instinct with fraternity, devotion, courage, and deathless determination."[29] In the context of the United States during World War I, this had all sorts of problematic moral and civil rights implications. Yet the true potential damage of propaganda only would be realized two decades later, with the rise of the Nazi regime in Germany.

The Committee on Public Information proceeded with such power and swiftness that it was often at odds with other branches of the government, including the Army, Navy, and War Departments.[30] At times, Creel's attempts at censorship were so excessive that the *New York Times*, generally supportive of the Wilson administration's policies, suggested that American news was better known in Germany than in the States.[31]

For many who study the history of propaganda and disinformation, Creel's Committee on Public Information represented a turning point in states' understanding of what propaganda could, or should, accomplish. As a founding moment in twentieth-century disinformation, Creel's "Fourth of July Fake" points to larger, almost universal, truths that would later characterize propaganda and large-scale efforts to influence mass opinion.

The first lesson relates to how states' attempts to control the media erodes journalists' trust in sources of information, often in ways that are irreversible. In May 1917, a month before Pershing's troops sailed, Creel had locked horns with newspaper editors over the administration's censorship—or, if you prefer, "war reporting"—guidelines. Although the Committee on Public Information claimed that these guidelines were to be voluntary and self-imposed, they carried a strong whiff of potential retribution. "Censor Creel" had also, reportedly, been personally calling newspaper editors to try to shape editorial opinion pieces.[32] The press would, throughout the war, accuse Creel and the committee of suppressing bad news and putting a positive spin on events.[33] So a month later, when Creel attempted to issue statements suggesting that the brave Navy boats ferrying America's soldiers had valiantly fought through a sea of the Kaiser's U-Boats, the press was disinclined to believe him. His words had lost credibility; his motives were already suspect in many political and media circles.

The second lesson is about how disinformation, or even the appearance of it, corrupts truth by stoking an audience's skepticism. Creel's accounts to the press and the public turned out to be *true*. Yet, because the original story had been called into doubt, the public ended up frozen in its skepticism. It made sense, at some level, that Censor Creel would embellish the story to get the public fired up for the war effort. Having been primed to doubt something, the public then wanted to doubt it.

The final early lesson is that efforts at public deception often "boomerang" on communities and societies that tolerate or support such actions, creating doubt where a society may want certainty. Creel's goal was to build public support for the Wilson administration's war effort. Give its explicit role as a propaganda outfit, the Committee on Public Information faced challenges in convincing people that anything it said was true—even if it were factual. Further, the corruption of mainstream, private information sources produces its own kind of boomerang effects in democracies. The incident created an almost generation-long ripple effect that undermined the public's trust in the press.[34]

Ultimately, the "Fourth of July Fake" was just a minor incident in the overall sweep of the history of America's involvement in World War I. Yet, Creel's work time and again over the course of the war suggested a vast set of possibilities for how those in power might manipulate truth and public opinion, ones that would be developed by careful practitioners after the war. The lessons from World War I would reverberate over the next century, from the rise of the Nazis, through the Cold War, and on into the digital era of information warfare and cybersecurity, to January 6, 2021, and beyond.

THE SKEPTIC'S PROCESS

Almost as soon as sophisticated thinking had sprouted about how to carry out population-level campaigns to manipulate attitudes, a critical counter-tradition began to form, one that also has trickled down through the years to our time.

Walter Lippmann had been trained at Harvard (class of 1910) by some of the nation's leading philosophers; within a few years of graduating from college, he had already made a national name for himself by founding *The New Republic* magazine. Like Creel, Lippmann's early career blurred journalism and politics; he made his living through news work, but his informal advising work and his social circles commingled politics and politicians. Lippmann had been a socialist, then a more realist progressive, and in any case always a liberal.

By 1917, Lippmann, who by now had a reputation as a leading liberal voice, had become utterly disgusted with how Creel and the Committee on Public Information were carrying out the business of democracy in war time. He began approaching top Wilson advisors to address what he perceived to be the excesses of the administration and the Committee. Lippmann would write to one high official: "So far as I am concerned, I have no doctrinaire belief in free speech. In the interest of the war it is necessary to sacrifice some of it. But the point is that the method now being pursued is breaking down the liberal support of the war and is tending to divide the country's articulate opinion into fanatical jingoism and fanatical pacifism."[35]

There were factions within the high-octane world of American propaganda efforts, and Lippmann joined a newly created effort, formed outside (and rivalrous with) the Committee on Public Information, to shape the postwar situation in Europe. In July 1919, Lippmann donned an Army uniform and, having been designated "Captain Lippmann," was sent to Europe to serve in the Military Intelligence Division. Despite being just a captain, Lippman operated at the highest levels, advising the White House and the Secretary of War, and participating in the propaganda efforts that would set up future postwar treaties and agreements. He would be part of the effort to prepare the world for a new order through the Treaty of Versailles and the League of Nations.

It is perhaps one of the great ironies of media history, therefore, that America's foremost early scholar of the press and public opinion crystallized his own most penetrating, enduring, and skeptical insights by working within a propaganda organization himself. A kind of inverse character to the figure of Creel, Lippmann saw up close the foibles and failures created by the propaganda-driven universe, and his trepidations would only grow through his writings in the years to come. In an astonishingly productive half-decade period, Lippman published a kind of trilogy of books, *Liberty and the News* (1920), *Public Opinion* (1922), and *The Phantom Public* (1925), which traced the trajectory of his increasingly bleak thinking about the relationship between information and democracy. Modern society, in his view, had increasingly run out of the informational tools to manage itself successfully. More and more, modern societies were running according to a kind of destructive illusion about citizens within democracies and their plausible capacities and roles.

During World War I and its aftermath, Lippmann had seen the press report an avalanche of false news and fake facts. Part of this early "post-truth" environment came about through the work of the various national combatants' propaganda machines. But Lippmann also came to believe that, even under better conditions, the press could not be expected to produce accurate pictures of the world. "Everywhere to-day men are conscious," he wrote in *Liberty and the News*, "that somehow they must deal with questions more intricate than any that church or school had prepared them to understand."[36] Neither the press nor the citizens were equipped to handle the questions of domestic industrial policy, war and peace, trade and tariffs, or any number of complicated issues. Lippmann believed that the ideas about democracy that had been formulated by both the Greek philosophers including Plato and Aristotle and the European Enlightenment thinkers including Locke (and his heirs in Jefferson and Madison) had outlived their usefulness.

In 1922, just a few short years after concluding his political propaganda work for the Wilson administration, Lippmann published his masterpiece, *Public Opinion*. The book is a devastating critique of many things he had only recently been fighting for.[37] Today, the book stands as one of the most influential works on media and its relationship with democracy ever written in the United States. Its publication would spawn new fields and ways of thinking, including much of advertising and the field of public relations.[38] Generations of social scientists and philosophers would find its deep skepticism a real challenge to democratic theory.

For Lippmann, his experiences conducting propaganda on behalf of the Wilson administration led him to the startling and near-nihilistic conclusion that modern democracy could not work at all, under any conditions that he could imagine. As dangerous and deluding as propaganda is, the human mind itself—which must face the task of making sense of an increasingly sophisticated and complex society—could create just as many illusions. These were what Lippmann would call "pictures in our heads" or "stereotypes."[39] (We might today call them "stories" or "narratives.") No citizen, no matter how well informed, could be expected to keep up with the dizzying array of issues at play in a large, modern democracy. Yet democracies were continuing to operate under the false premise that their people could operate as "omnicompetent citizens," capable of providing rational, well-informed inputs to policymakers and leaders. Humans try to align what they believe to be true—the pictures in their heads—with the vast, mostly unseen, environment around them. They therefore operate in a "pseudo environment," a combination of the mental fictions they have produced and the real world around them.

In a small community, it might nevertheless be possible for citizens to play an informed and constructive role in a democracy. They might know enough to make good decisions. But in the ashes of World War I, with

Figure 2.2 British gunners fill shells with propaganda leaflets as they fight against Nazi forces in Holland in January 1945. In both World War I and World War II, the information side of warfare involved vast operations to persuade the other side to give up or turn against their leaders. The digital information warfare of the twenty-first century builds on a long tradition. No 5 Army Film & Photographic Unit, Palmer (Sgt), War Office Second World War Official Collection.

complex modern technologies coming online and citizens and their leaders facing hundreds of important decisions each day, the old model of
the omnicompetent citizen had collapsed. Democracies were essentially
operating now as a kind of fiction.

In *Public Opinion*, Lippmann provided a well-crafted list of the reasons
why citizens had neither the knowledge they needed, nor the underlying
facts required to produce knowledge: "The artificial censorships, the limitations of social contact, the comparatively meager time available in each
day for paying attention to public affairs, the distortion arising because
events have to be compressed into very short messages, the difficulty of
making a small vocabulary express a complicated world, and finally the
fear of facing those facts which would seem to threaten the established
routine of men's lives."[40] In this list, we see the root causes of many familiar, contemporary issues and problems afflicting twentieth-century society, including disinformation, xenophobia or prejudice, soundbite culture,
the limits of language, and basic human desires that feed confirmation
bias (the tendency to favor information supporting our existing beliefs
while ignoring contradictory evidence). Lippman essentially articulated
the research agenda for media and communication studies scholars for
the next one hundred years, which was to figure out how these six areas of
distortion, compression, and bias might affect humans and society.

Yet the solutions Lippmann offered in *Public Opinion* have left many
readers unsatisfied. Lippmann ultimately gave up on the idea that the
press can fill the void in democracy. He believed that asking news media
practitioners to inform society in any kind of deep and accurate way was
simply too much of a burden. But Lippmann nevertheless held out the
possibility that the world of expertise, of organized bureaus, agencies,
and proto-think tanks, could do the deeper work that the press failed at,
and citizens needed. The vision for such a knowledge machinery is a bit
vague, and critics have never quite been satisfied with those portions of
thinking in *Public Opinion*.

In the end, Lippmann too rejected this experts-based solution to disinformation. Within a few years after writing *Public Opinion*, he had become
even gloomier, and had essentially given up on articulating any particular
solution to the problems of the death of the omnicompetent citizen, the
manufacturing of consent—the use of propaganda to manipulate public

opinion—and the pervasive pseudo environment in which we all find ourselves. His follow-up book, *The Phantom Public*, suggests that there will never be a convincing or definitive answer to the problem of how individual citizens can participate intelligently in the collective business of democracy.[41]

Lippmann's ideas were so bleak that critics at the time did not know what to make of them. The work stirred the great American philosopher and social theorist John Dewey, with whom Lippmann is often juxtaposed, to write his book *The Public and Its Problems* (1927), which argued that democracy should be measured by its ability to produce grassroots deliberation and productive communication among citizens, not necessarily by its rational outcomes or institutions for knowledge-based decision-making.

Lippmann did, however, speculate on some abstract principles that might signal, at least, a process of public debate that had a prayer of succeeding, particularly in complex situations where there is no right answer. *The Phantom Public* contains some insights that have powerful resonance in the context of thinking about media governance—democracy, information, and propaganda—in any era, including our own. Ultimately, Lippmann chose *procedure* over articulating substantive rules for what is good for democracy. Procedure, rather than any specific objective, is how we are to judge the quality of media governance. Translated into contemporary problems of content moderation, a process-based approach emphasizes public transparency and the possibility for revision, rather than striving for ironclad rules.

Lippmann suggests that, in any public debate, over any issue, the procedure by which the public makes decisions determines the quality and merit of the decision. Lippmann leaves us with three rules for judging democratic decision-making. The first rule is about transparency, or "public inquiry," for determining whether one side in a dispute has served the public properly: a given side must not hide anything and must be willing to let the whole of their claim be subject to scrutiny. This "means simply that where the public is forced to intervene in a strange and complex affair, the test of public inquiry is the surest clue to the sincerity of the claimant."[42] For example, let's take the decision to go to war, perhaps the gravest of all decisions for a society. Has the public been given as full an accounting of reasons and motives as is possible? This is not to say that the public will not endorse a bad decision, but the first test is public inquiry and transparency.

The second rule for judgment relates to the right of revision of decisions. Can the decision be modified or reversed? If so, what is this process for amending and revisiting the situation? In the previous example, does the decision to go to war mean consenting to a "forever war," or can the decision be revised? Finally, Lippmann's third rule says that revision cannot be willy-nilly or indefinitely postponed; there must be "due notice," where the rules for revision and the timeline are known in advance, set down according to a procedure.[43]

While Lippmann had no grand solutions, he could see how certain principles must be present for any participatory democratic system involving knowledge and information to have a chance. These ideas map very well onto any content moderation regime. Transparency, capacity for revision, and orderly procedure for iteration—these are minimalist principles, but solid ones, that seek to order a chaotic new environment. From questions of truth and media to content moderation, these ideas have enduring merit. For policymaking, perhaps the most important is the core idea of "public inquiry" and transparency—all sides should explain themselves fully and be allowed to put the evidence out in the open for all to inspect. In terms of future regulation, particularly in the social media space, the ideas of proceduralism and public inquiry are crucial, as there are frequently no right answers. Lippmann identified the central democratic ingredients for creating any rules around expression, speech, and the flow of information. These rules must create publicity—allowing all sides to inspect the evidence—and have an orderly and predictable way of modifying decisions and rules.

As he moved out of his brooding intellectual stage in the 1920s, Lippman's deep ties to power and his growing reputation as an incisive public philosopher made him the most influential newspaper columnist in the United States. He again participated in covert and overt propaganda work during World War II, and served as an adviser to President Franklin D. Roosevelt,[44] and, two decades later, to President Lyndon Johnson. He died in 1974, having participated in one role or another for every twentieth-century Democratic presidential administration in his adult lifetime.

THE INFORMATION SCIENTIST

Over the course of his life, communications researcher Harold Lasswell would write, coauthor, or edit sixty books and more than three hundred articles—more than four million words in total. Wherever questions of ideas, political movements, and propaganda lurked, Lasswell seemed to be there, beginning with World War I and stretching into the early Cold War. He spent his career mostly at the University of Chicago and Yale University, but he took on a wide variety of other jobs and advising roles, including as the director of War Communication Research at the Library of Congress, from 1939 to 1946.[45] Born in 1902, and therefore too young to participate in World War I directly, he studied under the legendary political scientist Charles Edward Merriam, who had served as America's propaganda chief in Italy during World War I. That fateful connection would prove important, as Merriam encouraged Lasswell to undertake a sweeping set of interviews and fieldwork across Europe to study how propaganda efforts were conceived, executed, and received.

This work formed the basis of his dissertation, which was published in 1927 as a book titled *Propaganda Technique in the World War*. As Lasswell defined "propaganda," the term has a specific analytical meaning: "[It] refers solely to the control of opinion by significant symbols, or, to speak more concretely and less accurately, by stories, rumors, reports, pictures and other forms of social communication. Propaganda is concerned with the management of opinions and attitudes by the direct manipulation of social suggestion rather than by altering other conditions in the environment or in the organism."[46]

Lasswell's research provides one of the most definitive catalogues and analyses of various attempts of the countries involved in World War I to influence the population of one another, including the efforts of Creel's Committee on Public Information. President Wilson himself, Lasswell notes, proved the master propagandist of the war, with his speeches constantly urging discord among the Germans and their allies, persuading enemy populations to revolt and join the forces of freedom and humanity.

What were the general communications strategies employed by World War I propagandists? Lasswell notes that messages that attempted to demoralize the enemy or make victory seem impossible were commonplace—

and used on all sides. The various sides attempted to convince their own populations, and other sympathetic ears on the other side, that the enemy had started the war and stood in the way of a godly peace. Many of these messages contained religious overtones, framing the fight as for God and against Satan. Combatants spotlighted atrocities, both real and fabricated, to emphasize the inhumanity and moral degradation of their enemy. Propaganda campaigns manufactured false reports of the imminent collapse or defeat of the enemy to sustain the will of their populations and weaken the will of their opponent.

All sides also experimented with new ways of delivering propaganda to their enemies including through planted newspaper stories and forged documents, leaflets, and pamphlets. At one point, combatants experimented with literally shooting mortar rounds that exploded into a flutter of leaflets. But as one observer pointed out, there was something slightly absurd about shooting explosive rounds at one moment and then spraying the enemy, using the same mortars, with leaflets that proclaimed that all men are brothers; and so the airplane (and sometimes the air balloon) became the preferred delivery vehicle.[47] In 1918, the Allies delivered an estimated five million leaflets more than one hundred fifty miles behind German lines.[48]

Through his comprehensive empirical analysis of these techniques and outcomes, Lasswell derived some deep, generalizable insights. In an academic article based on his dissertation work, he put forth the theory that propaganda is primarily about shifting attitudes. It "involves the presentation of an object in a culture in such a manner that certain cultural attitudes will be organized toward it. The problem of the propagandist is to intensify the attitudes favorable to his purpose, to reverse the attitudes hostile to it, and to attract the indifferent or, at the worst, to prevent them from assuming a hostile bent."[49] Such attitudes might relate to factual information or understanding of events, but they also might relate to how people feel about other people and their sense of risk, fear, or grievance.

In his work relating to World War II, Lasswell would go beyond observation and theory to develop more concrete proposals for responses and countermeasures for misinformation and the fog of propaganda. In a democratic society, Lasswell believed, we must nearly always tolerate propaganda, even as we attempt to counter it through what he termed "instant reply." The right of reply, Lasswell argued, was "deeply entrenched in the folkways of democracy." He found antecedents for this practice in the court system, in administrative affairs, in newspapers, in so many walks of life.[50] When we don't like what someone says about us or those we care about, we always reserve the right *to talk back*. Democracies are about the possibility of pointed dialogue. This was a key point for Lasswell: However democracies decide to fight propaganda, they must do so democratically, rooted in the traditions of a society organized around openness and consent.

In Lasswell's 1941 book *Democracy Through Public Opinion*, he sketched out a system organized around the "instant reply plan," by which private news and information sources might submit judgment calls to advisory councils.[51] Unusually, he also insisted on a strict one-to-one, immediate form of reply in all forms of media so that, for example, a text like Hitler's *Mein Kampf* should only be allowed to circulate if it had an explicit reply within the body of the book itself.

Lasswell himself acknowledged that this proposal was largely unworkable unless it were reduced to the practice of labeling. "Much as we require descriptive labels on commodities for sale, we may call for propaganda labels on anti-democratic material," he argued, continuing, "and the label might name the place where a suitable antidote can be obtained."[52] This he called the "instant label plan," anticipating a mass phenomenon that social media platforms would begin carrying out seventy years later, following the 2016 U.S. election.[53] Lasswell left the details of how this might be carried out, and by whom, with what authority, a bit vague, but his ideas would inform a larger debate about how libel law should change in response to the rise of mass communications through radio and television.[54] In short, the instant label plan argues that informational dangers to democratic systems must be met with an active response.

Although Lasswell's system and theory for dealing with propaganda in a democratic society might be unsatisfying in its particulars, his writings are remarkable for struggling with the core issues that bedevil the modern communication environment.[55] He not only was one of the first people to see how propaganda really worked, but he also posed questions and offered solutions to certain mass communications problems that society is facing now, in the third decade of the twenty-first century.

Figure 2.3 The social scientist Harold Lasswell pioneered the study of propaganda and misinformation and analyzed early techniques of mass manipulation. Harold Dwight Lasswell Papers (MS 1043), Manuscripts and Archives, Yale University Library.

Yet even among academic social scientists now, relatively few know much about Lasswell beyond recognizing his name as a venerable citation in the fields of political science and psychology. It was his work that advanced the core "5W" framework for understanding mass communication: "Who says what, in which channel, to whom, with what effect?" It's a series of questions that can help define and evaluate any given piece of communication. That model has been updated by scholars many times since it was first articulated, and the era of networked and social media—of mass self-communication—has greatly complicated it. But the 5W formulation was one of many dozens of powerful intellectual tools and ideas that Lasswell created over his career.[56]

Our own era of disinformation has seen renewed interest in Lasswell's work. His quest was always for more data about the communications in which people were engaged and how these messages affected them psychologically and politically, a familiar concern in our own day. He knew that his understanding was limited; he admitted that regardless of whatever solutions and theories we might propose, there first needs to be a lot more understanding of how propaganda and disinformation work, of their origins and effects. "We need a better knowledge of the whole process of communication than we have at present," he wrote in 1941, "if we are to act wisely on behalf of democratic ends."[57] We need more transparency, more data, more knowledge of what is going on—all resonant points as we interrogate the behavior of social media platforms.

MODERN MITIGATION

The early theorists of propaganda and disinformation did not get everything right, nor did their solutions perfectly apply to novel technological ecosystems. It may seem odd to contemporary sensibilities, but many of the earliest analysts of propaganda were not necessarily against it, as they saw mass media as a necessary tool for managing society. Such mixed attitudes were common, and there was a robust debate about the line between useful education for a society and propaganda.[58] Many—including Lippmann and Lasswell—even flirted with propaganda operations and perfecting techniques themselves. Scholars have noted that these were men of power and influence, and they were not the most thoroughgoing skeptics of propaganda.[59] But they nonetheless identified an essential way of prioritizing activity toward combatting malign messages and campaigns. Transparent procedures, public labels, and careful attention to democratic values, namely respecting citizens' judgments, were all paramount. Top-down removal and censorship should be a last resort in extreme circumstances. The line between political speech and disinformation is frequently difficult to discern. Therefore, keeping trust in the ongoing deliberative process is of the highest value.

In the twenty-first century, an academic subfield structured around the concept of "information correction" carries forward this early central insight and spirit into the digital and platform era. Few issues in the current academic fields focused on online platforms have seen more critical inquiry from researchers than how best to limit the impact of mis- and disinformation. Researchers are particularly interested in how to make people more discerning about the information they consume. While industry has experimented with many practical solutions and techniques to the problems of disinformation, researchers have focused on more fundamental questions about information processing in the human mind. Without a fuller comprehension of mental mechanisms, any interventions may sit on shaky grounds.

The emerging psychological research on interventions has, at various times, split into two camps, or schools of thought, on these questions. There are two areas of disagreement: what's the root problem, and where do you intervene? In the first instance, scientists have come to believe that human beings online are simply not paying enough attention and not using their reasoning faculties. From this perspective, belief in corrupted information is, in part, explained by a kind of mental laziness, slackness, or just zoned-out relaxation. This would make some intuitive sense, as social media platforms are designed for fast consumption of highly engaging content, with rapid flows of messages, images, and videos flying by the mind. In the prior media era, we had a relatively strict separation of channels for news and entertainment, for fact and fiction. Now, they are blended together. According to these researchers, the place to intervene is "downstream," at the point of consumption; the solution lies in activating the brain as it engages with information.

Researchers David Rand of MIT and Gordon Pennycook of Cornell University—frequent collaborators—believe that a susceptibility to misinformation derives from a breakdown in the brain's information processing. There is a longstanding idea in psychology that the human mind has two systems for processing. System-1 thinking uses intuition to make rapid judgments whereas system-2 thinking exercises deeper reasoning. The Nobel laureate Daniel Kahneman popularized this idea with the phrase "thinking, fast and slow" (the title of his book.)[60] Building on this idea, the likes of Rand and Pennycook say the problem is that humans are not exercising enough system-2 thinking as they consume media. Rand and Pennycook therefore propose that the solution to disinformation lies in increasing people's reasoning and dialing up their motivation to sort truth from falsehood.

In a major 2021 study published in *Nature*, a team led by Rand and Pennycook concluded that finding ways to get social media users to think about the concept of accuracy improved their abilities. Sometimes, all it takes is asking users to rate something based on accuracy first. The key, though, is to get them to do something more than just scroll through information.[61] Rand and Pennycook, among many others, continue to pursue this line of research, which has broad implications for how social media companies design their user interface, contextualize information, and provide features that might improve reasoning.

A second school of thought believes accuracy nudges and increasing reasoning are not sufficient to solve the problem of disinformation. Rather, these researchers believe that people's deeply held identities—for example, their personal beliefs, geographic location, political identity, demographic categories—are the real factors driving the public's inability to discern and judge misinformation. Social scientists sometimes call this "motivated reasoning," or "myside" bias.[62] Such researchers often point out that, in studies, political conservatives seem to be more susceptible to or accepting of misinformation that aligns with their underlying identity than political liberals.[63] This camp also believes you need to go "upstream," before people consume information, to prepare them and to get them to shift their mental framework as they go downstream and see things on social media.

Researchers such as Sander van der Linden of the University of Cambridge and Jay Van Bavel of New York University argue that we need a more holistic understanding of the problem of misinformation as a social phenomenon.[64] People are stubbornly dug in because of their identities, and the problem goes beyond directing more attention to accuracy. They suggest that the best solutions revolve around reaching people *before* they encounter strategies designed to trick or confuse them. The researchers think of corrupted or false information almost like a disease that might be prevented by "inoculation" or "prebunking." Teaching users how they might be deceived then generates resistance to future misinformation. We might, for instance, teach people about the kinds of tactics agents of disinformation use, including twisting arguments or facts, and using rhetorical tricks. Or we might engage in more specific forms of prebunking, such as when Twitter informed users to be on the lookout for voting misinformation just before Election Day 2020.[65] Such strategies have shown some promise. Researchers in this camp want to make a more news- and information-literate public, with a multilayer approach that includes fact-checking, inoculation and prebunking, and various efforts by media platforms to change incentives and neutralize bad actors.[66]

There is, however, an inherent risk associated with inoculation and prebunking. Namely, the approach presents a danger of making people more generally skeptical of all information—including valid information—and not necessarily more discerning of true and false information. We need a great deal more research about how to combat misinformation, and it may turn out that specific techniques may always need to be tailored to specific problems. Many different strategies, from accuracy nudges and fact-checking to inoculation and prebunking, seem to find support in the research data.[67] New insights continue to accumulate. For example, strategies that go beyond correcting messages and highlight the low expertise of misinformers seem particularly promising.[68] In general, fact-checks seem to work, and ongoing research validates this.[69] However, effect sizes— how successful fact-checks are in changing minds—are often small, and successes decay rather rapidly over time. And some research suggests that even effective corrections—when they lead people to change their mind on a specific issue—may not have much effect on people's broader political views.[70]

Even if we get the science right, there is the "What next?" question. Academic studies on how to tackle disinformation campaigns only rarely speak to the practical ways that social platforms might address such problems.[71] In this respect, the companies do themselves no favors, in that they increasingly lock down their data and do not collaborate with disinformation researchers. But public policy could incentivize more collaborations between social media platforms and disinformation researchers, especially if companies might fulfill their duty of care by showing the extent of their activities to regulators.

THE CORRECTION PROFESSION

While highly relevant to platform systems and labeling, the academic science on mis- and disinformation, and how to change beliefs generally, can seem a bit abstract to frontline practitioners in media fields who are trying to reassert the truth in public discourse, often under difficult conditions. Ask many such persons across the Global South, and you will hear more than a bit of disdain for the abstruse findings of cognitive psychology. Much mis- and disinformation proliferates despite efforts to mitigate its spread. The practical reality is that it corrupted information is common in certain cases, and someone may need to do something about it.

Corrections, replies, and counterspeech sometimes are particularly needed where press and knowledge institutions, such as universities, courts, and nongovernmental organizations, are not yet strong. Africa Check, a new kind of news and information organization headquartered at the University of the Witwatersrand in Johannesburg, is taking a novel approach to an old problem—that of false news, propaganda, and mis- and disinformation. Founded in 2012, the organization has helped to stand up a growing continental network, extending across Kenya, Senegal, and Nigeria. One goal is to provide empirical verification and fact-checking on statements made by influential public figures such as politicians; another is to strengthen the media literacy of the publics across four influential African countries.

The site, which operates in English and French, has roughly forty staff members who attempt to choose newsworthy, impactful narratives—for example, health misinformation in Nigeria, or political claims in Kenya—and give audiences an alternative, empirically based view on what is being said in public discourse. Reports can focus on the nitty-gritty statements of individuals—"Kenya President William Ruto Misses Mark in Claiming Country's Annual Food Import Bill Is KSh500 Billion"—but they frequently interrogate broader narratives by groups, for example, "Fact-checking the ruling party's claims about progress in South Africa."[72] Importantly, Africa Check also does trainings, media literacy campaigns, and capacity-building to bolster the region's quality of media and journalism. It has also built the Africa Facts Network, a consortium of twenty different efforts in the region.[73]

Noko Makgato, a journalist since 1998 who has both an MBA and digital marketing experience, took over the reins of Africa Check in 2019.[74] He has noted the challenges of trying to provide factual information for an entire continent—one that is poised to have the world's largest population by 2050. Africa Check must carefully consider cultural differences and needs in choosing what it responds to, and how:

Africa is a huge continent, right? So the idea is to try and learn as much as possible from our country officers in terms of the work that we're doing there and the impact that we think the work is having on the local front. In other words, the trick for us going forward is to not have one site with one approach, or one single way of doing things. It's to try and experiment with different things that are influenced by how those countries perceive misinformation or handle misinformation, and acknowledging how different types of misinformation are experienced differently in different countries.[75]

Makgato took over as executive director at a crucial moment in Africa Check's history, when the organization in 2018 began formally partnering with Facebook as a third-party fact-checker. That means that Africa Check's content has had a direct pipeline with Facebook and Instagram (both Meta companies). Africa Check's staff could view a shared dashboard queue of content that might be fact-checked and responded to as they see fit. Managers of the social platform could then use automated tools to take that content and apply labels, and link back to Africa Check to stories and messages that were disputed and circulating on Facebook. Facebook often lowered the visibility of the information that African Check had flagged on the platform (downranks it algorithmically), so that the misinformation had less chance to spread and cause confusion or harm. The company also notified any sites, including news sites, that were carrying the disputed claim, and even penalized sites that use Meta's advertising tools if they failed to take action on the disputed information. Africa Check's posts effectively "train the algorithm," as Makgato puts it, to find other instances of the -fact-checked claim across the media ecosystem. As promising as this process sounds, Africa Check was only allowed to create eighty to one hundred posts for Meta per month, a very small quota for four countries, especially during election season.

Further, Meta's announced rollback of (many of) its fact-checking partnerships in early 2025 has put this long-running work in jeopardy. Meta had provided monetary compensation to Africa Check for its fact-checking operations, as it had to a wide array of nearly one hundred fact-checking operations around the world.[76] The field of fact-checking has grown enormously over the years, increasing from 44 organizations in 2014 to 188 by 2019.[77] The formation of the International Fact-Checking Network (IFCN), supported by foundations and Poynter, a U.S. journalism-focused non-profit organization, has been crucial to help organize this growing global community around information-verification work in the public interest.

Makgato notes that the "African and Latin American model" for fact-checking has been different than the American model, which focuses more directly on specific claims and correcting the public record. The

Global South model involves audiences more explicitly as active participants. It focuses more on the "demand side," Makgato says. The goal is to
help inoculate the South African, Kenyan, Nigerian, and Senegalese public
audiences, so they "are able to actively take a decision not to become con-
duits of misinformation." The Global South model is less about providing
data and statistics, and more about engaging with people—to "take real
steps inoculating people against misinformation." Even on social media,
Makgato says, his organization's work is "really about trying to educate
the social media users . . . it's not about telling you what's wrong or what's
right. It's about context."[78]

For the past decade, the academic and media worlds have debated the
merits of the fact-checking movement—whether it works, whether anyone listens, and how it might be sustained and grown. Some commentators have feared that fact-checks might "backfire," making partisans dig
in their heels when confronted with factual rebuttals. Those fears have
subsided, as more scientific evidence for their effectiveness has accumu-
lated.[79] Practitioners on the ground, like Makgato, attest that they can
see results, especially as the partner platform provides feedback on user
ratings and number of viewers. "With any of the other work we do, getting a sense of its impact is very difficult; with this program, the impact
you feel is recognizable super early and super clearly—especially when
somebody's not happy about it," Makgato has said about the Facebook
relationship.[80]

Perhaps the two deepest critiques of fact-checking, setting aside issues
of sustainability and concerns over human psychology and fallibility,
concern scalability and the difficulty of matching, or logical targeting,
of the fact-checks to those originally misinformed. First, given that the
world is full of half-truths and misinformation, how can a small team
of humans possibly do more than scratch the surface? Particularly in
regions such as those covered by Africa Check, where there is a great need
for more independent journalism capacity and reliable, well-resourced
knowledge institutions—agencies, courts, civil society, universities—fact-
checking may play an important role on a given issue, adding a minimum level of baseline ground truth, or at least an alternative channel
for verification of major claims by leaders. But the scalability problem
stands, despite the growth of fact-checking across the world. The world's

population continues to grow, more people are adding their voices to the digital public sphere, and the volume of information online multiplies.

And second, the difficulty of targeting the information to those most "in need," those exposed to the misinformation, is perhaps the most vexing issue. People exposed to a politician's misinformation-riddled speech initially may be difficult to reach when the journalist's fact-check surfaces days later. Matching those persons originally exposed to the false information to the corrective information is difficult. Further, there may be whole areas of media and communications that are not visible to fact-checkers, and they have no recourse or pathway to reach misinformed persons. Africa Check, for its part, solicits offline information tips from its audience, and then attempts to take fact-checking directly into communities through traditional broadcast channels. "Our strong push through our inoculation work is really through radio," Makgato says, noting that Africa Check regularly runs thirty-second public service announcements on community radio stations that alert citizens to particular kinds of misinformation.[81]

This general educational mission is especially important in the Global South, he notes: the "assumption, as I think is probably the case in Europe, the U.S. and other parts of the world, is that people live the majority of their lives online. . . . That's not really the reality of the majority of Africans."[82] In developing countries where flyers, posters, brochures, and other print media still play a sizable role in the information environment, online solutions may not be sufficient to move the needle in terms of correcting beliefs. Scholars studying misinformation in the Global South have also noted particular dynamics that require careful and intentional strategies, including citizens' greater reliance on messaging apps; low state capacity in terms of news and official institutions; low state capacity for managing downstream effects of disinformation-driven social media crises and flashpoints, such as communal violence outbreaks; and low levels of platform accountability, as companies may have few local ties and local research communities and journalists may not be engaged in critical scrutiny that draws sufficient attention from the multinational companies.[83]

Contemporary social media platforms are in large part giant targeting engines, with elaborate technological tools that allow advertisers to

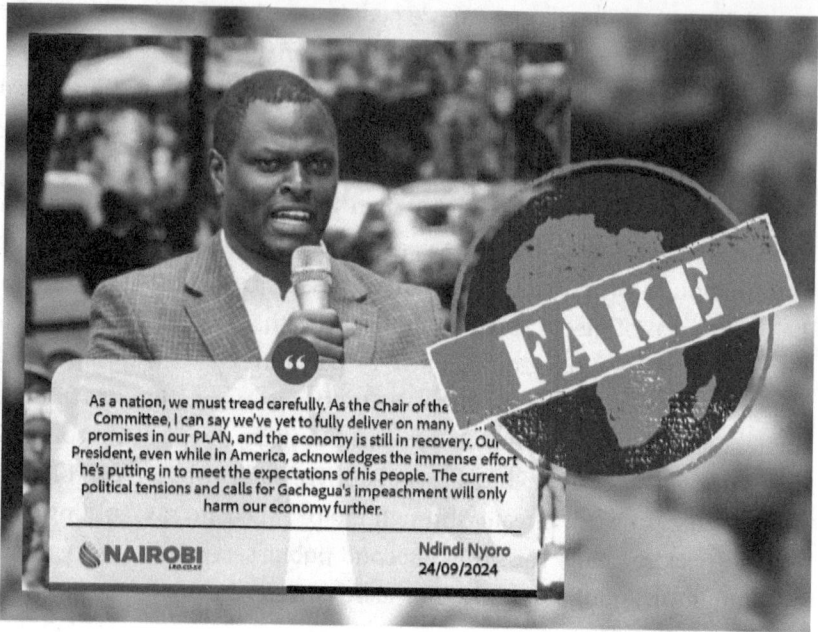

Figure 2.4 An example of an Africa Check–created correction and label on a fabricated quotation misleadingly attributed to a Kenyan politician. https://africacheck.org/fact-checks/meta-programme-fact-checks/fake-graphic-kenyan-mp-ndindi-nyoro-didnt-say-calls-impeach.

reach would-be consumers of anything—goods, services, products, ideas, causes. The technical capacity to track down mis- and disinformation is growing, as forms of advanced machine learning and generative AI provide more comprehensive and sophisticated tools for counterspeech in the public interest. Social platforms could provide their users with a variety of labels and contextual nudges, such as "source alerts";[84] and they have even experimented with alerting people that they may have been exposed to harmful information. Still, the challenges of addressing counterspeech-at-scale and targeting/matching are substantial. Funding for fact-checking and public interest journalism is sadly lacking across most societies, even in wealthier Western countries. Nor does any of this begin to resolve the quandary presented by the increasing popularity of encrypted messaging tools (as will be discussed in a later chapter), which are nearly impossible to monitor systematically. It has nonetheless become abundantly clear that the status quo cannot continue if free societies are to survive intact in this moment of technological transformation.

DISINFORMATION LESSONS

Counterspeech against mis- and disinformation must continue to solve for a practical efficacy problem: Can it make a difference and change beliefs in the real world? In terms of creating pathways for counterspeech, there are several existing general models, including Fairness Doctrine-like policies (regulating balance) in media messages, allowing open comments from the crowd on news and social sites, and fact-checking (empowering professionals).[85] Although the idea of restoring the Fairness Doctrine for social media has been discussed and proposed by prominent leaders, it would face numerous practical and legal challenges and remains an unlikely pathway, as policy scholar Philip Napoli of Duke University has pointed out.[86] The problem with open commenting is that there is no guarantee that misinformation will be met with countervailing views, and comments are often supportive and sometimes just ordered or ranked for users by popularity (in long comment threads, the reliable information may be buried.) Further, with fact-checking, as mentioned, it is exceedingly difficult to deliver counterspeech to the persons exposed to the original message. For these reasons, experts continue to look for mechanisms that unite people of disparate views to come together to settle on counterspeech claims, thus forcing people to update their beliefs and guaranteeing efficacy. X's Community Notes, for example, tries to get persons of different viewpoints to agree on a common corrective note, although functionally that system has had problems with getting agreement in a timely way.[87] In general, scholars have called for more "bridging" mechanisms that funnel disparate people into more deliberate and cooperative tasks of producing counterspeech together.[88] In 2025, Meta declared it will adopt a Community Notes-style approach for its social platforms, but it remains to be seen if the company can figure out new ways to scale this often-cumbersome, user-driven process to its billions of users.

It would be wise to pursue a multipronged strategy given the urgency of the moment. Social media platforms should supercharge their fact-checking efforts and support for independent journalistic partners who perform this function. We also need to incentivize platforms to accelerate their labeling and counterspeech-related activities to deal with mis- and disinformation. More structured bridging experiments using crowd-sourced mechanisms should be tried. Finally, these companies need to make much more data accessible to independent researchers (and journalists and watchdog groups) through a regular auditing process to help monitor efficacy. The toolbox should be creative and sufficiently flexible to deal with the fast-moving environment.

Whatever new rules and regulations may look like, we would do well to draw on Lippmann's emphasis on proceduralism and public inquiry and Lasswell's idea of active response. Rules should promote transparency, capacity for revision, and orderly procedures for iteration. Social media platforms are complex systems where governance is often a matter of probabilities, estimates, and provisional truths; in many cases, there are no right answers. Enlisting the public to support new rules will require a focus on transparency, not on tools and rules that look like forms of censorship. Democratic systems undermine themselves through censorship; they empower themselves by "walking the walk," allowing bad speech but strenuously opposing it.

In studying the early modern propagandists and disinformation practitioners, Lasswell and Lippmann articulated fundamental truths that have not changed with subsequent technological innovations. Humans inherently live in a "pseudo environment," often composed of mental shortcuts and stereotypes; because of this, they are subject to manipulation. Modern democracies are likely to fall short of rational decision-making, given this aspect of human fallibility. The problem of the complexity of modern society and a lack of citizen knowledge is inherent to the problem of mis- and disinformation. It is the central problem to be managed, not solved.

Lippmann's persistent skepticism about fully "solving" the problem of disinformation, while depressing at one level, is also a useful tool: In modern, mass-media societies, we must start with skepticism about whether citizens are adequate to making informed decisions. We should not assume that a democracy will be an informed democracy; rather, we should recognize that citizens may not have sufficient knowledge and will make bad decisions. As Lasswell observed, publics are not typically manipulated through overt messages, but rather through waves of subtle messages that condition people to think about certain subjects with certain attitudes. (For example, a message that doesn't tell you outright that a political leader is a liar, but rather raises questions about some alleged incident in the leader's past.) Ultimately, propaganda and disinformation are forces to be managed and mitigated, not necessarily stopped in their tracks.

Lasswell proposed bringing the existence of this manipulation and its mechanisms to the public's attention, making them aware of what is being said. The spirit of his "instant reply plan of democratic defense" was exactly that: Democracies should work to expose and spotlight deceptions, for the purposes of citizen education. The advice is especially pertinent and resonant for our age of social media, when much activity, organizing, and tactics are taking place first out of sight.

In the United States, with its free speech traditions, any attempt to remove or diminish the visibility of disinformation or propaganda encounters charges of censorship. As an alternative, most of the large, mainstream social media companies have traditionally embraced approaches that sometimes include labeling, fact-checking, and downranking. (Two prominent exceptions are Twitter/X, a backslider under the new ownership of Elon Musk; and Telegram, a hybrid social media-messaging app, that has embraced a laissez-faire approach since its inception. It remains to be seen what Meta (Facebook, Instagram) may actually do following its January 2025 announcement rolling back content moderation measures.) Many platforms have built elaborate policies, terms of service, and community guidelines or standards. They claim to do their best to enforce them, although the limited resources the companies typically allocate to these issues suggest otherwise. It is essential that their practices be exposed to greater public scrutiny, with their decisions and decision-making patterns subject to regular, critical evaluation by researchers, regulators, and the public. But where companies commit resources and energy to such efforts, government and the public need to give platforms proper validation of socially responsible management through an orderly, audit-like procedure according to new U.S. law.

3

HATE AND HUMAN RIGHTS

An invisible atom bomb exploded in our information ecosystem, and the world must act as it did after Hiroshima. Like that time, we need to create new institutions, like the United Nations, and new codes stating our values, like the Universal Declaration of Human Rights, to prevent humanity from doing its worse. It's an arms race in the information ecosystem.[1]
—Maria Ressa, Nobel Lecture, Nobel Peace Prize 2021

It is unclear if social platforms themselves have driven people, or invited them, to be more malicious and hateful, or whether the ease and anonymity of such platforms has just exposed the human heart in its natural state of not infrequent depravity. In other words: Is social media driving hate speech, or just making humanity's worst instincts more visible?

Fighting hate globally is often a volume game. Consider a representative recent period: In the first nine months of 2023 alone, Meta reported having taken down 27.6 million posts on Facebook for containing hate speech. The company claimed that in mid-2023 of every 10,000 posts it saw, roughly one or two contained hate speech; this is down from ten to eleven per 10,000 in mid-2020.[2] Meanwhile, YouTube reported having shut down ten million channels between July and September of 2023; among those were 26,000 channels that contained hate or abusive speech. YouTube removed 187,000 individual videos for the same reason over that period, out of 8.1 million total videos removed.[3] For its part, TikTok removed 136.5 million videos in total, with about three million videos among those removed containing hateful speech or behavior.[4]

The business of fighting hate is a very ugly one. Although Meta's rules are now in flux following its announced policy reversals in January 2025, the company has traditionally defined hate as "direct attacks against people—rather than concepts or institutions—on the basis of what we call protected characteristics (PCs): race, ethnicity, national origin, disability, religious affiliation, caste, sexual orientation, sex, gender identity, and serious disease." But human expression is a complicated business, and so companies often must spell out exactly what they mean in documentation that reads like a nightmarish sewer of animus and dehumanization. Meta has banned dehumanizing speech in many forms, including human-to-animal comparisons such as: "Animals in general or specific types of animals that are culturally perceived as inferior (including but not limited to: Black people and apes or ape-like creatures; Jewish people and rats; Muslim people and pigs; Mexican people and worms.)"[5] TikTok has had similar policies, banning content such as "demeaning someone on the basis of their protected attributes by saying or implying they are physically, mentally, or morally inferior, or calling them degrading terms, such as criminals, animals, and inanimate objects" or "denying well-documented historical events that harmed groups based on a protected attribute, such as denial of the Holocaust or the genocide against the Tutsi in Rwanda."[6] YouTube also provides some grim examples of forbidden expressions: "'[People with protected group status] are dogs' or '[people with protected group status] are like animals.'"[7]

The large social media platform companies have regularly reported that their machine-learning classifiers—algorithmic filtering systems that analyze patterns in text, images, or other content to categorize posts as safe or potentially problematic—catch more than 90 percent of violating hate speech before users report it. Watchdog and civil society groups, however, continue to find gaping holes in the companies' enforcement patterns, despite the sheer volume of content taken down. These problems with enforcement persist even though leading companies have allegedly developed some of the best natural language processing (text) and machine vision (video) technologies in the world. Meta additionally employs 15,000 persons globally to work on content review, while TikTok claims to employ 40,000 such persons and YouTube's parent company, Alphabet/Google, employs some 22,000.[8] Yet policy rollbacks and major cuts in key trust and safety positions continue to undermine the ability of social platforms to mitigate systemic problems of hate and abuse.[9]

Hate speech online stands as one of the great human rights problems of our time. In every age, malign actors have demonized people based on their identity and characteristics. But the ability to do it anonymously, amplified by algorithms, and aided by online mobs that operate across platforms, is something altogether new. This chapter focuses on this problem in terms of its effects on the well-being of individuals and communities and the consequences for people's sense of agency and ability to participate in public life. Of course, hate speech is frequently intertwined with calls for violence, or what is often called "incitement." The following chapter will look more closely at incitement, while this chapter explores hate speech more as a tool wielded to wound people's well-being and agency and achieve social and political control.

As I will argue, promising avenues for addressing hate speech involve the wider adoption of international human rights law and its standards across global platforms—and more vigorous enforcement of these standards. Further, the use of next-generation AI technologies holds the promise of automating more of the "first read"—the initial level of filtering—of content and messages, allowing more scale and more subtle understanding of messages across cultures and languages. Humans will always need to be in the loop, and different cultures will have varying thresholds and tolerance levels, but technologies that support defensive strategies are being developed rapidly. All of that said, addressing this problem through policy requires a deeper understanding of how the concept of hate speech and the free speech tradition relate, as well as a sense of the global dimensions of the issue.

NOT EXEMPTED FROM ASSASSINATION

An intellectual woman of multicultural background, diminutive in stature, brown in skin color, gay in sexual orientation, a journalist by trade, and long a ferocious critic of one of the world's most powerful men. One cannot make up the profile of Maria Angelita Ressa, nor can many imagine the volume of hatred she has endured.

A Filipino-American journalist who came to prominence as the founder of Rappler, an investigative site in the Philippines that relentlessly interrogated the regime of its strongman President Rodrigo Duterte, Ressa is

perhaps the global truth-teller par excellence of our time. The Nobel
Peace Prize awarded in 1921 to Ressa and Russian journalist Dmitry Mura-
tov for their "efforts to safeguard free expression"[10] confirmed what many
already knew about the importance of her work as a model, and locus of
debate, that clearly defines some of the most pressing public issues relating to global communications platforms and media.

At one point, the Princeton graduate and former CNN journalist, who
had returned to her home country of birth and early childhood to practice journalism and cofound Rappler, was receiving an average of ninety
hate-oriented comments on Facebook *every hour* as she attempted to carry
on amid an onslaught of death and rape threats.[11] The Duterte regime
was not happy with Ressa's and Rappler's journalism. For opposing the
regime, she was made to pay dearly.

Ressa's example was one of many globally, particularly around the late
2010s, that began to raise serious questions about the social platforms'
laissez-faire approach. It's one thing to say that Americans can have free
speech—where the courts, police, and authorities may protect persons
with the rule of law (however imperfectly). But what about in communities where that is just not the case, even in theory—where hate speech
frequently leads to personal harm, without consequence? Judging from
Duterte's own words in 2016, the Philippines qualified as just such an
extrajudicial place. "Just because you're a journalist, you are not exempted
from assassination, if you're a son of a bitch," he said.[12] Human Rights
Watch estimates that tens of thousands of mostly poor people were murdered extrajudicially during Duterte's reign, activities that spurred the
International Criminal Court (ICC) to charge Duterte with "crimes against
humanity" and jail him in The Hague.[13] Indeed, it was after Ressa's Rappler began reporting on the regime's extrajudicial killings as part of its
"drug war" that the networked threats began across Twitter and Facebook, among other platforms. Pro-Duterte writers began organizing campaigns to have Ressa arrested—and worse. Fabricated legal charges and
lawsuits, revocation of a license to operate as a media outlet, and various
kinds of offline harassment followed. These actions then became more
fuel for a hate-filled campaign online.

A large-scale computational analysis conducted by the International
Center for Journalists (ICFJ) of messages directed at Ressa online found

that 40 percent of the 400,000 tweets analyzed (December 2019–January 2021) attacked her personally; further, 34 percent of messages in the category of personal attacks "could be classified as misogynistic, sexist and explicit abuse. This includes abuse targeting Ressa's physical appearance (emphasizing her skin condition [eczema]) and manipulated photographs depicting her head associated with male genitalia."[14] Troll armies and coordinated bot networks relentlessly attacked through the years. Twitter was filled with sexually explicit attacks; analysts who looked at the full dataset of posts found a slew of obvious red flags—messages filled with words such as "pussy," "go fuck yourself," "witch," "whore," and "bitch." This is to say nothing of various other vile, racist messages.

Time and again, when social media companies headquartered in the United States were asked to intervene, according to the ICFJ report, company managers did little to stop the hate and harassment. While the blame is also squarely on the online harassment perpetrators and the Duterte regime itself, Ressa has suggested that social media companies bear a great deal of blame for allowing the flood of hate to persist: "The only way it will stop is when the platforms are held to account, because they allow it. . . . They have enabled these attacks; they should not be allowing this to happen."[15] It is worth noting that, according to Ressa, some of the most brutal online attacks took place over Facebook Messenger, which because it is a private encrypted messaging app cannot be systematically analyzed or exposed to independent scrutiny.

The firehose of online hate that Maria Ressa experienced set the context for her ultimate physical intimidation by authorities and arrests. The regime planted various kinds of recurring stories and "metanarratives"— ongoing messages with frames of reference that portrayed her as a CIA-controlled plant and unscrupulous traitor—that prepared the conditions for further attacks. As with many conflicts around the world now, the information environment was a key battleground for public opinion, with Duterte's allies mobilizing sympathetic followers to participate in widespread acts of online hate and disinformation—which then justified actions by authorities and real-world violence.

In 2019, Ressa's situation drew worldwide public attention—and undoubtedly, too, the attention of the Nobel Prize organization—as she was dramatically arrested twice in a six-week period. Images of the

Figure 3.1 Maria Ressa, cofounder and CEO of Rappler, shared the Nobel Peace Prize 2021. Her reporting in the Philippines has made her a target of hate speech and threats, as well as arrest and government harassment. She has become a prominent advocate for requiring that global communications technology companies curb online harms. Photo by Jay Dixit, licensed under CC BY-SA 4.0 (https://creativecommons.org/licenses /by-sa/4.0/deed.en).

diminutive but fearless journalist, her arms being held by police officers, were seen around the world, her trademark wire-rimmed glasses framing a serene expression of mixed defiance and chagrin.

LISTENERS OR SPEAKERS?

The United States has its own highly distinctive vocabulary for understanding and articulating issues of speech, press, and expression. The focus is the speaker's prerogative to speak one's mind. Under this theory, the listener is not a big consideration: If you don't want to hear it, you don't have to listen. More than a few around the world (and around the United States itself) have, over the decades, pointed out the hypocrisy that such rights have not been available to all races and sexes at various historical periods, including the present In any case, few if any countries now allow such wide-open and robust discourse to flourish, with such an extraordinarily high bar for libel and virtually unfettered opportunity to say almost anything about groups of persons and against public persons. For a time, perhaps hitting a fever pitch in the late Cold War, American elites believed that exporting this philosophy of First Amendment "fundamentalism" or "exceptionalism" was good for the world, opening up closed societies, empowering dissidents in authoritarian societies, and generally chipping away at tyranny.[16] And no doubt it has been good for the world in many cases.

Yet recent history has radically complicated America's free expression export business, with some around the world even calling it a kind of "digital colonialism" or a form of "imperialism."[17] Some of this rhetoric comes from quasi-authoritarian and antidemocratic figures, and governments waving a protest banner reading "cyber sovereignty," but it also comes from thoughtful civil society and political leaders who fear existing fissures and internal conflicts in their countries will be exacerbated beyond control. In recent years, the global community outside the United States has engaged in a complex conversation about the proper limits of certain types of speech, particularly hate speech and classes of language that demonize groups and may incite harm.[18] This conversation is grounded in the language of human rights, with its particular history and distinctive notions and vocabulary. Meanwhile, the United States has largely stuck to its own more austere and limited vocabulary of (nearly) "anything goes." The result has been a substantial disconnection, precisely at the moment that U.S. communications technologies have scaled across the globe; most of the users and growth for many platforms such as Facebook, Twitter (X), YouTube, and others is international, not domestic.

Many of these globalized American technology companies have found themselves plunged into the complex politics of other societies—with their very different histories and vulnerabilities—unable to cope with the vast differences in norms and rules, cultural expectations, and legal theories. Most of the major U.S.-based internet-based communications platforms, such as YouTube, Facebook, and Twitter, began with First Amendment fundamentalism in their DNA,[19] even if they eventually began to back off free speech absolutism as business necessity required doing so in countries where laws said otherwise. Although some contend that there may be theoretical compatibility between international human rights law and the First Amendment,[20] the question is often a practical one about how specific cases might be seen in light of each framework's overall direction. The default direction of the First Amendment is to protect speakers' individual rights, to live and let live; human rights law is very much attuned to the listener of speech and is focused on protecting them from harms. Increasingly, social media platforms have been embracing international law and human rights concepts as a basis for their decision-making, but that embrace remains incomplete at best.

If there is a single battlefield of contention exemplifying tensions at the heart of expression and rights, it is hate speech, which is not defined in American law and which—to the extent it is a coherent category of speech—U.S. courts have generally protected under First Amendment principles. International law itself does not strictly define hate speech either. To grasp these issues deeply, it is necessary to understand the history of these ambiguities and the ideas that help frame current debates and conundrums, focusing on conceptual clashes and the interplay between human rights law and the First Amendment. Reviewing contemporary examples of particularly difficult social media content moderation cases around the globe also can reveal how difficult these calls can be in practice.

First Amendment jurisprudence relating to hate speech has as its one of its touchstones the 1969 U.S. Supreme Court decision in *Brandenburg v. Ohio* (1969), where the Court ruled that government cannot punish speech unless it is "directed to inciting or producing imminent lawless action and is likely to incite or produce such action."[21] Beyond *Brandenburg*'s incitement test (which will be explored in chapter 4), however, there is an additional legal restriction on hate speech that constitutes "fighting words." What many people consider to be hate speech may be punished in the United States if it is used in the context of a fighting words scenario. The classic example is the use of the "N-word" by a white person yelled angrily at a Black person in a face-to-face setting. The 2020 case of *State of Connecticut v. Liebenguth* tested exactly that scenario and whether a perpetrator would be criminally liable for disturbing the peace.[22] In 2014, a white driver who had received a $15 parking ticket on his 1999 Ford Escort in New Canaan, Connecticut, began yelling racial slurs—twice using the phrase "fucking n___!"—at a Black parking official, adding at one point "remember what happened in Ferguson," a highly charged reference to the then-recent national controversy over the police-involved killing of Michael Brown, a young Black man, in Ferguson, Missouri. The aggressor's body language and gestures also indicated great anger, and while no violence occurred, the Connecticut Supreme Court agreed that he was criminally liable for what amounted to fighting words.

Thus, hate speech can be regulated in the United States, but only if it is used within the context of an already unprotected category of expression (namely, incitement to violence or fighting words or scenarios involving true threats). There are now emerging questions about how such unprotected categories might translate into analogous situations online. In a 2018 civil case in Montana, *Gersh v. Anglin*, a federal judge ruled against a neo-Nazi leader who called for his allies to "troll storm" a woman, who was then verbally abused and threatened online and doxxed (the release of her personal email, social media profile, and those of her family including her twelve-year-old son.)[23] The neo-Nazi in question, Andrew Anglin, who ran the *Daily Stormer*, perhaps the most well known site in that racist and bigoted movement, targeted a Jewish real estate agent who had a falling out with a family member of another prominent neo-Nazi. The real estate agent then was besieged by such statements as: "We are going to ruin you, you Kike PoS [piece of shit]. . . . You will be driven to the brink of suicide. . . . We will be there to take pleasure in your pain & eventual end"; "Worthless fuckin kike"; and "You filthy piece of trash. You are threatening an old lady. You worthless piece of shit. I hope you die, you worthless cunt. You stupid ugly bitch."[24] *Daily Stormer* readers were directed to the agent and her acquaintances, with readers urged to "tell them you are sickened by their Jew agenda."[25] The case was resolved when Anglin stopped defending himself, so the case did not proceed to further levels of appeal. But Anglin was ordered to pay $14 million in damages.[26]

As horrible as this type of online speech can be, we need to ask more questions about what to do where language is clearly hateful but falls just short of direct incitement to violence. The scale, speed, and networked nature of internet platforms gives a power and force, and global dissemination capacity, to such hate—following Maria Ressa's ideas about online violence—that did not exist previously in human history. Such words also have a kind of permanence in digital space that is quite different from bitter words exchanged in a parking lot. Non-inciting hate speech needs to be thought of in new ways, and we need to encourage social platforms to take such language more seriously, beyond the traditional framework for evaluating incitement and fighting words.

CONDITIONS AND RESTRICTIONS?

In the international context, through consultation with human rights experts in 2013 in what was called the "Rabat Plan of Action," the United Nations High Commissioner for Human Rights established relevant definitions related to speech and incitement: "'Hatred' and 'hostility' refer to intense and irrational emotions of opprobrium, enmity and detestation towards the target group; the term 'advocacy' is to be understood as requiring an intention to promote hatred publicly towards the target group; and the term 'incitement' refers to statements about national, racial or religious groups which create an imminent risk of discrimination, hostility or violence against persons belonging to those groups."[27]

Whether authorities can restrict such inflammatory messages in advance—exercising "prior restraint"—of inciting action, as opposed to punishing it afterward, is a related but even more vexing question. Former ACLU President and law professor Nadine Strossen contends that the very concept of a hate speech law is incoherent and existing examples are "irreducibly riddled with ambiguity, conflicts, and confusion." Having done her best to "track down and read every 'hate speech' law that has been enacted or proposed," Strossen claims that they are "ineffective, and perhaps even counter-productive, in reducing the potential harms that are feared to flow from constitutionally protected 'hate speech.'"[28] That said, she does emphasize, following American jurisprudence, that speech that causes "specific imminent serious harm" can be banned, but it must pass a very strict test.[29] In her view, merely insulting or smearing the dignity or reputation of a group—a race, a religion, a gender, or other category—is not enough to satisfy any strict test.

For social media companies, patterns of behavior and cultural context have become increasingly important in making decisions on borderline cases of hate. Certainly, for a society already embroiled in a violent civil conflict, it is possible that the standard might be quite different than rules necessary for a peaceful and stable environment. Yet as David Kaye, the former UN Special Rapporteur on Freedom of Expression and Opinion (and an American law professor) has noted, the concept of hate speech is also subject to widespread abuse by governments around the world and therefore must be defined extremely narrowly, with clear justifications and legitimacy from authoritative legal bodies (and not arbitrary whims of persons in power): "Its vagueness and the lack of consensus around its meaning can be abused to enable infringements on a wide range of lawful expression. Many Governments use 'hate speech,' similar to the way in which they use 'fake news,' to attack political enemies, nonbelievers, dissenters and critics." There is another, double-edged dimension to this term, as Kaye notes. The "phrase's weakness ('it's just speech') also seems to inhibit Governments and companies from addressing genuine harms, such as the kind resulting from speech that incites violence or discrimination against the vulnerable or the silencing of the marginalized."[30]

This latter point of weakness—creating a distinction between "mere" speech and "real" action and thus obscuring the causal connections between the two—continues to generate much contention. To be sure, all of this can seem rather dry legalistic debate. There are the policymakers and the legal theorists who fight over definitions, but there are also the frontline professionals who are deeply emotionally and physically involved in hate speech issues. Many in those frontline roles are increasingly arguing that the online and offline worlds are functionally collapsing, as viral hate speech on platforms has a kind of pervasiveness and punch (a kinetic energy that is itself incitement, even if not explicit) that is genuinely new in the world, forcing us to redefine the categories inherited from centuries past. Legal theorists such as Danielle Citron have emphasized for more than a decade now that online spaces are a new frontier for the civil rights movement, as so much hate speech and harassing activity seeks to undermine persons based on their identity.[31] Law professor Mary Anne Franks has noted that allowing hate speech and harassment curbs participation in the public square, reducing the ability to have a voice in issues for many citizens. Women and marginalized persons are especially vulnerable to being pushed out—forced to withdraw for their safety and well-being—from online spaces because of hate speech, veiled threats, and other forms of networked harassment.[32]

One of the most vocal exponents of the view that we need a global reconsideration of hate speech is Maria Ressa herself, the 2021 Nobel laureate. Having endured wave after wave of threats, received many arrest warrants from the Duterte regime, and witnessed widespread violence against activists and journalists in her country, Ressa has concluded that the new digital environment, pervaded by toxic content, erases any speech-action distinction: "There is no difference between online violence and our physical world. They are one in the same. Online violence is real world violence. If you can make people believe lies are facts, you control them. This is why we have the rise of tyranny all around the world."[33]

Other regions of the world, such as Europe, are moving quickly in line to regulate speech according to such principles. There is much more room to maneuver already in European law. After all, Article 10 of the European Convention on Human Rights states the following:

1. Everyone has the right to freedom of expression. This right shall include freedom to hold opinions and to receive and impart information and ideas without interference by public authority and regardless of frontiers. This article shall not prevent States from requiring the licensing of broadcasting, television or cinema enterprises.
2. The exercise of these freedoms, since it carries with it duties and responsibilities, may be subject to such formalities, conditions, restrictions or penalties as are prescribed by law and are necessary in a democratic society, in the interests of national security, territorial integrity or public safety, for the prevention of disorder or crime, for the protection of health or morals, for the protection of the reputation or rights of others, for preventing the disclosure of information received in confidence, or for maintaining the authority and impartiality of the judiciary.

The expansive possible exceptions embedded in the caveats of paragraph 2 of Article 10 stand in stark contrast to the First Amendment's terse wording, which only specifies that "Congress shall make no law . . . abridging the freedom of speech, or the press." Many observers have long anticipated the potential for the increasing "Europeanization" of global regulations (sometimes called the "Brussels Effect"), including in the communications policy sector, because of the collective market power of the European Union's twenty-seven countries.[34]

Ressa's statement that "online violence is real world violence" is a powerful indictment of the way many social media companies and countries, and the international system itself, currently conceive of hate speech.

There is growing evidence to support the view, even if some of it remains anecdotal.[35] In her Nobel acceptance speech, Ressa was very direct about U.S. capitalism's role in exacerbating the situation: "Our greatest need today is to transform that hate and violence, the toxic sludge that's coursing through our information ecosystem, prioritized by American internet companies that make more money by spreading that hate and triggering the worst in us."[36] Ressa's shot at Silicon Valley and its many global communications platforms—a critique echoed by digital and human rights activists around the globe—is a stark reminder of the peculiar situation the global community now finds itself in. With the exception of China (and increasingly Russia), American rules functionally became everyone's rules, despite there being no explicit referendum or even much thought on the matter, until recently. Countries have local laws, and social media companies often say they abide by them. But the scale is enormous, the reality is messy, and much content violating local law sees no content moderation.

There are several historical trends that help to contextualize this peculiar situation. The first is, obviously, a tectonic shift in the media and communications landscape. There has long been concern about the ethics of multinational businesses and their practices in other countries, particularly the developing world where large Western corporations can wield undue influence and power. But for the first time, we see issues of business ethics and communications and media ethics colliding in a major way. A borderless media world may have begun with the rise of cable and satellite television. Yet for the most part, until the rise of the social web, roughly dating to Facebook's founding in 2004, most countries had media gatekeepers that were largely domestic actors and firms. There were many exceptions, for sure, with the syndication and reprinting of news—for example, the BBC, Agence France-Presse, the Associated Press, and various outlets that served global language communities. There were regional media spillovers across borders. Still, public discourse within national borders was not primarily governed by such cross-national organizations in most countries.

This globalization of communications media is happening at the same time that the world has become more economically interconnected, making it profitable to advertise brands across borders on media platforms.

Further, these trends are unfolding at the exact moment that, according to experts, we are seeing the "fragmentation of global policy- and law-making," as it appears increasingly impossible to forge consensus agreements on issues such as climate change, trade, and economics.[37] Possibilities for new global agreements on communications media seem distant.

Many of these tensions between competing notions of free speech have deep, complicated roots. They are at the heart of a huge global debate among professional experts, advocates, and scholars, who are largely split down the middle on these and related questions.[38] There is a significant amount to be gained by considering the genealogy of these concepts. How exactly did human rights law, as applied to freedom of expression and speech issues, come about? How does it compare with the First Amendment and its interpretation and development, and how are the two related? The answer is that it is difficult to disentangle them, and the real lines between the two remain contested and blurry at best. Their early histories are bound up together. It is worth noting that in her Nobel Peace Prize acceptance speech, Maria Ressa contended, provocatively, "An invisible atom bomb exploded in our information ecosystem, and the world must act as it did after Hiroshima." The dawn of the nuclear age indeed forced a great spiritual reckoning and brought with it a revolution in moral thinking, one whose theory has yet to be brought fully into practice.

MAGNA CARTA FOR HUMANKIND

The quest for human rights began in a moment of crisis, perhaps the greatest the world has ever seen. It was just a few days before Christmas 1945, and Eleanor Roosevelt received a letter from President Harry S. Truman summoning her to duty as a delegate to the fledgling United Nations. Much of the world was smoldering, having endured mass destruction from World War II. There were displaced and homeless people across Europe and Asia, and humankind was beginning to understand the legacy of the Holocaust.[39]

Amid the ashes of these events—particularly the Holocaust and the atomic bombings, events that began to completely redefine understandings of human morality and its limits—President Truman struggled to keep a coherent agenda, as economic troubles began to plague the economy again. Eleanor Roosevelt, meanwhile, remained a revered, if controversial and outspoken, figure, who advanced the legacy of her late husband while simultaneously advocating more overtly liberal views on politics. She had a long record of campaigning for international causes, including participation in the League of Nations and pacifist movement.[40] Consistent with her past causes and political profile as an ardent supporter of the New Deal, her advocacy around domestic policy was too liberal for the Truman White House of late 1945.

And so the plan among Truman advisors became twofold: Hitch the administration's star to the Roosevelt legacy on the international stage, by appointing Eleanor Roosevelt as a delegate to the United Nations, while at the same time getting her out of meddling in domestic politics. Hence Truman's appointment letter, addressed to Mrs. Anna Eleanor Roosevelt, 342 Madison Avenue, New York, NY, making her the only woman on the U.S. delegation attending the first session of the General Assembly of the United Nations. She ultimately accepted, and in relatively short order boarded a ship bound for London where, at Methodist Central Hall in Westminster, representatives from nations around the world were called to order for the first time on January 10, 1946.

For the next two years, in a feat of determination and leadership that has few, if any, parallels in diplomatic history, Eleanor Roosevelt became the living embodiment of a certain strain in U.S. political ideals: one rooted in an expansive view of the Constitution, the Declaration of Independence, and the "four freedoms" that her husband had articulated in his early 1941 State of the Union address—freedom of speech and expression; freedom of worship; freedom from want; and freedom from fear.[41]

As part of the American delegation to the United Nations, where she would be appointed chair of the drafting committee of the Universal Declaration of Human Rights, Eleanor Roosevelt made it her mission to see the Four Freedoms ideals translated into a wider framework for global action. After nearly a year of tireless consultations and endless days of debate, she and a select few others sat down to begin drafting the bill for the UN General Assembly. Her drafting partners were, among others, Pen-Chun Chang of China and Charles Habib Malik of Lebanon. Historians note the distinctive contributions of each alongside Roosevelt, as

Figure 3.2 Eleanor Roosevelt holds a poster of the Universal Declaration of Human Rights in November 1949. The Universal Declaration would serve as the founding document for international human rights law, a body of principles and ideas with which global communications technology platforms have struggled to align. FDR Presidential Library & Museum, http://www.fdrlibrary.marist.edu/archives/collections/franklin/index .php?p=digitallibrary/digitalcontent&id=2610.

Chang channeled human rights through a Confucian lens and Malik drew on his perspective as an Arab and Christian to emphasize individual rights and make human rights more formalized as protection against the state.[42]

As the United Nations first undertook its work in the mid- to late 1940s, leaders had to grapple with a world in which a colossal number of persons, on a relative basis, had no particular rights by virtue of active citizenship within a nation state. There were an estimated sixty million refugees globally following World War II, out of a global population of approximately two billion. Many millions were stateless.[43] On the minds of many advocates such as Eleanor Roosevelt was the need for rights that transcended borders.

Article 7 of the Universal Declaration created the modern framework for addressing hate speech, which would be further detailed in subsequent international law (as will be discussed): "All are equal before the law and are entitled without any discrimination to equal protection of the law. All are entitled to equal protection against any discrimination in violation of this Declaration and against any incitement to such discrimination." The language captured more subtle forms of hate speech, as it included incitement to discrimination, not just incitement to violence. Even as the drafters focused mostly on protecting speech, they were keenly aware—given the mass racial and ethnic violence that the world war brought—of the need for equivalent limits on forms of speech that would seek to do direct harm.

On December 10, 1948, the UN General Assembly adopted the Universal Declaration of Human Rights. Eleanor Roosevelt, using all her powers of persuasion, had won her battle. She had publicly touted the Declaration as a "Magna Carta" for the world, although privately she confided to a family member that it was an imperfect document that reflected compromise. As approved in 1948, Article 19 of the Universal Declaration states: "Everyone has the right to freedom of opinion and expression; this right includes freedom to hold opinions without interference and to seek, receive and impart information and ideas through any media and regardless of frontiers."

It was an expansive vision, and one that, originally, contained no explicit limits. It was the First Amendment on the global stage. Eleanor Roosevelt nonetheless seemed to believe certain limits were logically implied by a free society, as she suggested in an address designed to bolster support for the Universal Declaration's passage: "Naturally there must always be consideration of the rights of others; but in a democracy this is not a restriction. Indeed, in our democracies we make our freedoms secure because each of us is expected to respect the rights of others."[44] The degree of respect for others in terms of speech was, for the time, left unsaid.

The chief frame of concern for Roosevelt and others around her was the threat of the totalitarian state, as exemplified by the vanquished Nazis and the increasingly activist and expansionist Soviets. For the time being, then, international human rights would place its emphasis on individual speakers anywhere in the world and their ability to voice dissent. But it also put in place the initial building blocks to address hate speech.

TO THE COVENANT

Following Eleanor Roosevelt's pioneering work around human rights in the mid-1940s, it would take nearly another two decades for the United Nations to try to put together a document of "legal value"—which Roosevelt lamented the Universal Declaration of Human Rights was not—that would achieve more toward the goals broadly articulated in the Universal Declaration and would articulate a more nuanced vision of speech and expressive rights.

The kind of simple, quasi-First Amendment fundamentalism found in the Universal Declaration would become more nuanced, but not for some time. Following its passage, the plan was to put together specific binding commitments through treaties that would flesh out the more abstract gestures. One such treaty would come to be called the International Covenant on Civil and Political Rights (the ICCPR, passed by the UN General Assembly in 1966), and it remains to this day the defining, touchstone document for all around the world debating and analyzing freedom of expression. For insiders, it is often referred to through shorthand—"the Covenant," a kind of quasi-religious text for speech rights.

The ICCPR's central contributions on speech rights involved limits that Roosevelt and her colleagues simply did not address with the Universal Declaration of Human Rights. The Covenant's language detailed four important caveats. In Article 19—codified into legal language in the 1966 ICCPR, but building on the 1948 Universal Declaration's original intent—the text states that everyone has the freedom of expression, although this right may "be subject to certain restrictions, but these shall only be such as are provided by law and are necessary: (a) For respect of the rights or reputations of others; (b) For the protection of national security or of public order (*ordre public*), or of public health or morals." The ICCPR also restricts, in Article 20, "1. Any propaganda for war shall be prohibited by law. 2. Any advocacy of national, racial or religious hatred that constitutes incitement to discrimination, hostility or violence shall be prohibited by law."

The legally binding covenant, passed by the General Assembly in 1966, was not ratified by the United States until 1992, and even then it was ratified only with formally articulated reservations by the U.S. Senate.[45]

In what amounted to a legally awkward compromise, the U.S. Senate's reservations began: "Article 20 does not authorize or require legislation or other action by the United States that would restrict the right of free speech and association protected by the Constitution and laws of the United States." The reservations conclude: "Nothing in this Covenant requires or authorizes legislation, or other action, by the United States of America prohibited by the Constitution of the United States as interpreted by the United States." These caveats have been much lamented by human rights activists, as they not only weaken the apparent commitment of the central democracy that drove the UN's human rights movement in the first place, but the reservations also invite other, less rights-bound countries to pick and choose which aspects of UN treaties they might like.

The Universal Declaration had solved, at least rhetorically, the problem of authoritarian or totalitarian control of speech, but it had not fully accounted for problems of disempowered minorities facing less top-down, less Nazi- or Soviet-style, infringement on speech rights. Other challenges existed, and new ones were emerging in the postwar era, that involved civil conflict and extra-legal or vigilante threats, as well as more complex forms of governmental suppression across the world. The ICCPR offered solutions for this more complex array of speech- and expression-related problems, ones that seem quite pertinent in the contemporary landscape of social media. As the principles of what became the ICCPR were debated in the 1950s, Eleanor Roosevelt herself tried to address these more complicated problems. She saw that the Soviet Union, among other authoritarian states, might use the pretext of hate speech restrictions to suppress dissidents; thus, she and her allies insisted that only advocacy (rhetorical or otherwise) that was directly tied to violence could be banned.[46]

Major social platforms have committed to the ICCPR principles, with many enshrining principles deriving from ICCPR—and the related UN Guiding Principles on Business and Human Rights—in their terms of service. Yet critics have found their embrace of these international legal principles woefully lacking; the companies often fall short in living these values and implementing them.[47] International bodies such as the United Nations have continued to engage with the companies to urge them to do more in terms of enforcement. There continues to be criticism of the lack of full compliance, and the United Nations has called out the problems associated with non-inciting speech, specifically: "Inadequate investment by social media companies in efforts to counter online hate speech, given the speed, volume and diversity of online postings. In particular lack of investment in tackling hate speech that does not reach the threshold of incitement, requiring multipronged approaches, beyond content removal."[48] For such non-inciting hate speech, the UN notes that there are a variety of tools: "Alternatives to content removal should be considered, such as labels, demonetization, limiting 'reach,' or counter-speech."[49] This is to say that the ICCPR provides an important framework for thinking about content moderation, but there may need to be tailored strategies that fit specific problems, and international legal guidance from the United Nations endorses nuanced strategies.

OLD RIGHTS, NOVEL CASES

Thus, the First Amendment was there at the creation of human rights. The ICCPR, a more technocratic fix to notable omissions, now spans much of the globe, but its general acceptance and moral impact are simply not that of the Universal Declaration of Human Rights. Human rights law as applied to speech and the First Amendment have been inextricably bound together from the very beginning, even as their relationship has grown increasingly complicated in the digital era. Do we need new rules altogether now? What would they look like? How might these be connected to values forged through a long and noble struggle, begun by Eleanor Roosevelt in 1946, however incomplete and unfinished? Understanding these deep roots can help us contextualize many of the broad trends and threats that characterize the social media era.

The hate speech cases that now continually pop up around the world are complex. Courts are trying to adjudicate ever more novel problems created by a globalized speech environment. Taken together, such cases remain a chaotic jumble of conflicting findings. Legal scholars are trying to bring order to the chaos. For example, the Global Freedom of Expression project at Columbia University is trying to create one of the first global databases where case law from different international jurisdictions might be brought together and compared. The project was launched by

Columbia University President Lee Bollinger, a leading First Amendment scholar, who has articulated a need to consolidate case law globally with the hope of creating more uniform standards. He has noted that free speech law in the United States evolved from a very local or state undertaking through to a set of national standards, first clearly laid out in the 1964 decision in *Times v. Sullivan*, which largely prevents public officials from suing critics—thus keeping political speech almost completely wide open in the United States. "Just as the course of history with respect to freedom of speech and press has been to move to national principles as issues have become more national in scope," Bollinger has written, "so too must that happen on a global scale as the issues have become global in scope." He identifies the grand intellectual project for the twenty-first century speech issues as "to evolve global norms about these rights and to determine which global freedom of expression norms are essential for this interconnected world."[50]

Consider the difficulties involved in just one relevant example of this struggle for global norms. In the 2019–2020 case of *Ein Prozent v. Facebook Ireland Ltd.*, a German organization, Ein Prozent, or "One Percent," decided to dox a journalist who had reported on the organization.[51] Facebook chose to take down the post and deactivate the group's account on the platform. Ein Prozent had also made various offensive statements about migrants and refugees, and in the judgment of Facebook's moderators, it qualified as a hate organization. The group sued Facebook, arguing that the company had violated a civil law in Germany mandating clarity and transparency in terms and conditions of commercial products. On appeal, the Dresden Higher Regional Court ruled in favor of Facebook, saying that it had defined hate organizations sufficiently and precisely enough in the platform's Community Standards and therefore had the right to ban the group. From the perspective of policing hate speech, the case is fascinating: The German court ruled that offensive statements made by Ein Prozent might be OK under German laws protecting free expression, but taken together, they could trigger proof that it was a hate organization under Facebook's Community Standards. In other words, patterns of speech and behavior added up to proof positive of the nature of the group: a hate group. It was not so much the hateful speech that triggered the censorship, but what it proved about the speaker.

The Ein Prozent case represents innumerable others that social media companies deal with daily, although it's rare that one rises to the level of the courts. Given that Facebook (now Meta Platforms) is a private company in the United States, users would have little basis on which to sue Facebook for such a decision, as the company itself enjoys protections under both Section 230 and the First Amendment to make its own content moderation decisions. But Germany and many other countries have different laws on the books, in this case for contract and commercial interactions. As mentioned, Germany also has a powerful law called the Network Enforcement Act (NetzDG), which obligates platforms operating in its market to take down certain forms of misinformation and hate speech within a short period, or face fines.[52] The ghosts of the country's Nazi past haunt many such decisions and related debates; Germany has on its books various laws that expressly forbid messages supporting Nazism and Holocaust denial, although as with all things online, creative workarounds and memes sometimes defeat such restrictions, and the country has seen a resurgence of hate groups who flirt with neo-Nazism.

Yet even in a case where the German state might be sympathetic—tamping down the messages of hate groups—the specter of foreign intervention in internal affairs looms large. In deciding that Facebook was complying with the law, the Dresden Higher Regional Court nevertheless noted wider considerations about Facebook's enormous content moderation and market power because of its pervasive use: "When interpreting the Community standards and the balancing necessary in this context, it cannot be ignored that, due to this quasi-monopoly position in the area of social networks, the defendant takes over the framework conditions of public communication to a large extent and thus enters into functions that were previously assigned to the state as a task of services of general interest."[53]

In other words, the court had to consider that Facebook was, in effect, tantamount to the German public sphere itself. That would mean the government needed to guard against abuse of power to censor. If speakers are censored, they may have no other equivalent venue for expression. The lines between public and private power begin to blur in such situations, forcing novel calculations by domestic courts and governments that rightfully view external communications power over their citizens with alarm.

Parsing hate speech from borderline-but-allowable speech can, obviously, be incredibly difficult, especially given cultural differences and nuances of expression globally. One of the more intriguing first cases to be decided by the Meta Oversight Board, which is composed of independent experts and stakeholders who can rule on appealed cases they select, involves an allegation of hate speech relating to a post by a user in Myanmar, posted in Burmese.[54] Not everyone agrees that having such an independent board monitor and second-guess content moderation decision-making is a good idea, as it can seem a distraction, give the company cover and ethics wash, and may ultimately prove a paper tiger. Still, many see it as a potential model that begins to modify what is otherwise a very centralized, top-down model of corporate decision-making over users. And some board members began the work hoping to make a difference. "I had expressed interest in joining the board because I feel, and still do," said board member and digital rights activist Julie Owono during the effort's initial phase, "that Facebook is doing a terrible job on hate speech in environments that are already very tense."[55]

The Myanmar user in question posted two now-iconic pictures of a dead toddler, Alan Kurdi, whose body had washed up on a beach in Turkey during the Syrian refugee crisis; along with the images, the user posted disturbing musings about Muslims, including, according to Facebook's initial translation, "[there is] something wrong with Muslims psychologically." Yet the Oversight Board's own Burmese language experts translated the same phrase as "[t]hose male Muslims have something wrong in their mindset."[56] The Oversight Board deemed this phrase as less derogatory than the one originally interpreted. The user also referenced vague disparities between "Muslim" reactions to events in France and China, which seemed to suggest (to the Oversight Board) some kind of comparative point on behalf of the user in Myanmar and not necessarily a categorical slur against all Muslims.

In the appeals process, the user had also claimed he intended sarcasm and asserted that Facebook had a misunderstanding of nuances within the Burmese language. After reviewing the full context of the issue, the Oversight Board indeed elected to reinstate the user's post, having determined that it was not "hate speech" under the Community Standards.[57] The board cited Article 19 of ICCPR among other international human rights standards in its review: "Considering international human rights standards on limiting freedom of expression, the Board found that, while the post might be considered pejorative or offensive towards Muslims, it did not advocate hatred or intentionally incite any form of imminent harm."[58]

At one level, this decision-making by the Oversight Board looks like a successful translation from well-established standards and laws to a particular case. However, it took three months, and all that time and energy hardly solved a pressing case of international concern. It was a single user, whose post was likely one of many millions that day that was on the edge between acceptable and banned speech, insult and sarcasm, random musing and intentional provocation. How much the lesson generalizes is anyone's guess, and given the idiosyncrasies, it's doubtful it extends much beyond that post. What is important context, however, is that Facebook's platform had been thoroughly exploited by Myanmar security forces (and other Buddhist nationalists) in perpetrating sectarian acts of mass violence in 2017, a fact confirmed by both the United Nations and an independent inquiry funded by Facebook itself.[59] Both morally and reputationally, the company has taken a significant hit because of its lack of content moderation during that event, when some seven hundred thousand Rohingya Muslims were forcibly displaced along with documented mass killing and genocide. Still, even in 2022, reports suggested that the company had not gotten the problems associated with content moderation in that region fully under control.[60]

All of this prompts a larger question: How much should political context—what Oversight Board member Owono might refer to as an "already tense situation"—matter in these circumstances? Certainly, there are many human and digital rights advocates who are torn on this point: It would be good to treat users and their speech "equally" and have procedures in place that are uniform. But is that very idea of uniformity under law missing the point, perhaps a hangover from the American quest to produce a standardized jurisprudence under the First Amendment? Few human and digital rights advocates would love to see the Facebooks of the world act imperiously all the time, but many might support ramping up content moderation temporarily, when lives are on the line in a civil conflict. Given Myanmar's recent history, is it worth endlessly parsing

the speech of a user who is clearly raising hostile questions and reinforcing stereotypes about Muslims? Such questions come down to moral
judgment that corporations are often ill-suited to decide.

ALGORITHMIC SOLUTIONS?

The rise of generative AI is allowing for better tools for reading user-
generated messages and interpreting them with more subtlety. Such tools
are beginning to change the field of trust and safety, and automation will
play a bigger role in curbing hate speech in the future, even as humans
will need to be in the loop to help settle disagreements and attend to
novel issues that are outside of AI training data. How such technologies
will be implemented precisely is unknown. Indeed, we seldom get a clear
look at how social platforms use algorithms to perform tasks, as they
are kept under wraps for a variety of reasons: they are trade secrets to
be kept from competitors; companies want to avoid giving information
that bad actors could exploit and game; and platforms may not want
public scrutiny.

One window into these complex processes came out of the U.S. Congressional (House) investigation into the events of January 6, where
investigators had subpoena power and were able to interview platform
managers. According to this account, Facebook used a novel strategy to
deal with hate speech and other forms of content that violated terms of
service. A centrally important aspect of the challenge in this context for
Facebook was the concept of probability. One approach, called "probable
violating demotions," was structured through mathematical formulas.[61]
Classifier algorithms cannot always be sure if what a user is saying is hate
speech, or just something borderline offensive or even crudely humor-
ous. Such automated systems must make a probabilistic guess. The Facebook team decided to create a kind of golden ratio: If something is 10
percent likely to be hate speech, it is then 10 percent less likely to be seen
in user's news feeds across the platform. This "break the glass" measure
then proportionally escalates, as the probability of a true instance of hate
speech increases. So if a post is judged 95 percent likely to be hate speech,
theoretically almost no one will see it on the platform. This is not a typi-
cal approach for the company, as content moderators will often link a

probability to a more fixed action (e.g., a demotion of five times, or an outright removal). But the general point is that companies experiment with different uses of probability to moderate content.

Yet as congressional investigators noted, the company's bottom line was often top-of-mind for leadership, making them unlikely to sign off on risk-prevention measures being implemented: "Many Facebook employees complained that leadership was often skeptical of potential interventions which might limit MSI [meaningful social interactions], growth, or user engagement."[62] One inherent problem that Facebook— and any other company doing content moderation—was working against is that cultural and political context is ever-evolving; language itself and the meaning of words, phrases, symbols, and images are slippery. For automated systems to catch up with this evolutionary process, they must be trained on new data. But that takes time. There is therefore leakage and slippage in all machine learning/AI systems. If a platform wants to catch, let's say, half of all genuine hate speech, it might have to cast a big net. This means a lot of valid, nonviolating speech and messages will get taken down in such a dragnet. There are major trade-offs. As will be discussed in chapter 5, perhaps this will change as generative AI and newer technologies allow greater precision in identifying and classifying hate speech, incitement, and the like. But how much computer systems can keep up with humans, who are creative meaning-making creatures at their core, remains unclear.

Yet demotion and downranking carry potential downsides. Because of concerns about a lack of transparency and explainability to the public— and concerns that demotion amounts to "shadow banning,"[63] inviting accusations of political bias—some companies have been moving toward increasing the threshold (high bar) for items that might constitute hate speech but making the consequence clear and definitive through removal or account suspension.

IS COUNTERSPEECH EFFECTIVE AGAINST HATE?

In the matter of online hate speech, solutions-focused research is still nascent in many ways, especially around the effectiveness of counterspeech.[64] The prevalence of hate speech is difficult to measure, scholars generally agree, and it likely constitutes only a very tiny fraction of all content on mainstream platforms.[65] That said, in surveys, fairly large segments of the public say they have seen abuse online or have themselves been targeted, and some of that undoubtedly involves attacks on identity and personal characteristics.[66] Some studies, using careful experimental methods, have found that varying the tone of the counterspeech is particularly important, and that empathy in particular might be an effective strategy in certain situations, in terms of changing the behavior of hate speech originators.[67]

Catherine Buerger of the Dangerous Speech Project has studied another promising approach, which involves prosocial online "bystanders" weighing in collectively against hate speech. These groups attempt to create and reinforce a social norm and recruit the "movable middle" of people online (persuadable users, not the online haters) to support anti-hate and positive speech.[68] As more migrants from the Middle East and Africa have become part of Swedish society, the country has seen a rise in anti-immigrant expression, and newspaper articles circulating on social media tend to attract negative comments full of hate. But a civil society group has risen up to try to change this dynamic. Buerger notes the success of the Swedish Facebook group #jagärhär (or "I am here," in English), a collective of many tens of thousands of users who band together to fight hate. The goals of the group are not to respond directly to the authors of hate speech but to flood comment sections with critical posts (e.g., saying hate is not OK or deploying facts and reason) or positive messages that, on Facebook, will crowd out the hate speech and push prosocial and civil comments to the top of the comment thread. The goal is also to activate more counterspeakers beyond the activist #jagärhär members.

The work of #jagärhär represents an "ideal" counterspeech situation, where there is an explicit and powerful constituency in civil society that is looking out for the digital commons, trying to bring civility to public discourse. But the question is scale, and whether it is realistic to rely on such extraordinary efforts to put out fires around the world. Large-scale quantitative studies that have examined dynamics between hate speech and counterspeech have noted that organized efforts to generate counterspeech often are reasonably effective in the long run, even if they initially may incite a backlash from hateful users. Feeding "the trolls" can lead to redoubled efforts by bad actors, but sustained counter-efforts can prevail in changing the overall tone of the conversation and cooling things down.[69] Ultimately, organized efforts may tip the norm-based balance back toward civility online.

However, our understanding of why people voice hate online may not always be correct. In a war or conflict, as we have seen, demonizing the other side has a strategic dimension—for motivating societies, discouraging enemies, and persuading potential allies to join one's side. But most online hate is not a tool in a war situation. Pervasive hateful sentiment seems to ooze from all corners of global societies, generated by grievances new and old, poor education, disinformation, and damaging socialization, and general racism, sexism, and religious bigotry. Victims or targets are numerous and often isolated; hate speech is not always part of a highly organized campaign, even if it is usually a networked phenomenon involving groups.

One of the founders of the research field analyzing the dynamics of interpersonal online relationships, Joseph Walther of the University of California, Santa Barbara, has begun studying hate speech through a wider lens, overturning popular assumptions about what drives hate speech and antisocial speakers online. He has noted that the assumption in both the research literature and popular discourse is that hate is intended to antagonize a target. But Walther believes that the motivation is better understood as an attempt to garner social attention: The audience for hate is primarily other haters, not targets.[70] In many cases, the authors of hate speech are looking for social approval from a networked community: They engage in a perverse atmosphere of "fun," congratulating one another with digital "high fives" and participating in online escapades, raids, and attacks.[71] Many originators of hate speech are merrily and sardonically participating in community-building, albeit in a deviant, often sadistic, way.

If Walther's hypothesis is valid, then solutions become very obviously about disrupting the antisocial "fun" and not as much about creating wider social norm shifts. There is no doubt that the social platforms, using design architectures such as how comments are organized on posts, can help prosocial forces fight against hate and promote counternorms of peace and civility. Yet thinking carefully about how to intervene in networks of hate or, better yet, make it difficult for them to form in the first place, are the place for companies and public policy to do more work. Walther believes that certain features or affordances of social platforms are in some ways the problem; these include the "ability to find an appreciative audience, easy access to targets, the publicness of messaging activity and its consequences for attitude reinforcement, and the variety of easy-to-deploy signals of social approval that social media users transmit at scale to reinforce others' messaging."[72] Social platforms might look not only to empower counterspeakers but also to create better-designed online architectures and enable features that emphasize prosocial behavior and tamp down on the trolls and haters.

A related research community has been thinking about similar techniques and issues of disruption and intervention: the groups who consider themselves part of the Preventing and Countering Violent Extremism (PVE/CVE) field. Persons in this sector often come from the behavioral or social sciences side of national security studies, and they are interested not only in fighting the likes of Islamist terrorists and neo-Nazis, but also figuring out what generally works in terms of counterspeech messaging and deradicalization. It should be noted that changing online behavior and changing actual mental beliefs of individuals are not the same thing. Measuring scientifically how deeply techniques may penetrate in terms of countering extremism—whether online strategies might serve to deradicalize people and create belief change—is very difficult. That said, there is some experimental evidence that counterspeech generally can, at the very least, not generate increased extremism, and in many cases shift behavior in terms of making an individual less likely to engage with extremist content. There is also evidence that such efforts may have limited effect.[73] More promisingly in this domain, researchers have had some success "redirecting" those engaged in extremist communities toward resources with NGOs who specialize in deradicalization (often groups who employ former violent extremists now committed to peace).[74]

VARYING GLOBAL PREFERENCES

The 2022 presidential race in the Philippines, which resulted in the election of a Duterte-supported successor, "Bongbong" Romualdez Marcos Jr., saw the acceleration of many of the same disinformation-related trends that had plagued prior election cycles—and that Maria Ressa had had to fight against.[75] Observers have called the country "patient zero" of election disinformation globally, even as it has produced a variety of innovative counter-disinformation strategies from civil society groups.[76] Further, some of those targeted by the campaigns of hate speech and disinformation in the Philippines have become influential voices as global advocates on these issues. Ressa has now embarked on a global "10 point" campaign to address the harms of social media, while the former vice president, Leni Robredo, who lost to Marcos Jr. in 2022, has also become an important voice on human rights in the digital age, as a survivor of disinformation campaigns that targeted her in highly gendered ways.[77]

The recent history experienced by the people of the Philippines matters enormously in terms of how human rights are expressed and understood on the ground. Although rights may in theory be universal, communities may interpret rights in highly distinctive ways, even within ostensibly similar cultural regions (see figure 3.3). Despite the ambitions of the Facebook Oversight Board—and other policy and content moderation teams from other global companies—to formulate decisions that are universal in character, much depends on cultural perspective, and data often bear this out. For example, as part of an ongoing project to evaluate global public opinion on social media content moderation, in 2023 my team at Northeastern University surveyed a nationally representative sample of persons in the Philippines and the United States to compare their views on issues such as how harmful speech should be handled.[78] In the surveys, the differences between the two countries were often stark when it came to policy preferences, even as they were surprisingly similar on how they viewed individual rights.

During the heated 2016 elections that took place in both countries, American and Filipino citizens in tandem began experiencing significant challenges relating to disinformation and hate speech in public life, when Duterte (May) and Trump (November) were each first elected. The resemblances are not accidental. Cambridge Analytica, the firm that illicitly used Facebook data to help the Trump campaign, reportedly first tested out its strategies earlier in 2016 in the Philippines election; because Filipinos are such active social media users and the country's communications

People in Asia are divided on whether it's more important to say one's opinion or to preserve harmony

% of adults in each place who say that ...

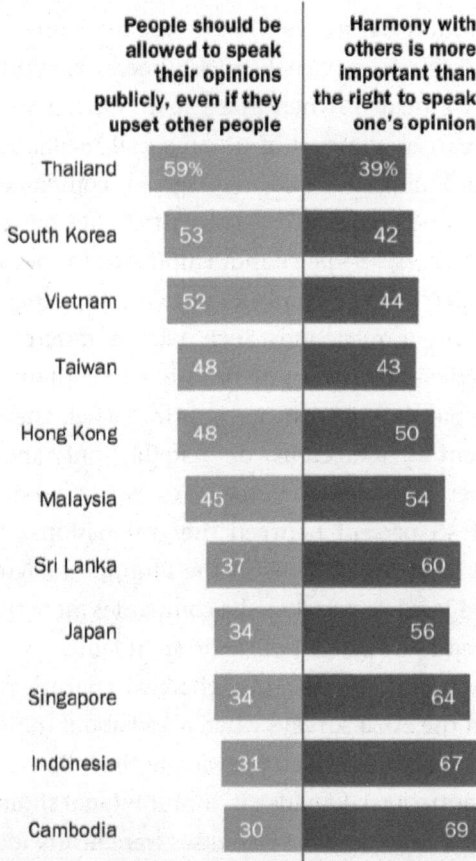

	People should be allowed to speak their opinions publicly, even if they upset other people	Harmony with others is more important than the right to speak one's opinion
Thailand	59%	39%
South Korea	53	42
Vietnam	52	44
Taiwan	48	43
Hong Kong	48	50
Malaysia	45	54
Sri Lanka	37	60
Japan	34	56
Singapore	34	64
Indonesia	31	67
Cambodia	30	69

Figure 3.3 Surveys by the Pew Research Center in 2022–2023 suggest that, even within global regions such as Asia, there is enormous diversity of opinion about the proper balance between free expression and societal values such as stability or harmony. "People in Asia Are Divided on Whether It's More Important to Say One's Opinion or to Preserve Harmony," Pew Research Center, Washington, D.C. (July 12, 2024), https://www.pewresearch.org/short-reads/2024/07/15/many-adults-in-east-and-south east-asia-support-free-speech-are-open-to-societal-change/sr_24-07-15_free-speech -asia_2.

regulatory environment has been fairly wide open and hands-off (similar to that of the United States), the South Asian country was thought of as a kind of "ideal petri dish" to explore new techniques that could be exploited later in Western countries.[79] The countries have had some similar experiences, in other words. But the degree of disinformation and violence on the ground during the Duterte regime scarred the Filipino public, and the two countries have distinct human rights histories.

In the surveys we fielded, when asked if it is better to "limit some harmful content than to allow all of it" on social media, 85 percent of respondents in the Philippines said they agreed, compared to only 57 percent of U.S. respondents. Asked if content should be restricted if it "causes distress on others," 84 percent of Filipinos said they either somewhat or strongly agreed, whereas only 44 percent of Americans indicated approval of such content restrictions. Such national differences were also evident when we asked about trusting decisions in content moderation. When asked if people should trust "authorities" when they restrict certain kinds of content as "dangerous" or "hateful," only about one-third (34 percent) of Americans agreed, compared to 79 percent of Filipinos—a substantial gap of 45 percent between the two nations. About three-quarters (76 percent) of respondents in the Philippines agreed that the government should regulate social media companies more than they currently are, compared to 47 percent of U.S. respondents.

Yet it is interesting to consider that the two countries' preferences seemed to align on the 2023 surveys when asked about individual rights and speech. Both groups were asked to evaluate the following statement: "No matter how controversial an idea is, an individual should be able to express it publicly." The two sets of responses were nearly identical, with 57 percent of Americans in agreement (24 percent said neither agree nor disagree) and 56 percent of Filipinos agreeing (27 percent neither agree/disagree.) The surveys asked the two publics to evaluate other such ideas, including, "Everybody should have full liberty to promote what they believe to be true" and "All individuals should have the right to openly express their ideas, no matter how prejudiced they might be." On these questions, respondents in the Philippines and United States were again roughly aligned, with a little more than half of each group expressing approval.

This 2023 cross-national survey data is just a snapshot in time of two nations, but it points to a potentially important distinction between how people may think differently about rights in theory and solutions to problems. The universal aspirations of international human rights law related to expression—to uphold ideals for citizens to speak their conscience and hold beliefs as they see fit—may be generally embraced by many societies. But that does not mean that societies will necessarily have harmonized views on policy, or what to do about harms such as hate speech and disinformation targeting other groups. Even within a discrete region or continent, views may diverge widely. Such policy views are likely to be shaped by national circumstance, particularly as societies undergo severe challenges relating to their online information environment, as the Philippines recently has.

FUTURE POLICY

The United States embodies the most wide-open speech environment and has some of the most permissive laws around hate speech. It also headquarters many of the most important global platforms. It would therefore be globally consequential if new American regulations were put in place that urged greater responsibility, and a more energetic response, by the relevant communications platform companies regarding hate speech. It would change the default and create a new baseline, or floor, for policy around the world. While hate speech, loosely speaking, may still be allowable under the First Amendment, addressing online harms from hate speech could be part of how social platforms regularly demonstrate their responsibility to regulators. Of course, individual cases may prove difficult, and algorithms and even human experts may miss damaging material, or even disagree about the risk it carries. There should be room for error. Under a new regulatory regime, it would not be absolutely required, perhaps, that any given speech act or message be taken down. But showing attention to the problems of hate speech is one way that a given company could demonstrate a duty of care and satisfy a more general requirement of social responsibility. Audits could establish a baseline for the degree of hate speech endured by certain communities, and companies could be brought to account about whether their policies and platform design facilitate a disparate impact on certain identity communities.

The Universal Declaration of Human Rights and the Covenant are, as we have seen, major accomplishments on the world stage, in part facilitated by U.S. leadership. Bringing their spirit into the age of social platforms and online speech is completely in keeping with American traditions, and in fact ensures that the protections that were so hard earned through the twentieth century can flourish again in this age of social and digital platforms.

4

ON INCITEMENT

[N]o danger flowing from speech can be deemed clear and present unless the incidence of the evil apprehended is so imminent that it may befall before there is opportunity for full discussion. If there be time to expose through discussion the falsehood and fallacies, to avert the evil by the processes of education, the remedy to be applied is more speech, not enforced silence. Only an emergency can justify repression. Such must be the rule if authority is to be reconciled with freedom.[1]
—Justice Louis D. Brandeis, *Whitney v. California* (1927)

Incitement to lawless action and legitimately protected, but fiery, political speech are often close cousins, and the difference can depend on the subjective experience and worldviews of those watching or involved. Hate speech can be terrible and contribute to violence, even genocide, as it has in the era of social platforms in such places as Myanmar and Ethiopia.[2] Hate speech contributes to a narrative of demonization; it is a tool of power and control. Incitement, by contrast, leads to some direct action. The question of whether a statement constitutes incitement often depends on how direct or how likely such an action is, given the inciting message. Incitement is also an organizing tool. Messages can incite calls for political revolution or resistance, civil disobedience or boycotts. Nonviolent but physically disruptive action might be incited by a social media post. But incitement is also the domain of terrorists and heavily armed groups, who often need do no more than speak in coded and bland language and symbols to activate some pre-planned strike.

By definition, incitement is potentially dangerous. So what do we do about incitement on networked communications platforms? What are reasonable expectations (from society and potential regulators) for the corporations handling such speech? We have reviewed the *Brandenburg v. Ohio* precedent for defining incitement, as well as the fighting words standard in the context of American law. Yet, we've also seen that there is a great deal of ambiguity in these definitions, and new dimensions introduced by the shift to online communication make definitional precision only more difficult.

In this chapter, I will argue that social media platforms need to do three major things to address the problem of incitement. First, social platforms should be required by law to do risk assessments around incitement and terrorism and to have on hand, at all times, sufficient personnel and technical capacity to handle reasonably foreseeable threats. As will be discussed, the events around the U.S. Capitol on January 6, 2021, underscore clearly the need for this kind of preparedness and capacity. Second, social platforms must embrace a version of what legal scholars are calling the "overt acts rule," which, in the judicial context, means taking into account what platform users are doing in the real world (as best can be discerned through investigation and research) where ambiguously inciting speech is in question.[3] Translated to platforms, this would mean that content moderators take a more "actor-based" approach to assessing the content and meaning of speech, devoting much more time to understanding how online speech may be related to offline, violent planning or activity.

Finally, working in tandem with legal scholars and governments, social platforms must begin to settle a long-running and highly technical debate about the feasibility, and legality, of monitoring encrypted messaging apps. In recent years, much violent organizing and incitement has taken place on end-to-end encrypted messaging (or hybrid messaging/social) apps, including Signal, WhatsApp, and Telegram. Is there a way to keep encrypted spaces safe, and to provide some content moderation, without breaking encryption? New technological and cryptographic innovations hold some promise. Yet before we can get to these three platform-related solutions, it is worth unpacking some examples and context for evaluating incitement in the contemporary environment.

NO EXPERIENCED SUPERVISOR ON DUTY

The Ellipse is a fifty-two-acre park lined with white elms that sits south of the White House; it is where, over the generations, Civil War and World

War II troops have massed and organized; where old-time professional baseball games were played, and religious sermons preached. It's also the place where on Jan. 6, 2021, a sitting president wearing black leather gloves, a long trench coat, and a red tie rallied his followers while standing beside the banner "Save America March." The goal was not to win a war but to overturn an election.

On January 6, 2021, President Donald J. Trump, at a privately organized campaign-style event, encouraged a large crowd of supporters at the Ellipse to march over at the to the Capitol building to protest the results of the election. His speech ended: "And we fight. We fight like hell. And if you don't fight like hell, you're not going to have a country anymore. . . . So we're going to, we're going to walk down Pennsylvania Avenue. I love Pennsylvania Avenue. And we're going to the Capitol, and we're going to try and give."[4] This coded incitement led to a highly dangerous situation involving violence against police officers, rioting within the Capitol building, and a narrowly avoided calamity wherein many top political leaders might have been killed by an angry mob. The world has seen numerous dangerous events in which networked technologies fueled violence. But January 6 had a special quality—a kind of tragic, chickens-coming-home-to-roost dimension—of showing that the United States, the key driver producing the world's leading technology platforms, could undermine its own democratic institutions, the oldest in the world, in a matter of hours.

The riot at the Capitol building in Washington, DC, on January 6, 2021, egged on by President Donald J. Trump, seemed an astonishing event, even if, in retrospect, many saw it as the logical culmination of a controversial term office by a highly unorthodox leader and his followers. It is worth viewing the event in a bit more context, as its particular details—and what happened behind-the-scenes on social platforms, leading up to and during the event—frame some of the central problems that likely need to be addressed through public policy and regulatory reforms, both domestically and globally. Almost all the public discourse about January 6 and the social media companies has focused on their subsequent decision to ban Trump's accounts on their platforms. But this misses larger, more systemic questions about how companies should be expected to behave and manage risk around disinformation.

On December 19, 2020, President Trump tweeted out messages to his followers urging them to protest the election at a Washington, DC, event on January 6, adding at one point "be there, will be wild." Thousands of extremist and paramilitary individuals and groups across the web, already highly organized around the president's cause and campaign throughout 2020, began to focus their attention on that geographic location and date.[5] Meanwhile, social platforms of many kinds suddenly faced a variety of dilemmas, ones that extended beyond anything they had ever bothered to prepare for. What became clear over the coming weeks, and in the aftermath of the January 6 riots at the Capitol, is that the lack of rules for running networked communications platforms—not just about what to take down or leave up, but even basic requirements for staffing and paying attention to problems—fundamentally damaged American society. Such conclusions are justified by indisputable facts documented in fine-grained detail in an unpublished (but subsequently leaked) report by January 6 House Select Committee investigators on the role of social media in the events.[6]

Although the images of the physical, offline January 6 riot are shocking, the account of what happened across digital space before and after that date is almost equally extraordinary. The ground had been "prepared," so to speak, well before the election. A subreddit (an interest-focused, volunteer-moderated discussion board within the larger Reddit platform) called r/The_Donald became a hub for organizing, helping to push the entire paramilitary and extremist community to a central platform site, TheDonald.win, where calls for violence—many of which might qualify as illegal incitement or even seditious activity—became a mainstay. Reddit did not shut the subreddit down until it was far too late, in the summer of 2020. By that time, online communities had become well organized, and preparations for protesting a potential defeat in the election were set in motion (coalescing around the "Stop the Steal" campaign, what amounted to an enormous disinformation campaign).[7] A mid-December event supporting the president in 2020 had become violent, and violence of some kind was widely expected during the January 6 events.[8] Although Twitter and Facebook took some actions, they were relatively modest in the run-up to the election in terms of actively trying to curb extremist organizing.

Immediately after the president's "will be wild" tweet on December 19, the social and instant messaging platform Discord had an unprecedented crisis: A server (an individual instance of the platform controlled by a user group) became, within hours, a giant organizing community focused on bringing weapons to the Capitol for the protest. Discord, known for its decentralization and laissez-faire content moderation, took the extraordinary step of shutting down a server called DonaldsArmy.US, which was organizing the paramilitary actions of supporters.[9] At this point, a variety of smaller "alt social" sites such as Gab, Parler, 8kun, 4chan, along with TheDonald.win, were becoming hives for extremist organizing, with cross-platform content such as plans, memes, and instructions virally cascading from site to site, group to group. Almost all these platforms lacked, according to investigators, "even a remotely adequate content moderation system"[10]—one where even a violent threat directed at an individual, which is illegal under federal law and carries no free speech protections, could freely be expressed, approved of by thousands of people, and kept visible and public indefinitely. The site Gab, with perhaps two million users and tens of millions of regular visits, had a grand total of one person doing content moderation on January 6.[11]

Throughout, persistent cries by figures on the political right to "protect" the First Amendment became a kind of blind, unreasoning excuse to allow violent threats and organizing to persist. Such radical free speech sentiments meant there were few acts of courage by platform managers. Congressional investigators subsequently interviewed platform owners and managers under oath and found that "even content that the owners of these sites themselves admit should be deleted . . . ahead of real-world harm" was not taken down, for fear of looking like they were not defending the First Amendment (as they conceived of it) for their platform users.[12]

The apparent negligence of even the more "responsible" platforms was also extraordinary, despite elaborate preparations for Election Day itself. Yet many of those measures were dismantled in the run-up to January 6. Some platforms were riven by internal tensions, as platform managers at Twitter, Facebook, YouTube, among others, feared accusations of partisan censorship if they took strong action against criticisms of the integrity of the presidential election. Balancing competing interests in

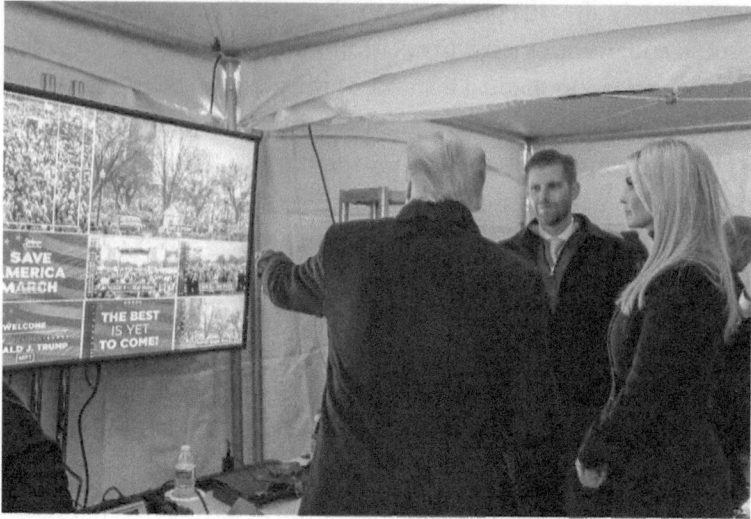

Figure 4.1 President Donald J. Trump, with his family advisors, reviews video screens as he prepares to speak to a crowd of supporters at The Ellipse in Washington, DC, on January 6, 2021. Highly organized through social media and online forums, the crowd would subsequently march to the Capitol and ransack parts of the building, while also threatening and injuring government and security officials. Courtesy, Donald J. Trump Presidential Library.

this regard is never easy, but time and again, platforms lacked the basic staffing and attention necessary to adequately handle the threat or the stakes for the country. Without resources dedicated, decisions to act, or not act, proved to be weakly considered, often reactive, or in some cases just the result of inertia, bumbling, or laziness. Nothing in the law necessarily required platform staff to make informed judgments based on well-resourced efforts, and they behaved accordingly, overwhelmed by the scale of efforts to undermine the election and often hapless in their attempts to mitigate harms, given the small teams on hand as events escalated out of control.

Twitter's experience was perhaps the most poignant, particularly given the president's well-known affinity for the platform and his constant use of it during his term in office. Because of prior incidents of violence that had unfolded during the president's term, Twitter had created a policy for "coded incitement to violence," or CIV. But the policy was essentially not in place on January 6, and even if it was, the platform dramatically underresourced whatever team would have implemented it. Instead, as with the Gab platform, Twitter had only a few staff who ended up in charge of content moderation on January 6, including at the crucial moment of violence at the Capitol—when it had become abundantly clear, hours prior, that an all-hands crisis was highly possible for the platform.[13] When a staffer asked about how to implement the CIV policy, there was no one home: The regular manager was attending a funeral, and the backup manager was based in Ireland. Indeed, "no experienced supervisor was on duty" as the world's leading democracy attempted to certify its presidential election, in the face of an angry crowd that had been publicly directed eighteen days prior to show up for a "wild" situation.[14]

As congressional investigators note, when the riot began intensifying Twitter faced a "barrage of posts that essentially 'live-streamed' the attack, with details that were specific enough to focus on individual breach points and different areas of the Capitol that the crowd had reached."[15] Hashtags that called for the assassination of officials, including the vice president, began proliferating. Investigators concluded that the platform was totally unprepared, based on interviews with those involved on the frontlines of Twitter. They didn't even have the technical capacity to address content violations at any scale: "Because there was not a CIV policy or special response team in place for the Joint Session—as would have been routine practice for other events with a risk of sociopolitical unrest— members of the Safety Policy Team were manually taking down violent tweets, including those including '#ExecuteMikePence,' using only the Twitter search function. This understaffed, ramshackle [approach] made the former employee feel like she was a security guard hovering over the Capitol, trying to defend the building as the crowd tweeted out its progress during the course of the assault."[16]

No interpretation of the First Amendment would plausibly protect content that is aiding a terrorist attack and insurrection, and yet Twitter equivocated. When federal officials reached out to the platform to inform them of the riot organizers who were using Twitter, the head of U.S. policy at the platform did not recognize the name of a semifamous extremist, well known to almost everyone monitoring far-right extremism and militant groups. "It is amazing to me that people like Ron Watkins still have Twitter accounts," one outraged government official wrote to Twitter's manager for U.S. policy in a January 6 email.

"Who is Ron Watkins?" the Twitter manager replied.

"For real?" the government official wrote back, adding colorfully that the active Twitter account in question was linked to the extreme, fringe platforms managers. "He and his dad run 8chan/8kun. They are widely believed to have taken over the QAnon conspiracy a few years ago . . . you should also check out [name redacted by Twitter's counsel]—she's the QAnon-brain-poisoned woman who was shot today for storming the Capitol."[17] It was clear that there had been little preparation at Twitter in terms of understanding the events that might unfold as the election was being certified—and who might orchestrate them.

But step back for a moment. This is what fighting inciting speech and disinformation often looks like in granular detail, on the frontlines of today: intelligent people in government, business, and civil society trying to cope with a kind of networked madness. Ideas that might otherwise seem fringe gather a kind of kinetic power by being passed repeatedly across networks of highly motivated, or perhaps just vulnerable, people. Bots, inauthentic accounts, and indeed platform company algorithms often amplify these messages, creating the illusion that the social facts (likes, comments, views, shares, digital trace data) favor messages, providing the veneer of approval. Narratives take shape and gather power, bursting across platforms, sowing confusion.

What is perhaps most damaging is the way in which much of this takes place in darkness, often in private encrypted spaces. Even on more open platforms, however, managers often see problems, but they do not prepare the public for what is about to happen, nor is there any mechanism compelling them to do so. Storms gather, but no one is warned. Instant communications technologies have sped up almost all aspects of disinformation, incitement, and terrorist tactics.

The events of January 6, 2021, illustrate the need for reform across three dimensions. First, it was clear that platforms such as Twitter did not have sufficient capacity in place to act in a crisis where terrorism is being incited and abetted in real time. Part of a platform's duty of care and commitment to social responsibility should entail, even require, preparedness. Second, on many open, mainstream platforms, actors and organizations/networks of groups were allowed to post messages that, if taken in the wider context of their offline activity, were clearly meant to incite violence. Communications platform moderators should be much more comprehensive in their assessment of what kinds of messages might be allowable.

Finally, because so much violent organizing and inciting speech presumably also took place (and continues to take place) in "dark" spaces on the internet—namely, on encrypted apps such as WhatsApp, Telegram, and Signal, as well as smaller, alternative platforms—a variety of technical solutions need to be considered that could help do at least some moderation in these spaces, even as encryption is preserved. Computer scientists have developed new ways to do this—for example, allowing messages to be reported by users and surfaced, scanning of messages after they have been unencrypted, and more—but the law has yet to fully catch up.[18]

Although there has subsequently been a great deal of backsliding in terms of company safety measures, there initially seemed to be a reasonable chance that the decisive tipping point in terms of regulating socially networked communications media was going to be January 6, 2021.[19] A wide array of peer-reviewed research has confirmed a strong, direct connection between social media and violence during those events.[20]

REPLYING TO NAZIS

In thinking about how to handle dangerous political incitement, it is useful to remember that this debate is not new. We must also take seriously the possibility of government abuse through surveillance and the threat of censorship, which has a long history. Balancing the values of safety, privacy, and freedom of speech is never a finished process. Even in the most extreme circumstances, the proper balance must be considered. We can return, in fact, to the social scientist Harold Lasswell and the debate going on about how to deal with the Nazi attempts to promote subversion and inciting propaganda, targeting allied nations and minority populations.

On March 23, 1939, the radio show *America's Town Meeting of the Air*, a production of the NBC Blue Network, was crackling across speakers in kitchens and living rooms, porches and bar rooms. The panel of experts assembled on air was chewing over questions of the limits of free speech and the dangers of censorship. The show had a studio audience in Town Hall, at 123 West 43rd Street in New York City, which was encouraged to cheer and boo, as the case may be, and to ask occasional questions of the panel.

The country was in a tense mood: War was brewing in Europe again; ten days prior, Adolph Hitler had declared the *Anschluss*, the annexation of the Federal State of Austria by the German Reich. Meanwhile, Joseph Stalin, General Secretary of the Communist Party of the Soviet Union, had carried out purges across a vast swath of Eurasia. Fascist, communist, and Nazi supporters had sprouted up all over Europe, and, increasingly, in the United States.

NBC's *America's Town Meeting of the Air*, which eventually ran for more than two decades, fashioned itself as a public affairs show for the country, a progenitor to the many such TV shows that would come about later during the mid-century period. Sometimes these radio "meetings" were framed around social issues, such as "What's wrong with American marriages?" (an episode sponsored by Home Brand Foods and Minuet Crackers.)[21] But in early March 1939, the question at hand was an urgent political one: What should be done about speakers and propagandists who want to promote Nazi, fascist, or communist doctrines? Should they be able to do so freely? The question was at bottom a constitutional one, but as the country steeled itself again for possible war, questions of free speech and censorship were again pressing down, as they had during the late 1910s and the creation of Creel's Committee on Public Information.

American society at the time was full of calls for censorship and suppression of enemy propaganda and its attempts to incite dissenting activity. Among the speakers on the radio program was Lasswell, a pioneering political scientist who had produced the most detailed studies of World War I propaganda.[22] He listened as the other panelists put forth their views. All agreed that free speech must be preserved—one speaker said the United States would be committing "suicide" if it gave up this tradition of free expression—but there were lots of ideas about how to check, or undermine, fascist or communist propagandists.

There was a range of suggestions for addressing such speech. A sitting congressman on the panel, J. Parnell Thomas of New Jersey, an opponent of the newly reelected president, Franklin D. Roosevelt, riled up the audience and got some digs in against the administration. Roosevelt's family members, Thomas asserted, had been speaking before communist front organizations. Thomas suggested that members of such front organizations should be forced into the open, fingerprinted, compelled to disclose funding sources; any noncitizens fraternizing with such groups should be deported. Still, Thomas noted that allowing them to speak openly is proper, and the "healing qualities of public opinion" will help to drown out the bad ideas.

Lasswell, for his part, suggested a more technocratic and targeted approach. He noted that, across many countries in Europe, the brown shirts (fascists) and red shirts (communists) had been banned, their speech suppressed. In the United States, Lasswell stated, no such ban is advisable. Rather, America needed an "instant reply plan of democratic defense" (as noted earlier in this book.) Where antidemocratic propaganda is spewed—even where there may be calls for rebellion or antidemocratic actions of various sorts—it needs to be met with counterspeech. If in print, Lasswell indicated, then equal shares of column inches must be dedicated to countervailing views; and the antidemocratic organization might be expected to pay for that extra print space. If over a radio channel, then the fascist or communist propaganda must be accompanied by time for opposing views.

It was the first time Lasswell had put forth such an idea, and he would spell it out in more detail a couple of years later in his 1941 book *Democracy Through Public Opinion*, where he would give it all capitals by calling it the "Instant Reply Plan" for dealing with propaganda that tried to incite antidemocratic activity. Lasswell generally believed in democratic mechanisms for addressing issues, and the instant reply plan seems to split the difference between unmitigated free speech and draconian forms of censorship. His bottom line was to tolerate inciting propaganda but make sure it was "labelled and liable to instant reply."[23]

The instinct for active response but speech preservation runs deeply through American legal and cultural traditions, and any new regulatory effort would do well to align with it, to the extent possible. Yet there are also some areas where clear lines and limits can be drawn, and these are also in keeping with U.S. tradition and legal thinking. It is worth recalling a few relevant standards that developed over the twentieth century. In the international context, the ICCPR tries to articulate standards for when government might rightfully act to punish or temporarily suppress expression when it involves libel, incitement to violence, or public health emergencies, for example. The ICCPR specifies that any censorship must be "by law" and "necessary"—two key standards. Censorship must be authorized by a governing body and actions should only be tailored to the requirements of a situation. These criteria for exceptions articulated in ICCPR—legality, narrow-tailoring, necessity for a specific purpose—look generally familiar in American law, as U.S. courts have decided over the years where the absolute limits are and what are legitimate government instances of restricting speech. Particularly when political speech is restricted because of the viewpoint or content, it is evaluated with great skepticism, or strict scrutiny, in the American legal system, following *Brandenburg v. Ohio* and subsequent jurisprudence. Both the American and international systems in theory agree that whenever government restricts speech, it must be narrow in scope, properly authorized, and fitted to a legitimate state interest or purpose. In terms of incitement specifically, as mentioned, edge cases involving fighting words test the limits of such legal frameworks; and there is a growing, and quite technical, legal debate, running all the way up to the Supreme Court, about "speech integral to criminal conduct," which is related to the "solicitation" of criminal conduct (which is not protected under the First Amendment).[24]

BREAK THE GLASS

Twitter's performance during the January 6 insurrection at the U.S. Capitol illustrates a glaring hole that Section 230 and its no-liability, no-obligation-to-respond philosophy have created. It is the problem of a lack of mandated preparedness and resources devoted in advance, and then in real time, to risky situations. It is the problem of allowing a fire department to have no hydrants and hoses. While it may never be easy to moderate illegal or policy-violating content instantly, most platforms have it in their power now, particularly with increasingly sophisticated automated tools (which are now advancing rapidly in the age of generative

AI), to address significant patterns of violent incitement and illegal activity unfolding over many hours. And they can certainly have more than a few people on hand. Social media companies have routinely begun tasking large, special teams to handle high-traffic moments such as sporting or political events, but nothing in the law requires them to do this—or to achieve any standard of basic effectiveness.

For platforms to be allowed to have no liability—even when they negligently underprepare and behave cluelessly or irresponsibly—is to invite more January 6 situations, in the United States and abroad. The question then becomes what kinds of rules and incentives might be put in place. The costs to companies to have more hands on deck, and to do more contingency planning, will be substantial. But in all major industries, safeguards increase over time, and it becomes an expected cost of doing business. Through modern history, across industries, it has often taken major disasters, fires, crashes, worker deaths, product-related fatalities, and the like to spur regulation. January 6 was the equivalent of a flaming oil spill in the information environment.

So, what kind of reasonable infrastructure and risk management procedures do social media companies need to have in place, to avoid liability? Facebook's response to January 6, like Twitter's, was inadequate, but its more sophisticated approach highlights important lessons and dilemmas that will need to be addressed in any future regulation.[25] As content moderators and managers know, it's not as if most users sign up for an account and show up at the moment of crisis, like some spontaneous angry mob in the town square. Networks of users have often been organizing, planning, and motivating one another, using memes, hashtags, symbols, and various forms of engagement to build solidarity and focus energies. And so while resources in the moment of crisis are crucial, it's often the case that crises, at least in digital space, can be defused or tamped down ahead of time.

The Facebook platform tried to take substantial measures around the 2020 election itself precisely to try to get ahead of events, even as it failed to fully implement policies and do more to prevent the "Stop the Steal" campaign from raging out of control after the election. Because of the company's notable failures in the 2016 election—allowing abuse of its platform by foreign actors and political campaigns alike, as well as fake news scammers—its leadership and staff were determined to prevent a repeat in 2020. And largely they did, through Election Day, at least. However, the "Stop the Steal" campaign stealthily gained momentum after November 2020, allowing a broad, networked set of actors to organize and gain momentum in the days before the election certification on January 6. The company had wound down important "pump-the-brakes" measures after Election Day.[26]

Under "break the glass" measures, the company tried many things: demoting the posts of people who repeatedly shared misinformation; removing share buttons or other "amplification levers" for certain kinds of content or recommendations for new political groups. The company's content moderation teams defined a group of "dangerous organizations" that were domestic U.S. actors who had strong inclinations toward violence, and they tracked them through the election and afterward.[27]

As part of their break the glass strategy used during the election period, moderators focused on both inhibiting leaders who were creating large, invite-only group chats (it turns out that a tiny fraction of persons in such groups did almost all the inviting) and trying to downrank or demote problematic posts and messages that persons saw across the broader platform.

What is clear is that humans will need to be in the loop in these systems. Brian Fishman, a key witness for the January 6 House Select Committee, was Facebook's lead on dealing with dangerous organizations. An experienced counter-terrorism policy expert, Fishman had the difficult task of trying to make a wide variety of judgment calls on how to deal with the likes of the conspiracy group QAnon and the "Stop the Steal" movement generally during the election and postelection period. The efforts of his team highlight a key movement in the field of content moderation to examine and focus on patterns of behavior as opposed to regulating or removing individual pieces of content, a kind of whack-a-mole approach that many veteran policy managers at companies have found mostly ineffective from a strategic standpoint, even if necessary at the tactical level. Fishman's efforts were "actor-based," in that they did not necessarily focus on moderating pieces of content, but rather on strategies that attempted to thwart movement growth and mobilization on the platform.[28]

Despite diligent efforts, though, Facebook faced an overwhelming task that, in retrospect, needed both more stringent policies and more resources as January 6 and election certification approached. As congressional investigators note, "The company removed thousands of groups, pages, accounts, and ads tied to QAnon and various militia groups and acted to reduce the reach and distribution of remaining accounts and hashtags on the platform. This number swelled well into the tens of thousands through the end of 2020 and the beginning of 2021."

Fishman noted that there is no substitute for humans being in the loop, as the complex systems that companies have built require sophisticated navigation during crises. Dangerous groups and individuals present novel and complicated problems that require re-engineering systems and deep know-how to track down and mitigate problems. There are often no "automatic" ways of dealing with malicious, creative networks of humans. As Fishman notes of networked platform actors, chasing them down demands careful, sustained work within the technological stack underneath the surface of the platforms:

None of those things are automatic, even though those systems are better than they used to be. They still require people to make smart judgment calls to deal with glitches in the software, to try to communicate that up to leadership in a way that is comprehensible to people that don't understand how all the internal tools work. And so, there's a lot of room there for error. And I think there is a perception outside of Silicon Valley that, like, tech companies have everything totally wired, and all you have to do is press a button on . . . a black screen with green letters, and all the sudden all sorts of perfect, sexy information drops out of the sky. But that's not the case. What really happens is a bunch of 25-year-olds go chase down that information and query four or five different systems and try to compile it in a way that is reasonable for their leadership so they can make good decisions, and it's hard. And so, you need people on call to do it.[29]

The perception that companies, with all their technological sophistication, have certain kinds of superpowers likely leads to policy inertia, as politicians and the public assume they can quickly solve problems if they need to. But the reality is that, even with most cutting-edge technologies, public policy mandating preparedness is likely necessary to force private companies to be ready to defend basic public safety. Reviewing the types of scenarios that unfolded on January 6—which echo many other events around the world where communications technology companies have been caught by surprise—it becomes clear that some kind of policymaking that requires readiness to deal with emergency events is advisable. The era of probability has arrived, and the tools for accomplishing interventions and disruptions of bad actors will always involve error and best guesses. But it is clear that some kind of public guidance to communications technology companies on what constitutes reasonable, good faith steps in terms of disrupting violent organizing is necessary. There needs to be some kind of risk assessment—a mapping out of possible problems, leading to preparedness steps for contingencies—done in advance, a standard that has become increasingly accepted and enshrined in international business and human rights law.[30]

OVERT ACTS AND ACTORS

The online world presents and facilitates novel types of harms. As with Fishman and his focus on network organizing and groups—actor-based analysis for content moderation purposes—there is a more general puzzle about when online platforms become what some have called "tactical spaces," allowing violent conspiracies and terrorism to be organized and where the venue itself becomes weaponized, even where individual messages or speech acts may be mundane.[31] Issues such as doxxing—maliciously disclosing someone's address, location, and personal details online with the purpose of encouraging targeting—also creates conundrums. Then there is the question of civil law. Can someone be sued for taking an action such as releasing someone's home address into a chat group, even if no harm eventually comes to them? Can someone be held liable for encouraging others to take action online, including through doxxing—what lawyers call a theory of "vicarious tort liability"? More such cases with similar fact patterns are bound to come into the courts, in both the United States and abroad, in the years ahead. Questions around the legal liability for organizing and inciting online mobs and aggressive patterns of networked behavior—and who is responsible, both criminally and civilly—are becoming more pressing with each year.

The overarching issue of incitement has taken on new dimensions, as algorithms, networks, and encryption change the game. Speed, scale, and the permanence of speech also change the nature of the problem. The issue of whether President Trump's actions on January 6, 2021, constituted incitement has been the topic of endless legal and political debate. While that issue may never be fully resolved, it raises a more general issue about how to understand ambiguously inciting speech and what might be justified in terms of curbing or filtering it. Legal scholars Alan Z. Rozenshtein and Jed Handelsman Shugerman have argued that courts should take into account whether the speech was correlated with an "overt act," or concrete activities that are "designed to increase the imminent risk of such lawlessness and violence."[32] The scholars make this case in order to establish the standard for legal liability in the courts—they argue proof of overt acts could be a requirement for charging people for otherwise ambiguously inciting speech acts. (In the case of the Capitol riot, they point to "Trump's order to remove the magnetometers that were preventing his armed supporters from joining the rally crowd; and Trump's attempts, as evidenced by Secret Service emails, to personally lead the mob at the Capitol.")[33] But analogously, social media companies might make similar assessments, confident that such analysis is consistent with First Amendment traditions. Further, any regulatory rules that urge and validate such action by the companies can be seen as well aligned with general free speech principles. Such a claim is deeply historically rooted, as Rozenshtein and Shugerman note:

Recognizing that an overt act can be the key fact for establishing liability for speech that plausibly, though not definitively, incites lawlessness or violence not only clarifies an important doctrinal point, but it also surfaces a key historical continuity. For centuries English and American law has struggled with two overlapping concerns: how to criminalize concrete conspiracies but not mere loose talk; and how to criminalize treason, insurrection, and politically aimed incitement but not merely heated but protected political speech. For hundreds of years—and across the crimes of treason, conspiracy, and incitement—the law has rediscovered the same solution: requiring overt acts.[34]

Under this theory, it would be well justified for a social media platform moderator to take down, label, or downrank content ambiguously inciting content that is related to offline or off-platform overt acts (whether speech acts or physical ones). This overt acts assessment would not likely be a regular analysis by platforms—the scale is too great to perform labor-intensive research and analysis—but the risks of violence are often perpetrated by small, organized groups across online space. In any case, if a new regulatory agency overseeing social platforms were to ask for evidence of duty of care with regard to incitement, it would be in keeping with deep, democratic legal traditions to take actions based on a combined analysis of speech and overt acts.

ENCRYPTION: THE NEXT FRONTIER

The use of encryption in messaging/chat apps keeps people safe from government snooping and exploitation by criminals. But it can also protect criminals trading in child sexual abuse material (CSAM) and terrorists exchanging tactical plans, as well as nefarious actors attempting to damage elections.[35] Encrypted communications platforms are one of the greatest amplifiers and risk areas in terms of incitement. Consider the use of encrypted messaging apps such as Telegram, which allows very large groups to see content—where messaging and the broadcast power of social media are combined in a kind of new way. Telegram messages, which are notionally encrypted in some parts of the app, can be broadcast to up to two hundred thousand persons who are part of a given "group." Some of this messaging activity has been linked to all sorts of dubious actions and behavior, from drug trafficking and child sexual abuse to war propaganda efforts and criminal activity of many kinds, including violent unrest.[36] In August 2024, such patterns of harm and unlawful activity on a platform led to the arrest of Telegram CEO Pavel Durov by French authorities.[37] Forwarding of messages to sizable groups in sequence has also been a problem on WhatsApp, among other platforms, leading to real-world violence.[38] Such functionality means users can get messages to huge audiences quickly, but platform moderators and external analysts don't have ready access to the messages. Messaging platforms have indeed modified the size of groups and limited forwarding functionality to deal with problems.[39] There have long been questions about Telegram's actual level of encryption (its level of security depends on what functionality and features are being used) but Signal, iMessage, and WhatsApp, for example, make breaking encryption nearly impossible.[40]

Why does encryption matter? As more of the world's networked communication is encrypted end-to-end—meaning that only the sender and receiver can see it, and not the company platform managers or any third parties such as law enforcement—there is reduced ability to moderate content, to identify and take action against true criminal and dangerous messages and material. For many years, there was thought to be no "in between" in terms of encryption—you either had it, or you didn't. That is why privacy advocates have consistently fought so hard to make sure communications systems can ensure maximum guarantees to users. Anything less, and it's a slippery slope—all manner of governments and hacker groups will be trying to exploit any back door or vulnerability. Even European courts, which have been more open to saying that encryption must yield to legitimate law enforcement orders, have noted that encryption protects human rights and shields citizens from abuses around the world.[41] As the legal scholars Charles Duan and James Grimmelmann have noted of encryption technologies: "Either they are intact or they are broken, and the starkness of the choice has made the positions of encryption advocates and critics seem wholly irreconcilable."[42]

However, cutting-edge research in the computer science and cryptography community is beginning to change the way many think about encryption, and it's possible that we will end up in a world where the options are less binary; there are newer mathematical and technological innovations that may end up presenting a spectrum of options, possibly allowing for targeted enforcement without weakening general security and privacy. It's part of a changing debate over encryption and content moderation.[43] Hard-core privacy advocates may object even to newer techniques, but the framework for debate is beginning to change. There has been a raging debate over "client-side scanning," which in 2021 Apple proposed to apply to images and content uploaded to the cloud.[44] The basic idea is that platforms create a database of violating images and content, and there is an automated system that looks for and filters such content. This technique is used by social media companies regularly to look for terrorism-related content and CSAM may be uploaded by users. But because Apple was proposing to do it on people's personal devices, there was an uproar by privacy advocates, and the idea was scrapped.

Perhaps the most promising technique is called "message franking" (a term that derives from the old-fashioned term for postage stamps). The idea is that messages can carry with them a digital stamp that facilitates the authentication of the message sender by the platform, but only under certain conditions where abuse of some kind is reported by the message recipient. At a technical level, the franking process involves the passing of encrypted "keys," which can only be used to unlock the identity of a sender with the recipient's active reporting and consent. This technique allows the platform to have authenticated evidence of some violation such as CSAM or criminal behavior. Message franking solves the bedeviling problem that the platform itself has no actual way of validating who sent a given message—even if a user reports some kind of major violation and surfaces the message. Under end-to-end encryption, there is no "proof" whatsoever. There will undoubtedly be debates about the implementation of message franking on platforms, if it happens, and there are legal questions.[45] But the larger point is that new technologies may come along that preserve the spirit of end-to-end encryption but allow for platforms to have some ground-truth signal about the specific users who may be engaged in problematic behavior. New regulations for content moderation could mandate such technologies as a standard, or perhaps impose requirements for message franking only after encrypted platforms show a pattern of neglect for inciting disinformation, CSAM, terrorism-related activity, and other criminal content. Creating standards for issues such as political disinformation—where the content may be technically legal as political speech but platforms may want to protect elections or other public interests—will be more difficult to resolve, however.[46]

VIOLENCE AND SPEECH

The line between protected political speech and incitement will be constantly subject to contextual factors and the sensitivity of societies and platforms at given moments. We cannot pretend that it is possible to draw perfect, or permanent, bright lines. What we can do, however, is establish an expectation that social platforms become accountable and responsible for communications distributed through their sites.

Making sure that the platforms do regular risk assessments and have sufficient technical and personnel capacity to respond to emergencies involving violence and harm seems reasonable. Yes, this will cost money, but technology companies have had more than their share of profits in recent years. It's time to expect more. Content moderators should moreover devote much greater energy to investigating actions taken off the platform, that is, they should incorporate "overt acts," both in real life and on other platforms, into their decisions. This will require a significant investment of time, but it should be a regulatory expectation that platforms devote greater resources to this due diligence. Much ambiguously inciting speech, paired with overt acts, can constitute an obvious case for removal. We need to support companies in adding context where violence and criminality are involved. Finally, the debate over encryption is moving rapidly toward a more subtle and sophisticated set of arguments over how to provide some amount of safety while also preserving privacy. Message franking is one technique that could begin to give platforms more tools for dealing with out-of-control users and dangerous communities organizing violence.

5

AI AND EPISTEMIC RISK

The original question, "Can machines think?" I believe to be too meaningless to deserve discussion. Nevertheless I believe that at the end of the century the use of words and general educated opinion will have altered so much that one will be able to speak of machines thinking without expecting to be contradicted.[1]
—Alan Turing, "Computing Machinery and Intelligence," *Mind* (1950)

Generative AI is producing altogether new categories of content, including harmful content. Fears over "deep fakes"—synthetically produced videos, audio recordings, and images—have saturated news reporting and public discourse over the past several years. But the rise of AI technologies and their overall effects on the media environment should be seen in a wider context; generative AI technologies will produce a diverse range of changes across this field.

For more than a decade, social platforms have relied on machine-learning algorithms and automated classifiers to estimate how to deal with user-generated content. Human theories about what is good and bad in content moderation ultimately are translated into code that drives and produces automated systems—often dynamic machine-learning systems. How tight or loose should the automated rules for removal or reduction be? What are the thresholds? What are the criteria? Whether the task at hand involves inoculation and prebunking, fact-checking, accuracy nudging, or corrections work; detecting coordinated bad actors; or counterspeech strategies of various kinds, there can be little doubt that better precision tools are greatly in need for locating problems and bad actors, identifying people in need of support, and targeting solutions.

The new era of generative AI therefore constitutes an extraordinary moment given the growth of new technologies that, for the first time, are beginning to provide the kind of scale and supple understanding of human language and communication that could be adequate to the size of the problems on global platforms. These technologies remain flawed at present, but they are clearly rapidly improving in some cases. Some industry experts who have spent years tackling seemingly insurmountable problems are beginning to see real promise in using generative AI for content moderation.[2] Machine-learning technologies have been used for years now in content moderation, but they mostly have been doing complex pattern matching. In effect, generative AI allows for an approach to interpreting user-generated messages that is more sophisticated than prior waves of more traditional AI.[3] "We have machines now that can do something that functionally is equivalent to a human reading a document and responding to what it said," says Dave Willner, a longtime industry expert who led teams at Meta and who was the head of trust and safety at OpenAI. He explains that this "means we have a machine that can directly address the core activity that a human moderator is doing instead of merely producing the result."

Better AI tools also may alleviate long-running concerns about the psychologically damaging labor that, to date, has been performed by (often underpaid) human moderators, who regularly must stare at hundreds of images of violence, sexual abuse, and general trauma-inducing content.[4] They also may allow companies to enforce rules in emerging spaces such as social virtual reality platforms, where existing content moderation systems may not work or even be appropriate.[5]

Humanity has recently crossed a major threshold, what for nearly three-quarters of a century has been called the "Turing test," named after the British mathematician and computer scientist Alan Turing. The general idea is that if a computer can fool humans into thinking it's human—impersonating a human, winning the "imitation game"—it has achieved a measure of human intelligence. If we can no longer tell the difference in conversation between a human and a robot—imagine both behind a curtain, or behind a computer screen—we have passed the threshold of the Turing test. Large language models (LLMs) and advanced machine learning had begun fooling humans years earlier, but computers surpassed the Turing test for the general public (at least English-speaking) in 2023, and so, objectively, we have entered a new era in modern human history.[6]

Generative AI creates almost unfathomable possibilities for confounding and disrupting human speech and expression online, for complex disinformation campaigns, and for general strategic manipulation of societies. It also creates new tools for regulating and managing the communications space.

This chapter is about these two sides—offense and defense—of the same technological coin. Generative AI may create chaos online, allowing millions of fake and manipulated images, videos, stories, and narratives to proliferate. Yet the same technologies may create new systems for better content moderation, allowing more context-sensitive work to be done at scale, down to local geographies, and across custom instances of decentralized social platforms. There are in fact three aspects of the problem to consider in terms of trust and safety and social platform content moderation. In terms of offense, we need to understand how bad actors might wield AI to disrupt societies and achieve financial and political goals.

Regarding defense, we should consider both what AI can do "behind the scenes" in terms of assisting large-scale content moderation; and what AI may, in the future, be able to do as agent bots (modbots or chatmods, as it were) are deployed to help enforce platforms' community rules and perhaps even to improve the information environment on platforms. For the burgeoning world of "federated" or "decentralized" social media— platforms such as Mastodon or Bluesky, which offer open protocols that allow for fragmentation and no centralized control—better AI tools may give local moderators more speed and scale, allowing flexible options for control and rules enforcement. My argument is that, while we might fear the potential chaos unleashed by AI in the short term, over the long run AI tools may finally provide the scale and subtlety that human moderators have long needed to be in a better position to get a handle on problems.

Still, there is an even greater longer-term problem that I believe must be addressed, and this issue will be created by AI at a structural or fundamental level. This is the problem of what I call "epistemic risk," which is the danger that AI tools will be used by bad actors to degrade the information environment. AI models, trained on data from this degraded environment, will create feedback loops, giving priority to lower-grade content. Given such a situation, I conclude this chapter by arguing that content moderation algorithms will increasingly need to favor high-quality

Figure 5.1 In February 2024, the Senate Judiciary Committee called CEOs of large social media and communications platforms, including Discord, Snap, TikTok, X, and Meta, to testify about how they are fighting against the sexual exploitation of children online. Generative AI technologies are allowing the easy creation of intimate images depicting real persons, as well as making it more difficult to detect and remove child sexual abuse material (CSAM) because of the proliferation of synthetic images. U.S. Senate Committee on the Judiciary.

content—professional news stories, material and posts from authoritative sources, and influencers and content creators whose work shows a higher-than-average degree of fact-based storytelling.

OFFENSIVE CAPABILITIES

There is a strong chance that generative AI will create headaches across many domains, making high-quality content moderation even harder in some respects. For example, the ability to detect CSAM is becoming more difficult as bad actors create synthetic images and videos, which can avoid automated detection technologies. Synthetic images often cannot be matched to existing known images that experts and company trust and safety teams share in databases, in order to catch criminals.[7] It will be an arms race, across all manner of fields and areas. Generative AI will lower the cost for disinformation and deception efforts, and it is becoming easy to create automated accounts, well-crafted, auto-generated messages, synthetic images, and deep fake videos.

As noted by Stanford's Alex Stamos, a longtime industry security expert, a central worry is that the cost of creating troll farms and other forms of information warfare and organized scams will now plummet, making it possible for authoritarian governments and criminals alike to be able to carry out disinformation campaigns rather cheaply. Put concretely, this means that "what once took a team of 20 to 40 people working out of Russia or China to create 100,000 pieces of English-language propaganda is now possible with a single person using freely accessible generative AI tools."[8] Security researchers have expressed grave concerns about what nation states could do with these tools, which include getting AI models to carry out complex, multistep advertising campaigns and algorithmic "gaming," where machines might be able to grasp viral levers better than humans can by interpreting vast digital signals.[9]

Several early crisis cases have illustrated the potential for such mayhem. For example, in Slovakia, an AI-generated deep-fake audio tape of a presidential candidate plotting electoral tampering and fraud may have helped to swing the election to a more pro-Russian candidate. The details of that 2023 situation remain murky, but the potential for mischief became vivid for many around the world.[10] Similarly, in January 2024, a robocall of a fake voice recording purporting to be that of President Joe Biden was broadcast to potential New Hampshire voters urging them not to vote in the primary election. That debunked audio, which was also AI-generated, turned out to have been created by a political operative, who faced subsequent criminal charges.[11] In all such cases, experts have worried that, although such disinformation might ultimately be corrected, there might not be sufficient time to get the word out, especially if AI fakes are disseminated very close to a key electoral moment—a kind of last-minute surprise.

Some social platforms have rules prohibiting deceptive "synthetic media," but new types of AI content have also proven difficult for detection algorithms and for content moderation teams trying to enforce policy. For example, as the *Wall Street Journal* memorably put it in a scan of social media in 2024, one can find things such as "Mickey Mouse drinking a beer," "SpongeBob in Nazi garb," and "Donald Trump and Kamala Harris kissing."[12] Given the satirical nature (and sometimes political cartoon-like qualities) of such content, it is unclear that companies, honoring legitimate political expression, should necessarily remove all such items. AI may provide new dimensions to the range of political speech, even democratizing the tools for satire and citizen voice and campaigning. Because social platforms have not trained their detection models on sufficient non-English-language and non-Western data, much of the AI-fakes detection technology is still very shaky, if not useless, in the Global South and across the developing world.[13] This means that the harms of AI may accrue more for poorer countries in terms of social media damaging elections, fueling mob violence, or leading to bad public health outcomes.

AI'S DEFENSIVE POTENTIAL

As Jason Matheny, the president and CEO of RAND Corporation, has noted, there is a major debate in the research community about whether AI will be, on balance, good for offense or defense in terms of keeping the digital sphere safe and trustworthy.[14] Sure, there are risks with AI, but can it also be a defender of the information environment?

Improving what is done "behind the scenes"—flagging, classifying, downranking, organizing platforms' content—with generative AI is already taking place. There appears to be strong industry support among trust and safety professionals to embrace these new tools, albeit with a careful eye on potential new risks.[15] In terms of reviewing and rating content, OpenAI has reported that its models perform as well as humans with light training, although expert humans still outperform models.[16] Meta's security team has noted that sophisticated bad actors who engage in what they call "coordinated inauthentic behavior," or CIB, still struggle in "building and engaging authentic audiences they seek to influence." The challenge for disinformers, misinformers, and scammers is not primarily content creation but audience creation. "While generative AI does pose challenges for defenders," Meta's security team wrote in late 2023, "at this time we have not seen evidence that it will upend our industry's efforts to counter covert influence operations—and it's simultaneously helping to detect and stop the spread of potentially harmful content."[17] How far such confidence extends through the industry, or whether the alleged advantage to defense will continue even for the most well resourced companies, is unknowable.

There are domains such as video livestreaming where companies now must rely on AI technologies to achieve any kind of timely action, before events can spin out of control. The shooter in the Christ Church, New Zealand, massacre in 2019 infamously livestreamed on Facebook his killing of dozens of Muslims in two mosques. That gruesome video was then quickly copied across the internet. As part of the immediate aftermath, there was worldwide attention to the lack of safeguards around livestreaming video technologies. Facing pressure, social platform and livestreaming video companies poured resources into early detection algorithms; governments and civil society have also formed working groups to coordinate quick response across platforms.[18] By 2022, when a somewhat parallel atrocity took place in Buffalo, New York, involving a racially motivated mass shooting, the perpetrator's livestream was quickly detected and shut down. Companies can now detect many types of incidents involving violence in a few seconds, although some complex situations such as self-harm and suicide remain difficult to address through automation.[19] Further, there are business decisions, which come with trade-offs, that companies could make to create barriers to using the technology. These include requiring accounts to have established histories and sufficient numbers of subscribers—making it less likely that a deranged person could just join and press the streaming button.[20]

CHATMODS AND MODBOTS

Traditionally, companies have taken three types of actions on user-generated content that is problematic: labeling, fact-checking, and downranking.[21] However, a new category of approach or treatment is looming: the use of "agents," or semi-independent AI bots that have a custom purpose for keeping social platforms safe and trustworthy.[22] LLMs such as OpenAI's ChatGPT, Google's Gemini, DeepSeek (China), Mistral AI

(France), and Anthropic's Claude have demonstrated the ability to engage reasonably successfully in human conversations and simulate human-like expression. The AI industry is generally predicting the broad use of AI agents across economic and social life in the years ahead.

So much user-generated content is, probabilistically speaking, in the "gray zone"—it's not clearly violating and in need of removal or harsher action. There are increasing cries from both the political right and left for opposite treatments. On the right: Don't touch speech; it should be free. On the left: Pay more attention to harmful speech. These countervailing trends and pressures push companies to the middle, in the direction of speech-preserving but responsive and activist measures. Therefore, one obvious tactic that could scale would be for platforms to engage with users leveraging LLM-powered chatbots, deploying a kind of interactive agent "referee" who might start conversations with users, warn them, attempt to de-escalate and turn down the temperature on heated discussions, and ask about motives and intentions. There have been experiments with AI moderators within various smaller and decentralized platforms, such as Discord and Reddit, where community moderators can use this type of software.[23] OpenAI is developing LLMs for content moderation.[24] Meta/Facebook has rolled out engaging bots, parodying famous personas such as Jane Austen;[25] Snapchat has offered a chatbot to individual users. Researchers have used LLMs to engage with people who believe in conspiracy theories, and there is promising early evidence that generative AI may be able to make a difference in steering people away from such false beliefs.[26]

Bots have been a part of social media for years, often deployed by users to do everything from entertain to deceive. What would be new, albeit highly ethically complicated, is a fleet of bots that are operating centrally on behalf of the large platforms, in police, referee, or service roles.[27] As scholars have suggested, positive, prosocial uses of generative AI on social media could include mediation, information assistance, counterspeech, and moderation of discourse among users.[28] There are obvious risks, as AI technologies might say or do things that cannot be predicted in advance. They are still prone to error for complex tasks such as fact-checking.[29] They also often carry biases that are a product of their training data—racial or gender biases, influenced by all kinds of stereotypes because of training their models on internet data of every kind. Still, research on automated moderation tools shows they may have the potential to help users follow rules and guidelines, even as platforms must pay careful attention to humanizing the systems and user perceptions of justice and fairness.[30]

It is not yet clear how the public would respond to the widespread use of such consumer-facing, company-supported AI bot technologies that attempt to enforce rules or encourage rule-following. As part of another research project, my team at Northeastern University conducted a three-country survey in 2023 of about one thousand persons, representative samples, across the United Kingdom, Canada, and the United States.[31] We asked about the use of AI technologies in content moderation, both current uses (the classifiers that have been in use for years now in many cases) and the emerging possibilities of generative AI.

In our research, we found that about half of survey respondents in all three countries said it would be acceptable for company chatbots to start public conversations with users who appear to violate rules or platform community guidelines. When we looked at what might predict such positive attitudes, it was generally correlated not with any particular gender, race, age, or demographic characteristic, but rather with whether persons had had experiences with consumer-facing chatbots before in other parts of the economy. Those survey respondents who had dealt with chatbots before were less likely to be worried in general about the use of these technologies on social media, suggesting that experience and social conditioning is important if platforms are to establish trust. That said, a strong majority in all three countries surveyed (80+ percent) worried that if companies deploy chatbots supported by generative AI and engage in conversations with users, the chatbots may (1) not understand context, (2) ruin the social experience of connecting with other humans, and (3) make flawed decisions. People are concerned about mistakes and the overall user experience. There was also significant concern that chatbots could introduce false information on platforms.

What is also interesting to consider is that survey respondents across the three countries appear accepting of the use of AI technologies in general to carry out "softer" interventions such as producing warning labels for potentially harmful or violating content. Yet they are much more skeptical of "harder" approaches such as account suspension, without human review, by AI technologies. These attitudes were consistent with our wider survey data, which suggests that people are OK with AI in the position of helper but not of final judge or arbiter.[32] Technology companies already regularly use what is considered traditional or narrow AI to perform such labeling, flagging, classifying, and suspension tasks. Our survey data therefore suggest underlying distrust of some existing practices of automating decisions about the fate of users. Perhaps the public is only now waking up to the reality that AI is already widely deployed behind the scenes, even if it has not yet been visible in user-facing forms such as chatbots.

Setting aside the ability of chatbots to perform the job reasonably well, there is a larger question about the potential loss of social and knowledge value for democracy as machines begin assuming the tasks of refereeing public conversations over issues in the digital public square. What would be lost? The answer, potentially, is public knowledge—about what people think, how they argue, the norms they battle for, and the preferences they reveal as they debate and deliberate. For sure, well-functioning AI chatmods might provide speed and scale to an often-overwhelming task of keeping hate speech, disinformation, and the like from spinning out of control. But what could be lost is a great deal of socially and democratically useful information and knowledge, as users argue back-and-forth. There is value in witnessing corrections—in experiencing reasoning processes and debate—by other humans.[33] As mentioned in prior chapters, experts on hate speech see great value, as well, in digital bystanders sticking up for others and participating in the process of pushing back against antisocial voices, as such situations help to reinforce prosocial norms.[34]

Given the fluidity of human language and meaning-making—and, as discussed, the emergent nature of much human thought and ideation—there is also the question of how AI chatmods in this context could reasonably be expected to make ethical decisions that do not cause potential harm. Ethical alignment between human moderator preferences and AI agents closely adhering to such values is inherently difficult given the emergent nature and context of much online discourse, where breaking events and novel ideas often first surface.

As potential tools for moderators without significant financial resources—especially those operating in decentralized or "federated" environments—intelligent modbots might prove attractive in many cases. Persons managing large Reddit groups ("subreddits"), or instances on Mastodon or Bluesky, may find themselves overwhelmed with the rigors of constant moderation, across thousands of users.[35] Being able to tailor a modbot in a way that carefully conforms and aligns to the preferences of the human moderator could relieve hours of arduous labor. Provided that there are ways to audit and refine such technologies, and humans are constantly in the loop, modbots may satisfy basic technological ethics requirements and be deployed broadly. Experts continue to worry that not enough is being invested in trust and safety tools for federated systems and advocate for investing more in open-source tooling of various kinds.[36]

Social media companies assert their corporate and fiduciary rights to keep their platforms safe and trustworthy. But as a chatmod engages in public or private with a user, serious questions arise about the ethics of such human-computer interactions. Many AI ethics codes have extended the standard principles underpinning bioethics: beneficence; nonmaleficence; autonomy; and justice. Some have also added explainability, or the obligation to be able to articulate reasons for decisions or generally how things work.[37] Prior "traditional" AI technologies have for several years now been significantly impacting users in all kinds of more invisible or hardly visible ways, from the decisions by classifiers that are not taken (false negatives) to over-enforcement (false positives.) It is not clear that AI as deployed in the past on platforms is at all conforming to ethical AI principles, especially given the way it has been used in recommender systems to prioritize extreme, false, or incendiary content. The harms created by current content moderation regimes are well documented, raising profound ethical questions.[38]

Yet the use of machine bot personas to intervene in social space in a more visible and interactive way presents new ethical considerations, raising questions about the treatment of humans by machines. Even if a human user is posting messages that are borderline abusive, what right, and under what guidelines, does a chatmod operate under as it pushes back on a human's expression? Does the action embody the beneficence,

non-maleficence, autonomy, justice, and explainability principles? All of
this will depend very much on the behavior and the responses of the
chatmod, as well as the policy framework used by the underlying platform. The decision to use a chatmod generates further ethical obligations
on behalf of the content moderator system. This is an area greatly in need
of more research from a human-computer interaction (HCI) and applied
ethics perspective. But as a baseline, it would be reasonable to expect
that social platforms (1) emphasize the clear identification of the agent
as nonhuman in form (consistent with previously mentioned human-
centered AI principles) and (2) instill the concept of humility by the AI
agent (the possibility of misunderstanding and being wrong, possibly
leading to an appeal to a human moderator).

The use of persona-like agents in social space may just be the beginning of the widespread use of AI-powered robots in human life,[39] a vision
that has long entranced science fiction creators. There are serious concerns about the viability of democracy under such conditions.[40] But
researchers are already looking into how democratic values might be better incorporated into the goals, the "objective functions," of AI models
deployed on social media platforms.[41] What must be remembered is that
all social interactions within democratic life have the potential to create useful human-to-human deliberation and learning. In an ideal sense,
social media companies might structure their platforms and moderation
approaches to maximize the building of a healthy, high-quality information environment and to help users better navigate this environment.[42]
Chatmods may advance such a mission in some respects. But human-to-
human interactions also contain intrinsic value, as social ties can help
powerfully transmit information, norms, and values. As AI agents erase
or manipulate such opportunities for humans to debate, disagree, con-
nect, and interact, social platforms may cut short aspects of democratic
deliberation that are vital.

AI AND EPISTEMIC RISK

There are major concerns about the increasing pollution of the online
information environment by mis- and disinformation, conspiracy theories, hate speech, scams, and various forms of clickbaity, low-quality

content.[43] So much of the web, and of social platforms, already feels like a toxic swamp. Enter generative AI, with its capacity to generate synthetic content and deep fakes at a vast scale. Scholars have noted that the proliferation of deep fakes, in particular, threatens the "epistemic" order—the way in which knowledge and information are traditionally created and disseminated throughout society.[44] If everything might be fake, what can be trusted? Might we enter a world where high-quality information and factual authorities are further degraded, by virtue of not being believed or perceived to be credible?

Many have noted our era is characterized by a certain "post-truth" quality; but imagine if this phenomenon were to accelerate well beyond the realm of partisan news outlets and scammers. Imagine agents of mass communication, so to speak, deliberately trying to make the situation worse. This is a situation characterized by what we might call "epistemic risk." By this I mean an ordering of knowledge and information in society that is substantially distorted by AI technologies that are not aligned with human values and preferences—where AI has helped to create a situation of mass confusion, and where AI technologies create feedback loops of mis- and disinformation. Because AI technologies "learn" through online training data, an online ecosystem that is thoroughly corrupted and polluted threatens to create a vicious circle.

There are three major areas where social media platforms and other related societal institutions (media and educational organizations, in particular) should focus efforts to mitigate such titanic problems: labeling; quality preferences; and literacy. One of the grand problems of the social media era has been what is sometimes called "context collapse" or "container collapse."[45] In online spaces, we often lack the contextual cues that traditional media provides about the identity of the news outlet or information source. Credible information, infotainment, disinformation, and all manner of low-quality content cascade by in a single social media feed, washing around without any visual or intellectual cues as to origin or validity. Such a situation is brought about by platform companies' obsession with having "frictionless" experiences that encourage endless scrolling and mindless engagement.

One speech-preserving solution that has become more popular since the COVID-19 pandemic has been the use of warning, contextual, and informational labels with content. While not a panacea for mis- and disinformation, such labels can provide orienting information for users, reinserting contextual cues about provenance and quality of platform content.[46] Generative AI holds a great deal of promise in this regard, creating the possibility even of more tailored and personalized contextual information such as veracity labels and explanatory guides.[47]

Furthermore, there needs to be a great deal of attention paid to labeling AI-generated information, and indeed, AI bots and agents themselves on social platform spaces. Experts are beginning to test out different types of informational and warning labels that might help users make better choices, much as nutrition labels may help people make better choices in their diets. It has become somewhat common among major social media platforms to label synthetic or AI-generated media, but to be effective such labels may require additional warning information, such as precisely how the content may mislead others if shared.[48] In the years ahead, there may be a much greater need for establishing the valid human personhood of online users, as so many AI-powered agents attempt to enter online spaces.[49] Such agents will have powers and capacities that far exceed the traditional bots we have seen in the online world, as agents may be able to act and learn autonomously and carry out sequences of steps to achieve objectives, further muddying the waters of the information environment.

It may end up that social platforms, having helped erode the foundations of the information and epistemic landscape, will need to do major repair work for their products to remain viable and trustworthy. They will need to help users in instrumental ways, such as providing labels, but they will also need to increase the overall quality of the environment by emphasizing information quality in their ranking algorithms. As social media moves from emphasizing the "social graph" (what the people in your network are interested in) to the "content graph" (the types of adjacent messages, video, and material that may be conceptually related),[50] users are losing even the cues of seeing that their friends, family, or people they follow shared something. The TikTok, Instagram, and YouTube algorithms are currently just recommending new videos based on an analysis of the content graph—the universe of things that might interest you, based on your history of engagement.

Companies should consider thinking much more about the quality of knowledge, or epistemic, worlds they are producing for users, particularly as AI technologies threaten to overwhelm information environments. Platform algorithms might evaluate more quality-oriented signals, such as (1) the ratio of posts containing verifiable information to those containing misinformation on a platform; (2) whether users become better judges of genuine expertise on the topics (as evidenced through their engagement-related behavior); (3) whether users curate their information environment differently with respect to who they follow, unfollow, or block; (4) whether users are exposed to (or seek out) a wider range of viewpoints on those topics that are still under legitimate dispute; and (5) how users alter their sharing behavior (e.g., reposting) with respect to misinformation (e.g., do they increasingly identify it as such?).[51] Indeed, some industry and academic experts have argued that favoring information quality over engagement metrics (likes, shares, and general interactions) might be justified on both ethical grounds and a business rationale of properly sustaining a valuable product over time, helping with retention of users.[52]

All these information quality signals relate to the epistemic health of the environment in which users are operating. AI technologies, ironically, can help online platforms make much better judgments about the quality of social feeds for users, as they can make sophisticated judgments at scale, helping human moderators and managers get a better sense of platforms and products from an information veracity and quality standpoint. All these measures will also require bringing users along in the journey of improving their environment, helping to educate them on what algorithms are doing in this regard and how algorithmic systems work in general.[53] Across the world, many users lack basic knowledge, even now, of how algorithms are mediating what they see and, ultimately, believe to be true and interesting. Whether it is deploying AI to help with good defense, deploying chatmods or modbots, or improving the epistemic position of users, there are a broad range of steps companies might take—of course, with extreme care and properly resourced human oversight and evaluation—to demonstrate socially responsible and responsive platform management.

6

CONTENT MODERATION FUTURES

Certain forms of knowledge and control require a narrowing of vision. The great advantage of such tunnel vision is that it brings into sharp focus certain limited aspects of an otherwise far more complex and unwieldy reality. This very simplification, in turn, makes the phenomenon at the center of the field of vision more legible and hence more susceptible to careful measurement and calculation.[1]

—James C. Scott, *Seeing Like a State* (1998)

Social platforms have, with some exceptions, accepted the responsibility for content moderation, largely to avoid liability and political scrutiny. Some have more elaborate terms of service and community guidelines than others. Some are more vigilant about enforcement.

The rise of what we might think of as "industrial moderation" among the social media platform companies has been extraordinary. Since the first message boards and interactive websites were created in the 1990s, the concept of human content moderation review has undergone considerable evolution. Section 230 of the Communications Decency Act, the landmark U.S. legislation that helped create the interactive web as we know it, was initiated because companies complained that they needed legal protections to perform content review. Section 230 allowed owners of interactive websites that host user-generated content to choose to moderate heavily, or not at all. Under U.S. law these websites' owners do not have legal liability as intermediaries (copyright and CSAM are exceptions).

Most content moderation practices on early websites and message boards were ad hoc. Rules of the road for company websites and terms of service were generally not well spelled out through the early 2000s.

Content review teams were often tiny, even for large sites.[2] The practice of human content moderation on the social web began in earnest well after the founding of Facebook (2004), YouTube (2005), and Twitter (2006).

Since then, moderation has significantly evolved with the growth and complexity of the platform companies and has been characterized by what may be seen historically as several different phases. In their founding years, social media companies took a laissez-faire approach, largely allowing users to post whatever content they wanted. Even as platforms tightened and clarified their terms of service, policing of content was intermittent at best. As time passed, however, platforms began to remove content more actively, often in response to takedown requests from governments or other third parties or from public pressure relating to violent or offensive speech. Human review teams began to grow in size and importance. The larger companies started out with teams of five to ten persons, but these soon began to scale to dozens and hundreds. Companies began to realize that they could only tackle the volume of necessary moderation by using third-party firms and outsourcing labor. The content review enterprise became large enough that new director and vice president roles needed to be created to oversee operations. In-house trust and safety teams grew, with the roles occupied by various kinds of full-time employees, including subject matter experts, researchers, and policy staff.

Eventually, after roughly 2012, companies began relying more heavily on automated systems for flagging content driven by machine-learning techniques. These automated systems facilitated such tactics as filtering and downranking content. In 2016, Facebook began partnering with third-party fact-checkers at media outlets, heralding the beginning of more active, but also more nuanced, moderation strategies. (As mentioned, Meta announced its intention to end this program in January 2025.)[3] Subsequently, many companies have begun using techniques other than removal or reducing visibility/downranking, giving their human review teams more tools and options for enforcing policies. One example is the use of gray warning screens (interstitial warnings) or "knowledge panels" where users can get other facts (such as from the CDC, FDA, etc.). Overall, the application of contextual, corrective, warning, source, transparency, or other kinds of labels has become more common, making it an emerging area of focus for companies and researchers alike.[4] In 2020, the concept of warning labels were a topic of mainstream public debate, as they were used in both the presidential election (i.e., labeling President Trump's tweets) and the fight against the "infodemic" associated with COVID-19. Companies elevated the importance of human review, moderation, and policy teams accordingly.

On the global stage, companies have also rolled out special structures that allow civil society groups, called "trusted flaggers," to help identify potentially harmful or violating content.[5] They also have allowed law enforcement in various countries to operate as Internet Referral Units (IRUs). Most companies operate according to country-specific content restrictions. Meta, for example, tracks all the content it blocks based on countries' claims that the content violates local law, even though the content in question may not violate the company's global Community Standards.[6]

In this chapter, we will examine some of the specific practices that platform companies use to carry out their industrial moderation. We will also review some of the competing global philosophies, as espoused by key individual leaders, for regulating online communication. I ultimately argue that the United States must assert new rules to ensure that freedom of expression and human rights can endure around the world, at a time when more coercive governance models threaten to overrun the internet and social platforms, and where "swing states" such as India and Brazil are looking for more help with governance of American companies on their territory.

INDUSTRIAL MODERATION

We have looked at where AI may take the field, but let's also review social media content moderation as a developing area of increasing professionalism over the past fifteen years or so. Tens of thousands of workers around the globe now spend their professional lives as part of content moderation and review teams and systems. Reviewers spend their days examining specific pieces of content that have been flagged by an automated system or reported by other users as violating terms of service in some way. The work of human content moderators is often performed quite rapidly, with reviewers being given a set amount of time (for example, ranging from thirty seconds to two minutes or more) to make an initial judgment about whether content should be categorized as "violating." Violating categories might include hate speech, nudity, incitement to general violence or terrorism, or some other threatening, obscene, or demeaning form of expression. Humans are monitoring categories of content typically governed by terms of service specified by the companies through user agreements.

By reviewing, rating, and (internally) labeling content in their work, reviewers are often (at larger firms) helping to train classifiers and the algorithms that attempt to detect certain kinds of violating content. In other words, moderators may be both making particular decisions on whether content should be removed, downranked, or labeled with a warning, and providing the "training data" for the platform to make future automated decisions. At larger companies, reviewers typically are extensively onboarded and given specific training in how to apply standards and make judgments, and these judgments often undergo quality control of some sort (a higher level of human review on the initial judgments.) At higher levels of company review, a policy team member may spend much more time reviewing a judgment. Upstream from a basic/line content reviewer may be a team of company policymakers, subject matter experts (SMEs) with the company's central review team, and a research team that is helping to refine the rules and terms of service. Content moderation therefore can represent a "journey" of sorts, escalating its way up a company's corporate chain as decisions become more difficult and consequential.

Frontline human reviewers (sometimes called "agents" in industry) are likely to be contractors at lower levels and in-house (company full-time employees, or FTEs) at higher levels. Lower-level agents sometimes participate in degrading or stressful work. Their mental health can be affected by seeing a large volume of disturbing and degrading posts. Social media companies have been criticized for outsourcing, sometimes overseas, to lower-cost labor markets, and sending content review functions to third-party firms. Companies have also been criticized for failing to recruit teams that have language and cultural skills appropriate to a given context—in other words, persons who can recognize inside cultural jokes and sarcasm, or who can understand coded messages and dog whistles.

Many of these entry-level content review jobs are not well compensated and might compute out to a lower-middle class job in the service sector (equivalent to a salesclerk or a lower-level retail manager).[7]

Increasingly, social platform companies are turning to automated computer programs to deal with problematic content. At least in theory, these programs have significant efficiencies compared to the slower work of human reviewers, and they may shield humans from some of the trauma of reviewing offensive and disturbing posts.[8] They can review thousands of new posts or messages in a matter of seconds or minutes, whereas the best human reviewers may only be able to review a few dozen posts in an hour. Computer engineers with expertise in, for example, computer vision (image recognition), natural language processing (text understanding), and machine learning (software that can learn from the past and apply that learning to new cases) are needed to execute automated content moderation. That engineering work can be expensive, but the capacity for scale is only possible through automation. Automated systems can also remove content proactively/preemptively (before it is posted). Unless a company is willing to hand-curate content in real-time, this is not possible with humans. Every minute, more than five hundred hours of video are uploaded to YouTube.[9] Every hour, tens of millions of tweets (messages on X) are posted. And every day, more than one hundred billion messages flow across Facebook's products and platforms.[10] The challenge for many social media platforms, even small ones, is the colossal scale of content review.

Computer-based reviewing systems have their own challenges. The models can be brittle in how they apply rules. Even the most advanced algorithms may have a high rate of "false positives" (flagging content for human review or automated removal without justification) or "false negatives" (failing to flag violating content). This can leave platform users frustrated and diminish user experience. Human reviewers may be particularly critical in fast-moving or crisis situations, where human expression and human events are evolving quickly. Where communication across a novel topic (e.g., a new breaking news event, such as a war, a scandal, or a disaster) moves quickly, algorithmic classifiers often are not trained and prepared to respond flexibly. Further, on political issues, where issues of free expression may be in play, it has traditionally been very difficult for algorithms to distinguish between irony and real threats, obscenity and free speech, and the boundaries of activism and extremism. A fluid understanding of cultural nuance has mostly remained a domain where humans and human judgment are absolutely necessary to generate well-justified judgments.

Other models blend crowdsourced moderation (from the users themselves) with professional or centralized moderation. As Robyn Caplan of the Data & Society Institute has noted, these approaches might be categorized in three buckets.[11] The first is industrial: A paid team conducts centralized content moderation, assisted more or less powerfully by features that allow human user reporting/flagging. This is the model adopted by Facebook/Meta, YouTube/Google, and (traditionally) X, formerly known as Twitter. Its primary advantage is its potential for consistency, but the trade-off is a user experience that can feel authoritarian. The second category relies on community effort. This model empowers designated community moderators, subject to central company decisions in edge cases. X (Twitter) has begun scaling this approach with its Community Notes feature, which allows crowd-curated contextual, annotation, or counterspeech messages to be appended to original posts that are problematic in some way. Reddit also relies on community moderators, who are empowered to monitor and moderate a given thread. While this approach empowers users and keeps them engaged, and lowers costs, it puts control in the hands of moderators, who may have different values or tolerance for risk than the company would desire. Finally, the third category takes what might be called an "artisanal" approach. Sites such as Vimeo, Medium, Patreon, or Discord have traditionally had small professional teams who typically make content moderation judgments on a case-by-case basis, emphasizing context. While this approach comes with significantly reduced costs—and may produce more nuanced judgements—it struggles to scale.

There is some emerging evidence that users may place more trust in the labels generated by algorithmic systems than in the judgments of human community moderators.[12] Another important public perception, amplified in recent years, is that tech companies, and therefore content moderation, reflect a left-wing bias. Research has largely not substantiated claims that conservative content is unduly censored; in fact, some research has suggested company algorithms or online environments generally may favor conservative political content.[13] Still another perception is that companies pay attention only to the bottom lines of maximizing user attention and advertising success, and their computer code follows these bottom lines. While this has been true traditionally, the reputational costs for technology companies have increased for failure to moderate and therefore engineers have been begun emphasizing safety and trust in terms of desired outcomes.[14]

YOUTUBE'S DENIALISM DILEMMA

The adaptive intelligence of humans has often proven the best tool to grapple with content that surfaces amid an environment of shifting cultural norms and fluid semantic dynamics—again, speech and expression can change rapidly depending on political context. Moreover, some judgments require deep knowledge of the state of the offline world. Some decisions are strategic in nature, in that they involve more than just whether a particular account or message violates terms of service. Content moderation decisions are often embedded in larger contexts that involve threats to core societal functions, such as elections and public health.

To put in specific context such judgments and the challenges for industrial moderation, consider the case of YouTube in 2020 and 2021. As with the other platforms, YouTube and its managers failed to grapple with the full extent of the movement that was building around #StoptheSteal and the violent forces amassing around election denialism.[15] What becomes clear from YouTube's experience is that successful industrial moderation requires getting many pieces right, from effective software updates to sharp judgments by human reviewers, from full awareness of external political events to appropriate upgrades in company policy relating to users. The devil's in the design and execution.

The parent company of YouTube, Alphabet (Google), employs more than twenty-two thousand content-moderation staff members, many of whom are dedicated to managing the video sharing platform—the world's largest such video site.[16] As with Meta's Facebook and its other applications, YouTube has entered the era of probability. It fundamentally structures its environment through algorithms, which are like living organisms that are fed on data. The model of what's in and out is updated as more examples are encountered and coded by humans and machines. But YouTube's algorithm, in particular, has garnered a lot of criticism over the years for allegedly driving users down "rabbit holes" of extremist content.[17] Accordingly, the company revised its recommendation algorithm thirty times in 2019 alone.[18]

YouTube's algorithmic classifier sorts content into three main categories. The first is nonviolating content: the YouTube classifier uses hundreds, perhaps thousands, of signals to flag and evaluate content, considering not just the images and words in the videos, but also how the community behaves around them. The algorithm considers shares, likes, dislikes, and more. (Companies such as YouTube/Google and Meta also sometimes survey users directly.) As the classifier sorts the millions of pieces of content uploaded per hour, most of them end up in the largest bucket, that of nonviolating content. The second main category is videos that are flagged as clearly violating content. These videos are removed from the platform. Penalties for people posting violating videos range from a warning to a one-week suspension, and finally, permanent suspension, depending on past history of violations.[19] The remaining videos fall into the third main category: "borderline" content, when the classifier is uncertain and cannot make a confident determination. Sometimes, the automated system passes along the decision for human review, and the video in question's "reach" is demoted to make sure that fewer people see the video in their search results and personalized recommendation section.

Following the U.S. presidential election in November 2020, YouTube basically allowed Trump supporters to post claims of election fraud with no intervention. The videos were cleared as nonviolating content. On December 9, 2020, following the certification of the vote by the fifty U.S. states, YouTube changed this policy and banned election fraud claims. Over the next month, YouTube removed more than two thousand new election denialism videos from the platform, but because the policy did not apply retroactively, any videos making similar claims posted before December 9 remained in circulation, gathering millions of views. As congressional investigators observed, the policy "provided YouTube the appearance of neutrality but allowed continuing damage to faith in the election process."[20]

It is also notable that YouTube did not strike or suspend any users for posting new election denial content between December 9, 2020, and the certification of the election on January 6, 2021. Why? Because YouTube normally has a thirty-day grace period when it implements new policy restrictions, on the theory that word needs to spread to users. So new election denial videos were sometimes taken down in the month before the January 6 riot, but users were not penalized.[21] The policy curbed the explicitly "bad" or violating ideas, to a degree, but the older ideas stayed because of the lack of retroactive policy. The actors promoting #StoptheSteal paid no penalty. YouTube did try to apply warning labels to some election fraud-related claims in videos, but the labels were mostly invisible to viewers. As congressional investigators noted, the labels did not make users confront prominent warnings or click through a warning screen or panel.

YouTube has struggled to maintain the policy relating to election denialism coming out of the 2020 election, although it kept the policy in place longer than most social media platforms. In June 2023, the company announced it would no longer restrict content that denied the results of the 2020 election.[22] YouTube also said it would restrict speech that materially discourages voting in the future. But it was, to say the least, difficult to disentangle claims about past alleged election fraud from claims about future elections.

HIGHER POLICY VISIONS

In the United States, much of the discussion on content moderation focuses on issues of free speech. But globally, policy leaders are working within a broader set of ideas, including issues related to higher-level telecommunications, trade, and industrial policy that shape the context for social platform governance and rules. Globally, it is a complicated game, like chess with multiple highly opinionated people trying to agree on mutual decisions together on each side of the board.

Consider first the "China model," which, depending on how one looks at it, may be either a strategy to promote "digital authoritarianism" or "cyber sovereignty."[23] Internally, China has a sophisticated content moderation and censorship regime that involves a vast apparatus tied to the Chinese Communist Party. It enlists an army of monitors to supervise the digital ecosystem of WeChat, Baidu, Weibo, and TikTok, among others. The model features heavy social control and surveillance by the government, and that requires huge technical and human resources—the kind that few other countries have or could pull off. But China is nevertheless pushing a more general model of national control that is worth exploring in some detail.

In terms of China's global political, economic, and technological expansion, the veteran diplomat Zhang Ming has been a key figure in advancing the country's model. Across the world, Chinese diplomats have recently been adopting a "wolf warrior" posture, assertively voicing criticisms and advancing their agenda through social media. But there has been another, more plodding strategy. As an "old school" Chinese Communist Party diplomat, the low-key Ming has headed the multilateral Shanghai Cooperation Organization (SCO), a transregional governance, political, and economic group that is led by China, but includes Russia and other nations across Eurasia—some 40 percent of the world's population.[24] The countries have some common historical linkages, including, as China likes to highlight, the ancient path of the Silk Road, which cut across the Eurasian landmass. China now imagines a "Digital Silk Road" to accompany its global physical infrastructure program, called the "Belt and Road Initiative."

China is the only other country, beyond the United States, that has built its own complete social media and information communications technology ecosystem. The platforms include an extraordinary collection of companies, from ByteDance (parent of TikTok) to Tencent's WeChat, to Baidu (online search technology.) By walling off U.S. companies from its market through its internet "Great Firewall," China has built a viable and vibrant alternative model that it hopes will attract allies, especially those in the SCO.

Ming, SCO's most recent past Secretary-General, learned his craft most recently as China's representative to the European Union. Having studied that body up close, he took the reins of the SCO to bring more intensive integration and order to the multilateral group.[25] Born in 1957 in Hunan Province, the epicenter of ancient Chinese culture and agricultural production, Ming has reflected publicly on his rural roots, seeing his life's story as reflecting the grand sweep of China's post-revolutionary history. The year after he was born, Mao Zedong's "Great Leap Forward" campaign began, resulting in one of the largest famines in world history. In his June 9, 2021 speech to the College of Europe, Ming recalled the reverberations of that event: "To tell you something interesting and sad, some 30 years ago in my country, when people greeted each other, instead of saying 'Good morning' or 'Good evening,' they would often ask 'Have you eaten?'"[26] Ming noted that some 850 million people have been lifted out of poverty subsequently, an unprecedented achievement. But the gains remain fragile, and Ming says that China's model must focus on "inward" harmony, consistent with its ancient values, to continue to make progress. He claims that it is "precisely this kind of civilization that prevents China from seeking expansion outside its borders. Or you can say expansion is just not part of China's DNA." Rather, according to Ming, China's rise seeks to preserve the diversity of great world civilizations, each in their own way.

The legacy of nineteenth- and early twentieth-century colonialist powers, particularly the British and Japanese, haunts China. Chinese Communist Party leaders believe that colonialist threats not only sapped the country's traditional powers and capacities in the past but that such threats are poised to return at any moment. The near-past of poverty and societal chaos still seem fresh. To understand China's global policies is to appreciate the duality of the country's position: deeply reverent for China's inward traditions and proud of its recent recovery, but so worried about falling backward that it is becoming forcefully assertive around Eurasia. While Ming's sentiments about China's deep traditions may be genuine, the country's regional ambitions bely the rhetoric about mere inward focus, and it is clear that regional expansion—including in digital space—is part of the Chinese Communist Party's agenda.

The SCO embodies what has been called the "Shanghai spirit" of cooperation among members, who have recently been focused on fighting terrorism within their borders. Outside observers note that such a focus on terrorism can also be a pretext for cracking down on dissidents and human rights activism online, creating monitoring and surveillance mechanisms.[27] The goal is to prevent the kinds of digitally fueled "color revolutions"—the various global themed political upheavals in the twenty-first century, such as the Orange Revolution in Ukraine (2004-2005)—that

Figure 6.1 Indian Prime Minister Narendra Modi and Facebook (Meta) Chairman and CEO Mark Zuckerberg appear together in California in 2015. Meta's apps are widely used in India, and the Indian government has sought to exert more control over communications technology. Around the world, the relationship between political power and tech power remains contentious. Prime Minister's Office, Government of India, licensed under the Government Open Data License - India (GODL).

the West has (allegedly) promoted in Eastern Europe, the Middle East, and Central Asia, from Ukraine to Syria to Iran and Kyrgyzstan.[28]

The SCO was in part designed as a counterweight to various Western peer groups, such as the G-7 or NATO, and one of its goals is to promote the strategy of "cyber sovereignty"—the idea that each nation should govern its digital public sphere according to its own dictates and citizens should only have the rights allowed under domestic law. China and Russia have been partnering on this agenda for nearly a decade.[29] This idea stands in contrast to the traditional Western conception of an "open internet" or "cyber freedom," which necessarily entails data freely crossing borders without filtering or interventions by local authorities. The principle of cyber sovereignty, what American government analysts have characterized as China's "intellectual lynchpin,"[30] is part of what scholars see as a broad array of "global counter norms" that are now proliferating across the world, with the SCO perhaps the leading edge of that trend.[31] The goal of the SCO is in part to lay the groundwork for heavy surveillance by government, with content moderation explicitly tied to political goals.

SURVIVOR RIGHTS AND MALIGN CREATIVITY

While Chinese officials like Zhang Ming are laying the groundwork for a broad shift in norms around sovereignty, both regionally and globally, leaders in the human rights community are trying to translate their core ideas into the digital age. Born in the region that would become Bangladesh, Irene Khan, the United Nations Special Rapporteur on Freedom of Opinion and Expression, lived through the country's war of liberation from Pakistan as a young adolescent in the early 1970s. That experience of conflict has stayed with her to this day, influencing the ideas in her leadership and advocacy work for the United Nations. She has tried to formulate original ideas that extend the concept of universal informational, digital, and media access rights. Her ideas stand in sharp contrast to the Chinese assertion that a particular nation necessarily has absolute sovereignty over the rights of its citizens.

Consider, for example, Khan's articulation of what she has called a "survivor right" during times of conflict, which is the idea that accurate information and the ability to access media and exercise free expression is crucial for the existential well-being of persons in wars and civil conflicts. Khan knows well this type of perilous reality, having lived through such a conflict:

I was about 12 or 13 in 1971 when there was a war in Bangladesh. . . . I remember that we were stranded in the middle of the city in Dhaka. I had a grandfather who was paralyzed. He couldn't move, and therefore the family couldn't escape. So, we lived through that war there. I remember a bullet once coming into my bedroom, and I was there sleeping with my sisters. We all had to jump and go under the bed, things like that. And you know what kept us alive there. Because we had family abroad. We had no means of communication. That was pre-digital age. We lived on BBC. . . . Of course, the local radio was full of propaganda, military propaganda, Pakistani military propaganda. We didn't trust it. And we heard all kinds of rumors, you know, in the bazaar, or on the streets, and we saw people. I remember seeing bodies lying on the street going to school. Horrible experiences for a young girl. And what we did was at night, we would turn on the radio and we would listen. That information, that access to information from outside the conflict from a source that we felt was verifiable and trustworthy, was so important for us as a family to know whether we flee, whether we stay. Should we go east or west? Is the military action taking place in a particular area or not? That's why I call it a survivor right.[32]

Notably, Khan advocates that social media companies need to take special care to hold strong against government requests to interfere with information rights during such times of strife, valuing the survival rights of citizens higher than state orders. In general, Khan argues for "'smart regulation' of Internet intermediaries to ensure their compliance with human rights due diligence, meaningful transparency and due process requirements, rather than viewpoint- or content-based regulation."[33] This "smart regulation" means that social media companies should not necessarily comply with requests from states that violate international human rights law; rather, states should bring their laws in conformity with their commitments to the United Nations charter and covenants, which nearly all nations are signatories to. A country's courts and judicial system, Khan has argued, are the appropriate places to render verdicts on whether social media content is illegal; politicians in executive branch positions should not make these decisions unilaterally. Further, companies should publicize any requests they get from government and should "refrain from making deals behind closed doors."[34]

Khan has also highlighted a pervasive pattern of "gendered disinformation" around the world and called for the principle of "gendered response" to such patterns of harm. Coordinated, gender-based campaigns often portray "women as weak, incompetent and sexualized objects, incapable of leadership." Gendered disinformation seeks to drive "women and gender nonconforming persons out of public spaces and places of power; and [silence] those who do not comply with gender norms."[35] Such situations require a distinctive set of responses, Khan argues, and social media platforms must reconsider their typically "one-size-fits-all" systems for performing content moderation and enabling users to report harms. Victims of online campaigns often find that they cannot successfully report complaints to companies. Khan suggests that with cases of gendered harms, companies must set up systems to listen more carefully and take steps so that women are not isolated and silenced by perpetrators.

Addressing the problem of gendered disinformation requires local contextual knowledge, with subtle understanding of language; companies often either miss coordinated attacks or do not recognize how profoundly damaging the effects are. The methods used to intimidate, shame, and harass women are not always detectable using automated tools such as classifier detection algorithms; perpetrators often use what we might think of as a mix of "dog whistles" (which are difficult to hear except by in-group members) and hurtful memes and symbols. "'Malign creativity,' using various forms of media and coded images that seem innocuous or meaningless without context, can evade automated detection and filters," Khan noted in a 2023 report for the United Nations. "The methods of fact-checking individual posts, providing access to authoritative information or labelling and 'nudging' that are used against [general] disinformation are much less effective in relation to gendered disinformation, which relies on deeply held existing prejudices and social divisions to build credibility for its false or manipulated information."[36] The idea of women's rights as a distinctive set of universal rights is core to Khan's vision, and these rights not only require fundamental respect by sovereign governments, but also require communications platforms to create a different toolkit to deal with the particular dynamics of gendered harms.

TAMING THE GATEKEEPERS

A complementary school of thought to Irene Khan's work—and to that of a broad array of global NGOs, multilateral institutions, and advocates in the human rights community—is emerging from the frenzy of regulatory activity and fertile intellectual debate within research and policy circles in the European Union, and its executive arm, the European Commission. There is the Digital Services Act (DSA), which is forcing new obligations regarding content moderation and transparency on large online platforms. Platforms can preserve legal immunity and avoid fines, so long as they immediately take down violating content, as defined by the European Commission.[37] The EU's Digital Markets Act (DMA), which focuses on economic concentration and the competitive environment, introduces a new element into the global dialogue about how to curb the excesses of social media. Together, Europe's aggressive policymaking is spilling over to other continents, creating what Columbia University law professor Anu Bradford has called the "Brussels Effect"—the trend of European rules to exert power in other global markets, as companies potentially synchronize their global efforts with the EU's rules as a new kind of prevailing norm.[38]

Europe's digital policy tsar and face has long been Margarethe Vestager, a Danish politician who has served as the Executive Vice President of the European Commission and head of its competition-related policies. The daughter of two Lutheran ministers whose parish was in rural Ølgod, Vestager has spent her career in politics since her early twenties, working her way up to the top of Denmark's political class before eventually being nominated to fill a European Commission position. She has made a name for herself as a withering critic of the likes of Google and Apple, bringing antitrust actions against, and issuing billion-dollar fines to, numerous global companies that have large market shares in Europe. *New York Magazine* once called her the "one government official around the world who really keeps tech executives up at night."[39] President Trump called her the "tax lady who really hates the U.S.," to which she drolly retorted, "I've done my own fact-checking on the first part of that sentence, and I do work with tax and I am a woman, so this is 100 percent correct."[40]

Vestager's central idea has revolved around the concept of "gatekeeping"—more specifically, attacking economic gatekeepers whose market power serves to exclude potential rivals and competition. The Digital Markets Act zeroes in on big tech companies, formally called "gatekeepers," that control significant amounts of access to goods and services, such as Google in search, Amazon in products sales, Apple and its apps store, and ByteDance (TikTok) and Meta (Facebook) in social networking.[41] The DSA identifies a class of very large online platforms, or VLOPs—those tech companies with more than forty-five million EU users.[42] "In the past, we had public squares, elected chambers, universities, and cafes," Vestager has written. "When the internet first arrived, it held the promise of expanding these forums globally. But the rise of large platforms got in the way, fragmenting our conversations into a constellation of opaque, walled-off spaces, thus posing a threat to our democracy."[43]

The digital services and markets rules (DSA and DMA) have different functions, but they are devised to be complementary and work in tandem. Pushing back on antitrust claims, the largest technology companies often note that their products and platforms are simply better; this is why

Figure 6.2 European Commission leaders Margrethe Vestager and Thierry Breton have pushed for new regulations on large social media and technology companies and sought to hold them to account for a variety of online harms and questionable business tactics. The Digital Services Act (DSA) and the Digital Markets Act (DMA) together are poised to reshape the regulatory landscape around the world. European Commission Representation in Cyprus, licensed under CC BY 4.0 (https://creativecommons.org/licenses/by/4.0).

consumers prefer them. But Vestager has relentlessly examined the subtle ways that platform companies promote their own interests, lock in users, exploit data, and generally try to maximize profits even at the expense of the public interest. A central claim of hers goes further to the epistemic realm: that the large social media and information communications technology companies distort the free flow of ideas and, through their architectures, close the range of ideas that are encountered. "Algorithms narrow down conversations to small groups of data-determined 'friends,' while gatekeepers narrow down online markets to benefit themselves," Vestager has asserted. "With such narrowing comes the risk that we will lose track of the broader world, and the broader market, around us."[44] Antitrust and market policies will, in her view, serve to bring about the changes in the information and cultural environment that Europeans desire.

Vestager was also there at the creation of the DSA, which more centrally focuses on platform content and customer safeguards. Her early work created the framework for the DSA, even as she handed more day-to-day control to rival Thierry Breton, the European Commissioner for Internal Market and a longtime French telecommunications executive. Breton, a more vocal and pugnacious figure, became the head of implementing and enforcing DSA policies, and his role has provided a complement to that of Vestager, who has technically been his boss.[45]

The DSA has a variety of measures in place that seek to force companies to act responsibly, including mandatory takedowns of certain types of content and ongoing data-reporting obligations. Some of the DSA would theoretically be compatible with U.S. law, although a looming clash with the United States and First Amendment protections and norms seems to be brewing. This clash has been set up because the DSA allows "illegal" content to be defined by the European Union and the national laws of member states, many of which have much tighter controls on speech that would be considered protected political speech, including hate speech, in the United States. The DSA's Article 16 mandates: "Providers of hosting services shall put mechanisms in place to allow any individual or entity to notify them of the presence on their service of specific items of information that the individual or entity considers to be illegal content. Those mechanisms shall be easy to access and user-friendly, and shall allow for the submission of notices exclusively by electronic means."[46]

Following all notices, platforms must have a process in place to respond and take action on such illegal content. Companies must respond in a timely way and then notify the parties involved of actions. The entire DSA process is very much in early stages, but critics have already expressed concerns about the feasibility of such regulations.

Overall, Vestager and Breton—who in 2024 each stepped aside or changed roles—reportedly had different general visions for all of Europe's tech regulation, with Breton embodying a more aggressive, Europe-first philosophy and Vestager wanting to level the playing field even as Europe freely trades with the United States and its tech companies. But together they represented a general worldview that says Big Tech needs a lot of critical scrutiny, many more regulations with which to comply, much less market power, and more competition. The new social media laws on the books have begun to exert force, and Elon Musk and the X platform—with its very loose governance standards—became a prime target beginning in 2024.[47] The DSA will be deeply involved in the regulation of specific content on the platforms, issuing notices for takedowns and asking for detailed reporting on all manner of content moderation activity.

EMPIRICAL INSIGHTS

There are no obvious solutions to all these problems of global speech and communications. One route is through continually increasing top-down regulation at the national level. Individual governments around the world are certainly looking at social media companies such as X (Twitter) and Meta (in addition to others) as potential targets of increased regulation.[48] Critics say that the chief drawback with this approach is that there is no guarantee further national regulation would necessarily lead to better outcomes in terms of putting power back in the hands of people and adhering to principles such as those embodied in the Covenant's Article 19. Already, the patchwork of global governance has left social media companies in the role of "speech police," responsible for moderating content but with little accountability to government or civil society.[49]

If more countries take individual action, it is not certain that the problem of undue platform power will get any better, and many countries with authoritarian tendencies may take the opportunity to clamp down on opposition. It is true that action by the European Union, through the Digital Services Act, has the potential to be collective enough to change company policies and make them global, but how that will affect other countries and global markets is not certain. In any case, social media companies often say that they comply with local law, but the degree of effort and resources put into content moderation can vary widely[50] and the scale of user-generated content on these platforms can result in lax enforcement without significant human intervention, language and cultural knowledge, and well-developed algorithms.[51]

Other pressures outside of the communications policy realm are also shaping the possibility of regulatory change. As the trends of political polarization and populism sweep the world, there is potential for the erosion of freedoms of assembly, press, and expression.[52] Framing the discussion of global, context-sensitive content moderation are the international relations issues of economic, technological, and regulatory competition among China, the United States, and the European Union, which may determine the kinds of free expression models that societies and governments adopt.[53] Drivers of these differing views include nuanced issues of labor, national control, and sovereignty.[54] As global communications platforms have come to dominate public squares around the world, there is evidence that, in many countries, citizens believe there is currently too much free speech.[55]

To assess the possibility for global alignment, my research team at Northeastern University in Boston fielded public opinion surveys in 2021 that could evaluate the appetite for free speech and regulation on social platforms.[56] There had been relatively little data, perhaps surprisingly, relating to how global public attitudes compare on regulating information communication technologies, although there is some empirical evidence about the need and demand for reform.[57] However, much of this research has largely focused solely on the West, particularly the United States.[58] More cross-national comparative perspective is certainly needed in the years ahead that uses identical survey instruments across countries, to allow one-to-one comparisons, as experts, policymakers, and scholars propose ideas for synchronization—the hope that global freedom of expression norms might evolve in the same direction.

We conducted surveys in four countries: the United States, the United Kingdom, South Korea, and Mexico. All democracies, the countries nevertheless hold somewhat conflicting values with respect to free expression and communication policy. Generally, respondents from the United States are more skeptical of content moderation, less trusting of government regulation, and more comfortable with laissez-faire free speech values than are respondents from the United Kingdom, South Korea, and Mexico.

Without a doubt, the four countries we studied have their own set of sociopolitical issues and unique histories that influence public opinion. Context and culture matter a great deal. For example, in the United Kingdom, the British public continues to debate the implications of leaving the European Union, and many believe that the 2016 Brexit vote was heavily influenced by misinformation campaigns.[59] South Korea is relatively open in terms of free press and expression, but the country is also sensitive to messaging about North Korea, which leads to selective censorship.[60] American society has meanwhile shown signs of increasing polarization over freedom of speech issues online.[61] Finally, in Mexico, criminal cartels have targeted journalists and independent sources of information, while the government often lacks accountability to the public on a variety of issues.[62]

Our findings highlighted to us how democracies and their underlying cultures may manifest different needs, and therefore expectations of social media platforms, where local values are translated and applied in nuanced ways. While there is modest support at best in the United States for stringent moderation tools (e.g., banning, content removal, etc.), publics in South Korea, Mexico, and the United Kingdom are more supportive of such measures and regulations. We asked three questions about how much participants agreed with freedom of speech-related statements and three questions about how much participants agreed with censorship-related statements.

Across all three questions about free speech, we saw strong support for freedom of expression across all four democratic countries. We phrased our questions to capture three dimensions of free speech: full liberty, controversial ideas, and expressions of prejudice. For example, we asked on a seven-point scale how much participants agreed or disagreed with the statement: "Everybody should have full liberty to promote what they believe to be true." Responses indicate mostly agreement across all four countries, although South Korea did have a large portion of undecided participants.

In contrast to questions about freedom of speech, we saw more divergence when participants were asked about their views of limiting or censoring content. We constructed our questionnaire to assess views of censorship in an escalating manner, so that the first question broadly asked how much participants agreed that "it is better to limit some harmful content than to allow all of it," the second question asked how much participants agreed that content should be removed if it causes severe distress to others, and the third question asked how much participants agreed that "people should trust authorities when they restrict certain kinds of content as 'dangerous' or 'hateful.'"

We also saw broad support for limiting some harmful content rather than allowing all of it (UK = 76.4 percent somewhat or strongly agreed,

South Korea = 80.6 percent, Mexico = 78 percent, and US = 68.6 percent). However, we began to see overall statistically significant divergence when we specifically asked about authorities restricting "dangerous" or "hateful" content or taking down content if it causes severe distress to others. South Korea in particular supports removing content if it causes severe distress (91.3 percent somewhat or strongly agree), and the United States is much less supportive (61.1 percent somewhat or strongly agree).

When asked about freedom of expression issues, Americans are more hesitant to agree with censorship measures, as compared to respondents in Mexico, South Korea, and the United Kingdom. The results of our public opinion questions on free speech and censorship suggest that Americans are more supportive of uninhibited free expression, and these results were expected given that American identity is often defined in terms of support for free speech and the U.S. Constitution's First Amendment. What was unexpected was the large divergence between the United States and the United Kingdom on issues of expression, given the two country's historical similarities. Continental European countries have long been seen as more restrictive on speech issues than the United States[63]—although these dynamics may be in a complicated state of flux—and the United Kingdom may be closer to the views of Europe than to the United States.

South Korean public opinion observed in this study may indeed be informed by the "collectivist" nature of that Asian nation's culture,[64] and the results here suggest that participants in the South Korea sample are much more receptive to curbing speech to limit potential stress, danger, or harm. Additionally, evidence suggests that on free speech and censorship, Mexicans are more in the middle between the United States on the liberal side and South Korea on the collectivist side.

In terms of what speech should be allowed in public discourse, and what might be banned, our findings point to several comparison points and paradoxes in the global politics of platform regulation and misinformation. For example, participants from the United States and the United Kingdom—similar countries along multiple dimensions with primarily English-speaking populations with a shared history—have strongly divergent views on many factors of freedom of expression, censorship, government regulation of social media, and content moderation. Although the British public is more supportive of government regulation of social media than Americans are, public trust in government has declined in the United Kingdom since the Brexit referendum.[65] Yet British trust in government is not yet at the same low levels as in the United States. Furthermore, the Brexit referendum campaign was characterized by misinformation, with many actors (foreign and domestic) using social media in new communicative ways that had not been seen previously in British politics.[66] This experience of such a historically important vote being affected by rampant misinformation has shaped the British public's views of social media, and freedom of expression on social media will continue to be a focus in British politics.

The declining trust in government in the United States since the 1960s,[67] particularly on the American right, is a likely explanatory factor in the low approval of government regulation of social media relative to the other three countries in this study. Many would contend that a healthy distrust in government is not necessarily a bad thing in principle,[68] particularly when it comes to issues of censorship and freedom of expression. American politics is also characterized by increasingly stark polarization, and previous evidence points to polarized views of social media regulation, content moderation, and freedom of speech.[69] The polarized nature of American politics helps explain why across many questions analyzed here, we see more disagreement in the United States when compared with the other three democracies. What is interesting, then, are the questions where we see large majority support, such as support for freedom of speech or the use of information warning labels as a content moderation tool.

Our findings for South Korea also had intriguing implications. South Korea has long been at the top of freedom of the press ratings in Asia,[70] but South Koreans were also relatively more supportive of various forms of censorship, government regulation of social media, and intrusive content moderation methods. However, as mentioned, South Korea is often regarded as more of a culturally collectivist country compared to Western cultures like in the United States.[71] In collectivistic societies, the needs and goals of the group as a whole may be more important than the needs and desires of each individual. Therefore, it may stand to reason that the South Korean respondents in our study supported restrictive or regulatory initiatives if certain content (e.g., hate speech) causes severe distress on

Figure 6.3 U.S. House Speaker Kevin McCarthy and X CEO Elon Musk talk in January 2023. Musk has resisted many forms of regulation, even as the European Commission has used new laws to begin challenging X's lax governance standards and threaten X with legal action and fines. Meanwhile, Musk become a key early player in President Donald Trump's second administration. Office of the Speaker of the House of Representatives.

others or society at large. When implementing any possible government regulation of social media or social media content-moderation regimes, the collectivist nature of South Korean culture and their traditions of supporting freedoms of expression may come into conflict with each other.

Further, Mexico presented a unique case study, and the results were unexpected. At one level the Mexican public supported free speech in robust ways. But participants from Mexico were also much more likely to support restrictions on "dangerous" or "hateful" content, although they did not support government regulation to achieve these ends. This may be reflective of the current state of Mexican press freedom where protection for journalists—and against "dangerous" or "hateful" content—is needed, yet there is limited government accountability in preventing and protecting attacks against press freedom.

Regarding issues such as moderating hate speech, the central reality underscored by our public opinion work is that companies operating cross-nationally must consider more deeply how to allocate resources to grapple with the diverse needs of global societies. The four societies we studied are diverse, but they represent only a small fraction of the diverse societies across the world. The United States is a clear outlier in many categories of public opinion with respect to social media. Whether or not the views of tech executives and engineers in the United States should prevail globally is a matter of ongoing contention, to be resolved only as more nations individually decide to formulate public policy accordingly (as Europe is increasingly doing), to support or roll back current platform rules for expression.

CLOSING THE GAP

Still, when it comes to industrial content moderation, the United States has mostly been on the policy sidelines, even as its technology companies are obviously front and center to the debate.[72] The rapid innovation being produced by America's tech companies continues to outstrip the policy ideas of many different schools of thought around the world. Consider Margarethe Vestager's own words in 2021 as the European Commission put together its massive, laboriously and meticulously crafted guidelines for regulating AI. The policy guidelines, based on consultation with thousands of experts, were "landmark rules" constituting "new global norms to make sure AI can be trusted."[73] These rules were, Vestager claimed on April 21, 2021, "future-proof."[74] On November 30 of the following year, OpenAI released ChatGPT to the world, rapidly upending many assumptions about what AI technologies might do. Vestager's European Commission report did not seem to have any grasp of this type of technology, even hypothetically. The *New York Times* reported that ChatGPT "blindsided E.U. policymakers."[75]

How exactly will the United States manage its continuing advantages in technological innovation, given an external world ever more eager to regulate that technology? Nathaniel Fick, the country's first Ambassador-at-Large for Cyberspace and Digital Policy, pondered that exact question during the Biden administration. A Gen X former Marine officer who fought in Iraq and Afghanistan, Fick went on to become a famous young author (*One Bullet Away* is a memoir of his military service),[76] a think tank leader, and a cybersecurity software executive. Since being sworn in as America's top technology diplomat on September 21, 2022, he traveled the world attempting to align allies on a coherent agenda that has a "North Star," as he called it, which is the "idea of a free, open, interoperable, reliable, secure global internet that is not balkanized, that does not tolerate things like shutdowns and firewalls and content control by authoritarian governments."[77]

While such a vision can sound like a variation on the old rah-rah "Internet Freedom" agenda that the United States waved around in earlier decades, Fick's articulation of America's role in the world seemed to acknowledge that, despite all the country's global technological clout, other countries now have options: "We have a group of states that are with us and will always be with us. We have a group of states that are against us and maybe in competition with us for a long time. And then we have a vast middle, a huge number of people and countries, governments [and] companies, in the world that at different points are going to have to align themselves one way or another. And forcing them to choose is less effective than giving them a choice and providing a choice."[78]

China and Europe offer policy and technology alternatives, and many countries are eager to become less reliant on the United States. That means a more nuanced approach is required—as well as a lot more listening.

Under President Joe Biden, the executive branch of the U.S. government called for both privacy protections for user data and greater accountability from social platform companies in terms of limits on targeted advertising, among other things.[79] Such updates to policy, Fick said, are crucial if the United States is going to make a legitimate bid to earn the trust of both traditional allies and those on the fence, who might defect to the likes of China and Zhang Ming's Shanghai Cooperation Organization model. Fick noted that China is engaged in a "full court press all over the world" particularly on "information and communications technology of all kinds."[80] Thus far, however, the United States has not offered a fresh, compelling vision. The election of Donald J. Trump to a second term in 2024 makes new rules, synchronized among allies, highly unlikely. In any case, the political analyst Ian Bremmer has noted the emergence of an increasingly "technopolar" world, wherein technology companies and technological innovation are a central source of power and legitimacy around the world.[81] These very technological forces are likely making the cohesion and power of international rules—of a liberal international order—more difficult over time.[82]

Ultimately, the visions of China's Ming, Europe's Vestager and Breton, and Khan's human rights advocacy on behalf of the United Nations depend very much on the next move of the Americans, including the likes of Fick (and similarly inclined successors) and the U.S. government writ large, Congress, the executive branch, and the courts. A U.S. conservative countermovement is now taking shape, one that would seek to export American libertarianism and push back against European-style regulation. Policy analysts Dean Jackson and Berin Szóka characterize this U.S. movement as a driving force behind a "larger geopolitical struggle against social media regulation."[83] It is a fluid situation, as it appears nearly every technological and regulatory model, not just those originating in the United States and Europe, is facing pushback: For example, the Chinese-owned company TikTok faces legal scrutiny and potential bans in more than twenty countries around the world, including India and the United States.[84] Much hangs in the balance, therefore, both domestically and globally. The fight over the future of information communications technology has likely never been more consequential, given the interconnected global system brought about by these very technologies.

7

A RESPONSE PRINCIPLE

The development of the ideal of freedom and its translation into the everyday life of the people in great areas of the earth is the product of the efforts of many peoples. It is the fruit of a long tradition of vigorous thinking and courageous action. No one race and no one people can claim to have done all the work to achieve greater dignity for human beings and greater freedom to develop human personality. In each generation and in each country there must be a continuation of the struggle and new steps forward must be taken since this is preeminently a field in which to stand still is to retreat.[1]
—Eleanor Roosevelt, Sorbonne, Paris, September 28, 1948

Addressing social media content-moderation issues is an essential part of addressing a larger phenomenon. Many scholars around the world believe we need to think more holistically about what we might call the "information environment." In other policy cases, such as environmental pollution and degradation of natural resources, or diseases spread among humans, we have had to, in a sense, "invent" a new field to solve a problem: in those cases, environmentalism and public health.[2] Societies have had to name the problem, uniting seemingly disparate issues and cases, to fix it. In the case of our current communications problems, it has been tempting to describe them as a "social media" problem. Or perhaps we specify it as a problem with mis- and disinformation and hate speech on social platforms.

This view is only partially correct. Such a diagnosis misses an array of interrelated factors that feed into, fuel, and shape social media, from underlying political and economic factors to how news institutions create content, the standards they uphold, and how public leaders choose to shape narratives that organize stories.[3] The central argument advanced here in *Governing Babel* has an important caveat. Improving how we address social media content moderation will have broad benefits, but there are deeper structural issues at work in the crisis surrounding trust in information. The collapse of the business model for high-quality journalism, for instance, is a central issue, as is the digital platforms' turn to exploiting user data to generate advertising revenue and the lack of data privacy rights. Beyond this, many global societies are facing even more fundamental issues relating to media access and their citizens' ability to meaningfully contribute to public discourse.[4] Philip N. Howard of Oxford University, who has founded the International Panel on the Information Environment (IPIE)—inspired by a similar institution focused on climate change—has articulated the need to establish "standards for a healthy global information environment."[5]

In this regard, consider the case, and the enduring ideas, of Jamal Khashoggi. In a northeastern corner of Istanbul, looming behind a concrete wall on a narrow suburban street, sits the Saudi Consulate, a mustard-yellow concrete building with gray steel doors emblazoned with golden, crossed scimitar swords. This is where journalist and dissident Jamal Khashoggi was murdered by Saudi security forces on October 2, 2018, an event that galvanized the global media and human rights communities. The final known images of Khashoggi, a fifty-nine-year-old man with a goatee, a balding pate, and glasses, show him walking into the consulate, a guard in a pale blue sport coat looking on. He had arrived there to arrange some paperwork so he could get married to a Turkish woman. But he knew well that his direct criticism of the Saudi regime, particularly Crown Prince Mohammed bin Salman, whose behavior he had called "impulsive" and "dangerous," could cause him problems at the consulate.[6] His willingness to appear at the consulate suggests that he did not imagine what actually happened: a group of assassins flown in from Saudi Arabia tortured him, killed him, dismembered his body, and then made his remains disappear.[7]

The forlorn consulate now stands as a kind of monument to a basic truth in our contemporary information environment. The world remains a dangerous place for speech. Journalists and human rights activists across the world are under siege.[8] The ability to shape opinion and to allow, or disallow, access to ideas has such fundamental value that there are people who will take immense, even desperate risks to own it. Khashoggi was a writer. And his murderers cut his fingers off. They did this knowing that he was not only a famous person connected with the *Washington Post*, with all its media power, but also a friend of the Turkish president in whose country he was living and working.

Of all the many things that have been said about Khashoggi and the meaning of his death, perhaps nothing was more poignant than the editor's note that accompanied his final column for the *Washington Post*. The editor, Karen Attiah, had waited to publish the column, pending news of his whereabouts. But when she realized the terrible truth, she published it: "This column perfectly captures his commitment and passion for freedom in the Arab world. A freedom he apparently gave his life for."[9] Khashoggi's last column is a clarion call to create new narratives to challenge the various sclerotic regimes that rule the Arab world. This was his final paragraph: "The Arab world needs a modern version of the old transnational media so citizens can be informed about global events. More important, we need to provide a platform for Arab voices. We suffer from poverty, mismanagement and poor education. Through the creation of an independent international forum, isolated from the influence of nationalist governments spreading hate through propaganda, ordinary people in the Arab world would be able to address the structural problems their societies face."[10] The call for a "platform for Arab voices" resonates with those who have long thought about media access issues and global inequalities in media and communication. In the 2011 Arab Spring, activists used Facebook and Twitter to great effect to organize protests in such places as Tunisia, Egypt, and Syria. But except for Tunisia, the protests and nascent democracy movement fizzled, turning into what some have called a tragic "Arab winter," with Egypt resuming a dictatorship and Syria plunging into a horrific civil war.[11]

Yet Khashoggi's call is about more than just some kind of technology platform developed in the Arab world. At a deeper level, his words reference the raw intellectual material necessary to structure high-quality public discourse. Khashoggi is invoking the social system that allows truth to emerge from noise and disagreement—what the Brookings Institution's Jonathan Rauch has called the "constitution of knowledge," which is produced by an array of strong underlying institutions, namely the courts, the universities and scientific institutions, and accurate journalism.[12] Khashoggi knew that social change cannot happen without such pieces in place.

In a famous *Harvard Law Review* article published in 1967, professor Jerome Barron provocatively argued that the spirit of the First Amendment could not be fulfilled if all access to public discourse was controlled by monopolistic commercial media.[13] There must be, he argued, ways for average citizens to voice their opinions and disseminate knowledge, if the right of the press was to mean anything more than a corporate right of large newspapers and television stations to say what they want without government interference. "A realistic view of the First Amendment," Barron wrote, "requires recognition that a right of expression is somewhat thin if it can be exercised only at the sufferance of the managers of mass communications." The general philosophy he endorsed was also sympathetic to ideas like the right of reply, and Barron would articulate the need for both media access and right of reply throughout his career.[14] The article helped touch off a multidecade school of thinking around more "collective" interpretations of the First Amendment, whereby the law should not just protect individual rights to be left alone from state interference. Instead, the government should also actively promote and subsidize opportunities for citizens to speak and be heard. Technologies that narrow people's views or continuously surface confirming information make such policies all the more urgent.[15]

In the United States, these kinds of arguments, which suggest that protecting the First Amendment requires positive elements beyond stopping interference, has generated a steady and ongoing debate, but not much concrete policy. Several commentators have emphasized the importance of upstream design through technology policy, specifically through government support for innovation and research in communications technology. It is worth noting that the internet itself began as a government research project. As Jack Balkin of Yale Law School has noted, "If the system of mass communications is designed correctly, better media access is built into the system and into the existing models of business competition. Greater media access occurs without having to fight over whether the First Amendment guarantees positive rights and, if it does, whether the judiciary is the proper institution to recognize and enforce them."[16]

But to pull back to the global context—and to the quest for understanding how our modern Babel might be better governed—social media

Figure 7.1 Prominent Saudi Arabian journalist and *Washington Post* columnist Jamal Khashoggi was murdered in Turkey by Saudi security forces on October 2, 2018. Seen here in 2010 sitting to the left of President Barack Obama at a White House meeting, Khashoggi called for a greater global platform for Arab voices, overcoming the influence of national governments in the Middle East "spreading hate through propaganda." https://www.flickr.com/photos/obamawhitehouse/3594694537.

and platform governance must confront the fact that the world's nearly two hundred nations face diverse challenges. In some places, social systems for knowledge production are weak, and mere "voice"—the ability to say something publicly, to speak truth—may not be enough. The risks of being ignored or, worse, having your fingers chopped off are real. What if there are simply no supporting institutions to buttress the voices of citizens? This points to perhaps the great challenge of our media and communications moment: Social platforms generate many of the harms, but fixing the information environment often requires that we fix more than social media.

THE CHALLENGE

Larger structural issues aside, social media content moderation is a crucial piece of the effort to improve the information environment. Platform governance requires leadership from many corners of the globe. There will be no one-size-fits-all paradigm. But major players must do their part and, collectively, send powerful signals that can become generally accepted norms.

The United States currently lacks a well-articulated vision, or even a minimum viable policy, for what social media platforms should be doing in the world as responsible private stewards of the public information commons. While Europe has begun to set standards for what a responsible and accountable communications platform looks like, the United States has not. The price of this lack of vision increases every day. Most of the world's major technology companies are headquartered in the United States, but the lack of a robust regulatory framework means that the U.S. government and its allies have few tools to support these companies when they need help standing up to authoritarian governments and bad actors around the world. This has created an enormous vacuum for human rights violators, of all kinds, to articulate their own local standards, cut their own deals, and dictate their own terms. As more countries and regions begin to grow their own communications technology platforms, the chance for the United States to contribute to recognized—and ethical—global standards slips away.[17]

The United States must also act to address harms within its own borders, as witnessed by the events of January 6, 2021. Bringing social media companies under some kind of regulation and finally holding them to account will force American society and its political class to begin reflecting more deeply on the underlying issues of economic fairness, racism and xenophobia, political polarization, and structural inequality that are stoking political violence. Solving the problems associated with social media will not fix every ill in society, but it will allow policymakers to focus on the substance of the issues, rather than merely reacting to how they are discussed online.

What is the logical next step for the United States from a policy perspective? One possible path is for the country to actively renew and translate its core traditions to deal with this latest crisis in media and communications. The United States should draw on deep traditions of thought extending back to Lippmann's and Lasswell's basic ideas that the conveyance of knowledge in a democratic society is always radically imperfect, and that propaganda and disinformation are often subtle and endemic. Bad speech is a problem to be managed through process and response, not solved. Yet current social media companies can do much more than they are currently doing to manage problems.

Certain pillars must uphold regulating speech in a democratic system. As we have seen, Lippmann emphasized that certain ideals must be adhered to for the public to give meaningful input and to support choices by government, particularly where there is confusion and perhaps no possibility of certainty about the truth. To extend these principles to our era: Should problematic content be left up and allowed to circulate widely? Should troublesome platform users be banned? Should an algorithm downrank certain content? In most cases, these will be judgment calls. In any case, there must be transparency of evidence, capacity for revision, and orderly procedures for iteration of new rules. The public will never have enough knowledge to judge the merits of most conflicts between users, companies, and regulators. But as Lippmann observed nearly a century ago, it is nevertheless necessary that we ensure transparency around the rules for decisions and certainty about the process for their revision.

Lasswell further developed the core idea that actors' attempts to undermine the democratic system of rules must be met with an active response, rather than censorship, as a matter of demonstrating what democracies stand for. In cases where individuals and groups are attacked, they must have some rights to access the forum and stick up for themselves, to argue back, and present evidence and counterspeech.

We might then ask how these ideas might be applied to particular platforms and speech environments. How are we to judge whether managers are doing a good job overseeing them? We can examine social media along three criteria. First, does the platform provide instrumental value in terms of helping users understand the origin, source, and context of information? Second, is it structured to create knowledge value, so that users can make good judgments and formulate true, justified beliefs? Finally, does the platform treat people fairly as they seek information, talk about things, and are themselves subjects of discussion? Overall, communications and media managers should exercise social responsibility as stewards of the information commons.

The growth of international human rights law should also be an increasing guide to regulators and courts. This body of law and its underlying principles are deeply intertwined with the First Amendment, and new regulations should continue to look for the myriad ways they are compatible. The United States needs to reinvigorate its engagement with this body of international law to advance the original ideals set out in the UN Charter and the International Covenant on Civil and Political Rights. There are strong foreign policy considerations that support this.

All these foundational concepts are abstract ideals. Putting them into practice means translating them into specific, actionable steps for platform accountability. While there is no single way to govern Babel, we might begin with the general outlines of a new public institution capable of oversight, tied to a central mission statement. This is precisely what the establishment of the FCC accomplished in 1934, near the beginning of the hundred-year journey that this book has tracked. Today, the United States should strongly consider a new regulatory body that would, on perhaps a quarterly basis, audit the behavior of social and information communications platforms and judge them on broad patterns of responsibility and response rather than on individual instances and anecdotes of outrageous posts or harmful speech.[18]

The regulatory body proposed here might proceed by sampling at random problem areas and patterns of incidents. This approach might help address the volume problem, in that an overall compliance system would likely prove unworkable given the scale of data and activity on the platforms. The timeline for review might be sped up around national elections and their completion, to ensure both that preparations are in place beforehand and that social platforms engage in sufficient active response to problems after the fact.

Such a public regulatory body should, to the maximum extent possible, favor active but speech-preserving responses to problematic speech, not removal or censorship. It should require that communications technology companies respond to patterns of hate speech, abuse, incitement, election disinformation, public health misinformation, and other content that generates patterns of harms that damage the public interest. But rather than making platforms liable for individual posts or specific instances—threatening to create an endless series of lawsuits, and a whack-a-mole situation everywhere—we should judge companies on the totality of their actions, specifically their good faith and diligence in responding to harms.

An effective policy might be generally organized around the concept of a "response principle." Does a given communications platform consistently demonstrate responsiveness to systemic harms and take measures that a reasonable person would consider sufficient? Does the approach help reduce harms as a direct outcome? Systemic harms might include things like widespread endangerment of children, election disruption, propagation of misleading information related to public health, or ongoing patterns of incitement toward lawless action. In this way, we might consider keeping Section 230 but adding new regulatory layers on top of it.

This type of direction is what the European Commission has been driving toward through the Digital Services Act, although that political body's alleged agenda—critics say it is pushing implicit trade protectionism in curbing the power of American companies—could lead it to overreach. Some technology analysts believe the DSA is likely to encounter considerable problems with enforcement, given how sprawling its rules are.[19] Early analysis of compliance data by the companies subject to the DSA shows something of a sprawling mess of rule-following, suggesting that micromanagement across such an inherently diffuse and chaotic domain may never be an effective strategy.[20]

In the model I am proposing, regulators would ask platforms, on a regular basis, how they addressed a certain set of problems (identified by journalists, watchdogs, civil society groups, as well as expert staff) and how they will mitigate such problems in the future. The regulation would be "effects-based"—in other words, the precise methods of response would not be specified.[21] Rather, it is the effects and outcomes of platform governance that would be of primary concern, and many approaches might achieve similar outcomes in terms of mitigating harms. Platforms would provide evidence, openly and transparently. The long series of hearings with technology executives before Congress in recent years, which has generated so much public attention, might ultimately be seen as a kind of precursor: This process would move to an agency setting; it would be made more regular, detailed, and formal; and it would go past the mere spectacle and grandstanding that congressional hearings have featured.

On a periodic basis (perhaps quarterly or annually), a governing body would then make a collective human judgment on whether the company has reasonably demonstrated a duty of care, showing due attention to the response principle. Tax subsidies might be provided to companies to add trust and safety professionals and related compliance professionals who could make the reporting process robust.

In general, policy scholars note that regulations require rationales, and clearly the rationales for broadcast regulation—the scarcity of the airwaves—do not apply to internet-based technologies. It is preferable, then, to ground new rules in the rationale that our new communications platforms present systemic risks to many facets of society, much as financial and health industries do, and to regulate them as systems that need to be managed responsibly. Another rationale could be that government has a legitimate right to communicate with platforms, but no lane with comprehensive oversight for such communication is otherwise available. A new regulatory body could serve as the chief conduit—perhaps the clearinghouse and data collection agency—as government and platforms communicate. There is an interrelated set of issues that all touch on the free speech rights of the companies and users, as well as issues of harm. Centrally, there is the issue of "jawboning," which is potential abuse of government power to coerce companies to remove or alter content or take actions against users. Jawboning has been the subject of significant controversy and litigation all the way up to the Supreme Court (in *Murthy v. Missouri*, for example, decided in 2024), and legal experts expect such government pressure to continue.[22] As much as jawboning is a vexing problem in the United States, it remains, as this book has suggested, an even bigger problem around the world. Standing up a U.S. model for transparency around government-platform interactions would be highly useful globally. A new regulatory body could document all such government-platform interactions, subject them to public scrutiny, and provide a legitimate lane for urgent communications around, for example, national security concerns.

It is worth recalling, as we have seen, that the FCC mainly regulated broadcast media through license renewal, and it hardly ever failed to renew a license. Yet the process kept licensees fairly well in line. This might be precisely the kind of regulatory situation we reconstruct for social media. Surely, there will be evolution in technology and more granular rules will develop, but this regulatory starting point has a strong chance of being effective in terms of getting companies to be more active, and it has precedent.

The largest companies such as Meta, Google, and TikTok have elaborate trust and safety and security regimes in place. They have rules and do enormous amounts of content moderation. Some produce voluminous reports about the millions of pieces of content they have "actioned on." But it is all voluntary. Their attention to problems is therefore selective. There are no specific consequences for failure. A new regulatory body would energize their efforts across the board, even if it merely audits selected areas and incidents. Indeed, a central principle of auditing is that the entity being reviewed does not know entirely where it will be evaluated. This uncertainty forces the company in question to exert effort across all areas.

The broader tools of response are rooted in American tradition. Their targeted application is becoming both more possible and more expansive as AI-supported platform management technologies grow more sophisticated. Should a company not demonstrate active response broadly in its approach, the general remedy should have teeth but remain speech-preserving. Regulators might consider, for example, pausing a company's ability to add new users and advertisers on the platform, a sanction consistent with speech-preservation but one that would motivate every company. The objective would be responsible management; the penalty for lack of compliance would be loss of growth opportunity. Sanctions would not, for the most part, inhibit or affect the free speech rights of the platforms or their current users. Companies might object, pointing out their existing users would be stopped from speaking to an expanded audience and reaching more people. But all regulations involve trade-offs, and if such penalty-triggered pauses on user growth are relatively temporary, it could represent a reasonable balance between speech and public safety.

All such regulation should unfold much as the FCC's rules did, through rulemaking over decades, accounting for new innovations in communications technology. Recent Supreme Court jurisprudence has made agency rulemaking more difficult potentially, but again, my argument attempts to take a longer view.[23] In any case, all of this regulatory action should be under the constant supervision of the courts. Such a model could be replicated in other countries around the world, providing a standard for corporate social responsibility in this space while also clearly communicating that censorship mandates for specific content are not acceptable. It would generally align with Europe's new rules, while providing more flexibility in rulemaking and regulation than allowed by the Digital Services Act.

Reviewing the hundred-year journey of American media thinking, norms, and regulation points us in a definite general direction. At the foundational level, the modern First Amendment was both used as a speech-preserving tool and deployed as an active instrument via international human rights law to help keep the world safe for democracy, to avoid further aggressive wars, and to fight the propaganda, hate, and disinformation that accompany such physical aggression, by allowing people the right to free expression. The concepts of counterspeech, right of reply, labeling, and active response have been core to solutions for harmful or bad speech, including disinformation and hate speech. Within this history, we can see solution sets that are, as Harold Lasswell said, "deeply entrenched in the folkways of democracy."[24] The basic idea of active response to speech-related harms, threats, and accusations is part of democracy's DNA, constituting elementary fair play.

It follows from history and the general direction of the founding period in media and communications in the United States that we should again require private companies managing speech to show a duty of care. In the late 1910s and 1920s, jurists and public intellectuals framed the problems for democracies in the era of modern communications, outlining the central traditions for dealing with harmful speech while not destroying democracy in the process. In the 1940s, the Hutchins Commission set out the idea of social responsibility for those managing the public's communications space. From the late 1940s to the late 1960s, the Fairness Doctrine had an important period of two decades in which no national broadcaster was sanctioned or micromanaged segment by segment, story by story; rather, the rule "began to function more as the spirit of responsible broadcasting than as the letter of the law," as former CBS

President Fred Friendly put it.[25] The rise of cable and satellite telecommunications and then the internet began to erode the logic of existing rules through the 1970s and 1980s. Beginning in the late 1990s, Section 230 itself was authored to allow websites to be active stewards of their information spaces.

A new era demands new thinking. We find ourselves in need of a new principle for organizing and governing speech, one that takes account of the hybrid realities and the global implications of any new set of rules. If the new information environment is to be equitable and sensitive to global conditions, it must be guided by conceptions that are much more flexible, adaptable, and public interest-oriented than our older, more libertarian conceptions, under Section 230 and a narrow reading of the First Amendment of unbridled competition of speech, expression, and ideas. Likewise, strict rules under some older broadcasting regimes, where companies are judged story by story, segment by segment, are inappropriate and unworkable; revoking licenses (the contemporary equivalent would be shutting down platforms) even in extreme cases will not work, either, as it would impinge on the rights of average platform users. Older communications rules such as the Fairness Doctrine also do not fit well with the complicated challenges of the present and future, even if their spirit should live on.

When we think about regulation, we are often trapped in the mental model of regulating, let's say, meat packing, oil drilling, or pollution from a smokestack—some kind of other industrial issue from past regulatory battles. Conservatives fear a nanny state. Liberals often want answers on every possible violation of rights. All recent past media regulatory history has as its fundamental unit of analysis the news story or the broadcast segment. Addressing the contemporary challenge requires that we adjust to thinking about the outcomes of networked behavior—we must think about general patterns and trends, and their consequences, not atomized pieces of content. This will mean necessarily lowering expectations for what regulation can do. Content moderation may not be able to effectively stop every borderline potential violation of hate speech or disinformation. Instead, we need to hold all platforms accountable for general patterns of behavior and associated harms.

In this phenomenally complex realm of human communication and expression, all we can expect is to bend the arc, set directions, and do our best to constantly direct behavior toward a North Star. The nature of human communication is too fluid, too contingent, too unpredictable, for rigid rules. Given the scale of the matter, we cannot create a system of micromanagement or censorship, neither of which follow from tradition. Such patterns of thinking are roughly consistent with policymakers' recent pivot away from overturning Section 230 entirely and toward notions of risk mitigation and assessment.[26]

TRENDING VALUES

New rules should also take account of what we might think of as a long "information justice" movement across the twentieth and twenty-first centuries, which has often taken place in the areas of norms, public opinion, and civil society.[27] Over the past century, we have seen the related press freedom movement, the broader human rights movement, and the rise of the "right to know" (the transparency and consumer rights movement, which paves the way for platform data transparency for third-party researchers and the public).[28] This information justice movement points in a definite direction, even as we have seen democratic backsliding and worrying censorship trends around the world over the past decade.[29] Legal scholars note that despite the definite rise of authoritarian forces across the globe in spots, there is a discernible long-term trend in terms of international human rights law, which has cascaded from country to country.[30]

We also have an increasingly robust tradition of expecting transparency and certain standards of behavior from multinational corporations as they operate across borders, including technology and communications companies. A ready-made framework called the "Ruggie Principles" may provide a basis for corporate governance for social media. The late John Ruggie was a Harvard professor who in the mid-2000s became the UN's go-to advisor for extending human rights law to businesses. His work led to the unanimous endorsement by nation states and many global corporations of an overarching set of principles called "protect, respect, and remedy."[31] These were approved by the UN Human Rights Council in 2011 as the Guiding Principles on Business and Human Rights.

Ruggie has summarized the principles as follows: "(1) states have a duty to protect against human rights abuses by third parties, including business, through policies, regulation, legislation and effective enforcement; (2) business enterprises have an independent responsibility to respect human rights: that is, to avoid people's human rights being harmed through their activities or business relationships, and to address harms that do occur; (3) where individuals' human rights are harmed, they should have access to effective remedy, and both states and enterprises have a role to play in enabling this to occur."[32]

Among the many obligations that global businesses agree to take on under the Ruggie Principles is the central concept of "human rights due diligence." Companies should conduct this review as they move into new markets or consider new products and services. This due diligence, which might include the related concept of a human rights impact assessment, means careful ongoing scoping and anticipatory research into what might happen, who might be harmed, how things might go wrong, and what kinds of contingency plans should be put in place.[33] Time and again, social media platforms have rapidly grown user bases in countries and regions where, it turned out, they did not have the expertise or capacity to properly manage such problems as outbreaks of communal violence or contested elections. These impact assessments are becoming a standard tool for technology companies as they enter even more uncertain territory by, for example, developing AI models.[34] Any new regulatory body could incorporate impact assessments as standard practice, as a way of establishing an expectation that social platforms show proof of active response.

We also must grasp the logic of our emerging technological moment. Generative AI changes the game not only for the risks it presents, but also for the capabilities it offers—and the new responsibilities it should demand. Increasingly, communications technology firms will hold in their hands the ability to govern their platforms much more comprehensively, even as AI also challenges some of their internal rules. The original logic of Section 230 held that it was not possible for websites to police user-generated content at the level of millions of posts. That is, it was not possible for public content-hosting websites to exercise the kind of oversight on users' content in the same way that a newspaper or radio station might control their content. Section 230 therefore offered platforms a "Good Samaritan" carve-out, even if they took down only some objectionable material where they could find it.

Now, in the moment of generative AI, when speech and expression are becoming more scalable commodities, the logic of Section 230 increasingly no longer makes sense. Platform companies can use generative AI with increasing sophistication to detect and respond to users' posts. Generative models currently are plagued by flaws, but the timeline for improvement suggests that we can expect a very different situation within a decade. This is not to say that humans should not be "in the loop," helping to ensure that enforcement is fair and equitable, and that the AI models themselves are trained properly. Rather, new rules should require that even more humans are employed to help in these content moderation efforts, with regulation driving a whole marketplace and field for ethical AI. As we have seen with the stories from January 6, 2021, a key component of active response to harms is having a lot of humans on board, capable of pivoting quickly and flexibly. This should be considered a feature and cost of doing business.

As with all other maturing industries, the sphere of media and communications platforms needs regular public reporting and compliance; this means establishing baselines and proving to the public that companies are taking things seriously. And once we have more regular insight into patterns of harm, we can begin to look at issues such as "disparate harm"—how different communities may be more negatively affected than others.

In short, the response principle offers an opportunity to consolidate a new set of expectations, a norm that could be broadly translated into local law across the world. This principle derives from the original traditions of media and communications governance thinking, namely, First Amendment jurisprudence, the Fairness Doctrine, the right of reply, the power of counterspeech, and various aspects of the long information justice movement, particularly relating to transparency and human rights impact assessments that have developed over the past century. But all these concepts must be translated into the emerging order of algorithms, platforms, and generative AI, and that will require agile rulemaking that adjusts to changing technological conditions.

URGENCY OF RESPONSE

The solution outlined in this book is something quite broad. History points us toward the skeleton of a structure, a kind of minimalist starting point, that allows us to build on the solid ground of democratic tradition. A fair and careful reading and analysis of the history presented here, both older and more current, strongly supports the idea of a response principle. Numerous other thinkers, policymakers, and scholars have put forward ideas for social media and technology reform that are more fine-grained and broader in their aspirations for societal transformation. A new U.S. regulatory body organized around the response principle could support over time the realization of more ambitious regulatory visions as technology advances, further rules accumulate, and policymaking continues from this strong starting point.[35] We should begin to anticipate a future where AI technologies and agents begin to saturate the online landscape,[36] where we need to preserve the autonomy of human voices and activities. Indeed, in the future, human-generated activity may represent a valuable and scarce resource in the machine-driven information environment.

There are myriad diverse visions for rules and regulations that could be facilitated under a response principle. There is no shortage of ideas for reform. For example, in his book *Cheap Speech: How Disinformation Poisons Our Politics—and How to Cure It*, Richard L. Hasen, now at UCLA, explores several ideas for protecting U.S. elections, including requiring platform executives to sign a sworn statement that they did not tweak algorithms to favor particular candidates and passing new data privacy laws to take away platforms' power to target messages.[37] In *The Networked Leviathan: For Democratic Platforms*, Paul Gowder of Northwestern University articulates a vision for more democratic governance of platforms, involving users and citizens deeply in oversight through "polycentric" public-private groups that would have power over decisions.[38] Ellen P. Goodman at Rutgers University has proposed a variety of new types of "friction" and delays in how messages proliferate on social media platforms, building in brakes for harmful viral content.[39] An emerging, and related, school of thought suggests that content moderation is largely a platform design problem—in other words, the way that features, buttons, interfaces, and algorithms are deployed have decisive downstream effects on what kinds of harms are produced.[40]

Many of these policy ideas could be subsumed under a response principle that allows social platforms to show evidence of active mitigation and a duty of care. The tools that platforms use might be flexible and suited to the purpose, depending on the problem and its context. Companies might fulfill their regulatory obligations in diverse ways, with flexibility as new technologies and innovations continue to change both problems and potential solutions.

There can be no final, steady-state answer for the problems created by social platforms and information communications technologies. Problems of public communication and speech take place in complex, adaptive systems; they are akin to the problems of public health, terrorism, or global finance. They are problems to be managed, not solved. But I do believe we need to establish a North Star principle of response to harms by platform companies, enforced under law, and to begin to develop constantly updated regulatory rules, under the careful supervision of the courts.

Perhaps new U.S. rules will provide a model and standard that can attract allies, preserving important aspects of innovation culture and the First Amendment while also acknowledging the increasing power of networked communications technologies to inflict harm and fuel undemocratic energies and forces. Or perhaps inertia will prevail, leaving Babel's current state of confusion, and growing clouds of moral and political darkness, to continue spreading across the globe.

ACKNOWLEDGMENTS

Many colleagues and institutions have generously supported my work toward the completion of *Governing Babel*. First and foremost, I want to thank Northeastern University, the College of Arts, Media & Design, and Northeastern's Ethics Institute, where I spent my interdisciplinary research sabbatical, for allowing me the opportunity to range widely as a scholar. I thank colleagues David Lazer, Ron Sandler, Briony Swire-Thompson, Garrett Morrow, Myo Chung, Meg Heckman, Matt Kopec, Brooke Foucault Welles, Kenny Joseph, Mike Beaudet, Jonathan Kaufman, Dan O'Brien, and Dan Kennedy, among many others. Zeve Sanderson, Daphne Keller, Tom Wheeler, Anna Lenhart, Jack Goldsmith, Joseph Walther, Dean Jackson, Justin Hendrix, Nate Persily, Alissa Cooper, Andy Sellars, Phil Howard, Beth Goldberg, and Nicco Mele have my thanks for ideas and comments as I developed the manuscript.

Research assistants Emma Klekotka, Kristen Kilgallen, Jess Montgomery Polny, Ray Christian Cristobal, Roberto Patterson, Lauren Vitacco, and Daniela Rincon Reyes provided vital help and ideas on various project phases, while librarian Brooke Williams helped proof this manuscript. Staff administrators Susan Conover, Ariel Rodriguez, Amelia Keany, and Tammi Westgate have my gratitude. Libby Phillips provided great help with manuscript image preparation. I would also like to thank Senior Vice President Mike Armini at Northeastern and Dean Elizabeth Hudson in the College of Arts, Media & Design. My thanks go to editor Audra Wolfe for superb help and, again, to Gita Devi Manaktala, Suraiya Jetha, Kathleen Caruso, Julia Collins, and Katie Kerr at the MIT Press for expert work, guidance, and wisdom. John Keller, Audiovisual Archivist for the

National Archives and Records Administration, at the William J. Clinton Presidential Library, provided crucial help.

Many conversations at the Knight Foundation's INFORMED Conference Series, the Stanford Trust and Safety Research Conference, and internally within the Internet Democracy Initiative community at Northeastern helped catalyze these ideas. My external work as a scholar has provided me with a lot of material and experience that helped me formulate my ideas for this book. Since 2020, I have worked as a research consultant for the John S. and James L. Knight Foundation, helping to document and analyze a large research network that has been seeded and supported. That network is dedicated to studying the intersection of media, technology, and democracy. My work in this capacity has led to an ongoing study of scholars across the United States, their work, and the patterns of connection among them, as well as the impact of their ideas. My thanks go to John Sands, Ashley Zohn, A. J. D'Amico, and Sam Gill, as well as Alberto Ibargüen. I have performed about a hundred interviews in this role, with both internal and external stakeholders. I also had the privilege of serving as a research consultant to the John D. and Catherine T. MacArthur Foundation in 2022 and 2023. I led a team that coauthored an extensive internal report about opportunities for impact in the mis- and disinformation field. My thanks go to Kathy Im, Jennifer Humke, Elizabeth Oo, Chantell Johnson, and Lauren Pabst.

The Stanton Foundation has funded work on local news that Mike Beaudet and I have continued to conduct at Northeastern. My thanks to Liz Allison and Laurie Slap. I also want to acknowledge my work as a research consultant to Twitter, Inc. (now X), on their misinformation team. I gained valuable insights from this experience, although my engagement was far removed from the day-to-day operations of actual content moderation practice. Both Twitter (pre-X) and Facebook (now Meta) made unrestricted gifts to the academic project on content labeling of which I have been a part. My thanks to Sarah Shirazyan, Peter Stern, Yvonne Lee, and Liz Arcamona at Meta; Sarah Vieweg, formerly of Twitter; and Sudhir Venkatesh at Columbia University.

This book began during the pandemic, when my spouse, Carrie, and our children faced health challenges that made me question whether spending time on another book was worth it. The intellectual journey to produce a book requires tremendous sacrifice from loved ones. I am not sure I can ever repay them for their patience, but I hope they know I will be forever grateful for giving me the space and support to write.

I dedicate this book to those journalists, scholars, media creators, social media professionals, and human rights advocates whose daily practice embodies and preserves the right to "seek, receive and impart information and ideas through any media and regardless of frontiers," as the UN Universal Declaration of Human Rights stated some three-quarters of a century ago. Passing these rights to the next generation, and into the next century, will require much work ahead from us all.

NOTES

INTRODUCTION

1. Erik Barnouw, *A Tower in Babel: A History of Broadcasting in the United States to 1933*, vol. 1 (Oxford: Oxford University Press, 1966), 3.

2. Akshay Verma, Richard Sear, and Neil Johnson, "How US Presidential Elections Strengthen Global Hate Networks." *npj Complexity* 1, no. 1 (2024): 18.

3. For a variety of wider scholarly perspectives on these events, see Shannon C. McGregor, Daniel Kreiss, Khadijah Costley White, and Rebekah Tromble, eds., *Media and January 6th* (Oxford: Oxford University Press, 2024).

4. Abdi Latif Dahir, "Uganda Blocks Facebook Ahead of Contentious Election," *New York Times*, January 13, 2021, https://www.nytimes.com/2021/01/13/world/africa/uganda-facebook-ban-elections.html; Fred Ojambo, "Uganda to Maintain Facebook Ban Indefinitely, New Vision Says," *Bloomberg*, January 22, 2022, https://www.bloomberg.com/news/articles/2021-01-22/uganda-to-maintain-facebook-ban-indefinitely-new-vision-says.

5. Kat Losdorf, "Social Media Fueled Russian Protests Despite Government Attempts to Censor," *National Public Radio*, January 24, 2021, https://www.npr.org/2021/01/24/960113653/social-media-fueled-russian-protests-despite-government-attempts-to-censor.

6. Allide Naylor, "Russian Government Claims TikTok Deleted Young People's Protest Prep Videos at Its Behest," *Gizmodo*, January 22, 2021, https://gizmodo.com/russia-claims-tiktok-deleted-young-people-s-protest-pre-1846112989; Andrew Roth, "Tens of Thousands Protest in Russia Calling for Navalny's Release," *Guardian*, January 23, 2021, https://www.theguardian.com/world/2021/jan/23/alexei-navalny-supporters-join-protests-across-russia.

7. Zeba Siddiqui and Devjyot Ghoshal, "Twitter Blocks Dozens of Accounts on India's Demand amid Farm Protests: Sources," *Reuters*, February 1, 2021, https://www.reuters.com/article/us-india-farms-protests-twitter/twitter-blocks-dozens-of-accounts-on-indias-demand-amid-farm-protests-sources-idUSKBN2A12J9/.

8. "India Activist Disha Ravi Arrested over Farmers' Protest 'Toolkit,'" *BBC*, February 14, 2021, https://www.bbc.com/news/world-asia-india-56060232.

9. Yana Gorokhovskaia and Cathryn Grothe, *Freedom in the World 2024: The Mounting Damage of Flawed Elections and Armed Conflict* (Washington, DC: Freedom House, 2024), https://freedomhouse.org/report/freedom-world/2024/mounting-dam age-flawed-elections-and-armed-conflict.

10. Vittoria Elliott, "Elon Musk's Twitter Takeover Set Off a Race to the Bottom," *Wired*, November 5, 2024, https://www.wired.com/story/elon-musk-trust-safety-industry/.

11. James Gleick, *The Information: A History, A Theory, A Flood* (New York: Pantheon Books, 2011), 7–8.

12. Geoffrey Nunberg, "Information, Disinformation, Misinformation," in *Information: A Historical Companion*, ed. Ann Blair, Paul Duguid, Anja-Silvia Goeing, and Anthony Grafton (Princeton, NJ: Princeton University Press, 2021), 496–497. See also *Oxford English Dictionary*, s.v. "information (n.)," accessed December 2023, https:// doi.org/10.1093/OED/2626286341.

13. "Thomas Jefferson to John Melish, 13 January 1813," *Founders Online*, National Archives, last accessed January 2, 2024, https://founders.archives.gov/documents /Jefferson/03-05-02-0478.

14. As quoted in Nunberg, "Information, Disinformation, Misinformation," 496.

15. Nicco Mele, *The End of Big: How the Digital Revolution Makes David the New Goliath* (New York: St. Martin's Press, 2013).

16. For a sense of the range of proposals and issues at play and potential solutions, see Philip Napoli, *Social Media and the Public Interest: Media Regulation in the Disinformation Age* (New York: Columbia University Press, 2019); Paul M. Barrett, *Regulating Social Media: The Fight over Section 230—and Beyond* (New York: Center for Business and Human Rights, NYU Stern, 2020), https://www.stern.nyu.edu/experience-stern /faculty-research/regulating-social-media-fight-over-section-230-and-beyond; Ellen P. Goodman, "Digital Information Fidelity and Friction," February 26, 2020, *The Tech Giants, Monopoly Power, and Public Discourse essay series* (New York: Knight First Amendment Institute at Columbia University), https://knightcolumbia.org/content /digital-fidelity-and-friction; Olivier Sylvain, "Discriminatory Designs on User Data," April 1, 2018, *Emerging Threats* essay series (New York: Knight First Amendment Institute at Columbia University, 2018), https://knightcolumbia.org/content/discri minatory-designs-user-data.

17. Tom Wheeler, "Crossing the Regulatory Rubicon: The Future of Digital Regulation Is Being Defined in Europe," *Brookings*, June 7, 2024, https://www.brookings .edu/articles/crossing-the-regulatory-rubicon-the-future-of-digital-regulation-is -being-defined-in-europe/.

18. Tom Wheeler, *Techlash: Who Makes the Rules in the Digital Gilded Age?* (Washington, DC: Brookings Institution Press, 2023), 117–118.

19. Tarleton Gillespie, "Content Moderation, AI, and the Question of Scale," *Big Data & Society* 7, no. 2 (August 21, 2020), https://doi.org/10.1177/2053951720943234; Tarleton Gillespie, Patricia Aufderheide, Elinor Carmi, Ysabel Gerrard, Robert Gorwa, Ariadna Matamoros-Fernández, et al., "Expanding the Debate About Content Moderation: Scholarly Research Agendas for the Coming Policy Debates," *Internet Policy*

Review 9, no. 4 (October 21, 2020): 1–29, https://doi.org/10.14763/2020.4.1512; Sarah T. Roberts, *Behind the Screen: Content Moderation in the Shadows of Social Media* (New Haven, CT: Yale University Press, 2019).

20. Scholars from a variety of fields have been drawing historical analogies and tracing the pre-digital roots of ideas and phenomena to help understand our social media age. For example: Heidi Tworek, "Disinformation: It's History," July 14, 2021, Centre for International Governance Innovation, https://www.cigionline.org /articles/disinformation-its-history/; Sharon McQueen, "From Yellow Journalism to Tabloids to Clickbait: The Origins of Fake News in the United States," In *Information Literacy and Libraries in the Age of Fake News*, ed. Denise E. Agosto (Exeter: Libraries Unlimited, 2018).

21. Fred W. Friendly, *The Good Guys, the Bad Guys and the First Amendment: Free Speech vs. Fairness in Broadcasting* (New York: Random House, 2013), 24.

22. This book's guiding metaphor, embodied in its title, follows a certain lineal tradition: The Babel story has long fascinated media and communications commentators. Consider, for example, Erik Barnouw's classic work of early modern media history, *A Tower in Babel: A History of Broadcasting in the United States to 1933, vol. 1*; or in a contemporary context, Jonathan Haidt's essay, "Why the Past Ten Years of American Life Have Been Uniquely Stupid," *Atlantic*, April 11, 2022, https://www.theatlantic .com/magazine/archive/2022/05/social-media-democracy-trust-babel/629369/.

23. "Most Popular Social Networks Worldwide as of October 2023, Ranked by Number of Monthly Active Users (in Millions)," chart, Statista, October 1, 2023, https://www .statista.com/statistics/272014/global-social-networks-ranked-by-number-of-users/.

24. MG Siegler, "Eric Schmidt: Every 2 Days We Create as Much Information as We Did up to 2003," *TechCrunch*, August 4, 2010, https://techcrunch.com/2010/08/04 /schmidt-data/.

25. For more on how this field has developed, see: Megan Knittel and Amanda Menking, "Bridging Theory and Practice: Examining the State of Scholarship Using the History of Trust and Safety Archive," *Journal of Online Trust and Safety* 2, no. 2 (2024), https://tsjournal.org/index.php/jots/article/view/173; Adelin Cai and Clara Tsao, "The Trust & Safety Professional Association: Advancing the Trust and Safety Profession through a Shared Community of Practice," *TechDirt*, August 28, 2020, https://www.techdirt.com/2020/08/28/trust-safety-professional-association-advanc ing-trust-safety-profession-through-shared-community-practice/.

26. Jonathan L. Zittrain, "Between Suffocation and Abdication: Three Eras of Governing Digital Platforms," first in Tanner Lectures on "Gaining Power, Losing Control," Berkman Klein Center for Internet & Society at Harvard College, 2020, YouTube Video, https://www.youtube.com/watch?v=xBfYsBbDve8; Zittrain, "Three Eras of Digital Governance" (September 2019), https://ssrn.com/abstract=3458435.

27. Bruna Martins dos Santos and David Morar, "The Push for Content Moderation Legislation Around the World," *Brookings*, March 9, 2022, https://www.brookings.edu /articles/the-push-for-content-moderation-legislation-around-the-world/; David Morar and Bruna Santos, "Is the DSA a New Dawn of Legislating Platform Governance

1

Globally?," *Lawfare*, November 30, 2022, https://www.lawfaremedia.org/article/dsa-new-dawn-legislating-platform-governance-globally.

28. Jack Goldsmith, "The Failure of Internet Freedom," in *The Perilous Public Square: Structural Threats to Free Expression Today*, ed. David E. Pozen (New York: Columbia University Press, 2020), 241–258.

29. Wheeler, *Techlash*, xxii.

30. Mary Anne Franks, "How the Internet Unmakes Law," *Ohio State Technology Law Journal* 16 (2020): 10.

31. Policy scholars' debate calls this "technological particularism," which is the way distinct waves of technology end up with their own, discrete sets of rules. See Napoli, *Social Media and the Public Interest*, 143.

32. *Moody v. NetChoice, LLC*, 603 U.S. ___ (2024), https://supreme.justia.com/cases/federal/us/603/22-277/; Zephyr Teachout, "The Roberts Supreme Court's Decision on *NetChoice* Was Righteous," *Nation*, July 2, 2024, https://www.thenation.com/article/society/supreme-court-netchoice-moody/.

33. Evelyn Douek and Genevieve Lakier, "First Amendment Politics Gets Weird: Public and Private Platform Reform and the Breakdown of the Laissez-Faire Free Speech Consensus," *University of Chicago Law Review Online* (2022): 1, https://lawreviewblog.uchicago.edu/2022/06/06/douek-lakier-first-amendment/.

34. Congresswoman Lori Trahan, "Fact Sheet: The Digital Services Oversight and Safety Act (DSOSA)," 2022, https://trahan.house.gov/uploadedfiles/dsosa_fact_sheet_final.pdf; John Perrino, "Platform Accountability and Transparency Act Reintroduced in Senate," *All Cyber News*, Stanford Cyber Policy Center, June 8, 2023, https://cyber.fsi.stanford.edu/news/platform-accountability-and-transparency-act-reintroduced-senate.

CHAPTER 1

1. John Milton, *Areopagitica: A Speech for the Liberty of Unlicensed Printing to the Parliament of England* (1644), accessed December 1, 2023, https://www.gutenberg.org/ebooks/608.

2. Friedrich A. Hayek, "The Use of Knowledge in Society," *American Economic Review* 35, no. 4 (September 1945): 519–530, https://home.uchicago.edu/~vlima/courses/econ200/spring01/hayek.pdf.

3. Section 230(c)(1) reads: "No provider or user of an interactive computer service shall be treated as the publisher or speaker of any information provided by another information content provider." See 47 U.S.C. § 230. For a comprehensive and penetrating account of the policy's history, see Jeff Kosseff, *The Twenty-Six Words That Created the Internet* (Ithaca, NY: Cornell University Press, 2019).

4. Lee C. Bollinger, "'The Free Speech Century': A Retrospective and a Guide," lecture, 2018 Clare Hall Tanner Lectures, Clare Hall, Cambridge, UK, November 5, 2018, video, https://sms.cam.ac.uk/media/2870813/.

5. For a sense of the traditional interpretation, see Michael O'Rielly, "FCC Regulatory Free Arena," Federal Communications Commission, June 1, 2018, https://www.fcc.gov/news-events/blog/2018/06/01/fcc-regulatory-free-arena. However, it is worth noting that President Trump's FCC Chair Brendan Carr has a different interpretation and believes that there may be authority for some regulation. See Kyle Paoletta, "Going Broad: Brendan Carr Wants to Test the Limits of the FCC's Authority," *Columbia Journalism Review*, December 16, 2024, https://www.cjr.org/analysis/brendan-carr-test-limits-fcc-authority.php.

6. Peter Noorlander, "International, Regional, and National Approaches to the Protection of Reputation and Freedom of Expression," in *Regardless of Frontiers: Global Freedom of Expression in a Troubled World*, ed. Lee C. Bollinger and Agnes Callamard (New York: Columbia University Press, 2021), 107–108.

7. "The Communications Act of 1934," *Justice Information Sharing*, U.S. Department of Justice, Bureau of Justice Assistance (n.d.), https://bja.ojp.gov/program/it/privacy-civil-liberties/authorities/statutes/1288.

8. Friendly, *The Good Guys, the Bad Guys and the First Amendment*.

9. Victor Pickard, *America's Battle for Media Democracy: The Triumph of Corporate Libertarianism and the Future of Media Reform* (Cambridge: Cambridge University Press, 2015), 68.

10. Pickard, *America's Battle for Media Democracy*, 95.

11. Pickard, 102–103.

12. Federal Communications Commission, *Editorializing by Broadcast Licenses* (Washington, DC: Federal Communications Commission, 1949), https://www.fcc.gov/document/editorializing-broadcast-licensees.

13. Federal Communications Commission, *Editorializing by Broadcast Licenses*.

14. Friendly, *The Good Guys, the Bad Guys and the First Amendment*, 24.

15. "Red Lion Broadcasting Co. v. FCC," Oyez, accessed December 18, 2023, https://www.oyez.org/cases/1968/2.

16. Thomas W. Hazlett and David W. Sosa, "Was the Fairness Doctrine A 'Chilling Effect'? Evidence from the Postderegulation Radio Market," *Journal of Legal Studies* 26, no. 1 (January 1997): 279–301, https://doi.org/10.1086/467996.

17. Bianca Cepollaro, Maxime Lepoutre, and Robert Mark Simpson, "Counterspeech," *Philosophy Compass* 18, no. 1 (November 30, 2022): 2, https://doi.org/10.1111/phc3.12890.

18. Cepollaro, Lepoutre, and Simpson, "Counterspeech," 2.

19. "Whitney v. California," Oyez, accessed December 18, 2023, https://www.oyez.org/cases/1900-1940/274us357.

20. "How Can We Help You Identify/Defeat/Prevent/Track Dangerous Speech Today?," Dangerous Speech Project homepage, accessed December 19, 2023, https://dangerousspeech.org/.

21. Alexandra A. Siegel, "Online Hate Speech," in *Social Media and Democracy: The State of the Field, Prospects for Reform*, ed. Nathaniel Persily and Joshua A. Tucker (Cambridge University Press, 2020), 56–88.

22. "What Is Dangerous Speech?," Dangerous Speech Project, accessed October 21, 2019, https://dangerousspeech.org/about-dangerous-speech/.

23. Catherine Buerger, "#iamhere: Collective Counterspeech and the Quest to Improve Online Discourse," *Social Media + Society* 7, no. 4 (December 2021), https://doi.org/10.1177/20563051211063843; Lucas Wright, Derek Ruths, Kelly P. Dillon, Haji Mohammad Saleem, and Susan Benesch, "Vectors for Counterspeech on Twitter," paper, *Proceedings of the First Workshop on Abusive Language Online*, Vancouver, Canada, July 30–August 4, 2017): 57–62, http://dx.doi.org/10.18653/v1/W17-3009.

24. Jerome A. Barron, "The Right of Reply to the Media in the United States—Resistance and Resurgence," *Hastings Communication & Entertainment Law Journal* 15, no. 1 (January 1, 1992): 20, https://repository.uchastings.edu/hastings_comm_ent_law_journal/vol15/iss1/1.

25. Kyu Ho Youm, "The Rights of Reply and Freedom of the Press: An International and Comparative Perspective," *George Washington Law Review* 76, no. 4 (June 2008): 1018.

26. "Miami Herald Publishing Company v. Tornillo," Oyez, accessed December 18, 2023, https://www.oyez.org/cases/1973/73-797; Youm, "The Rights of Reply and Freedom of the Press."

27. 47 U.S.C. § 230, https://uscode.house.gov/view.xhtml?req=(title:47%20section:230%20edition:prelim).

28. Youm, "The Rights of Reply and Freedom of the Press," 1017.

29. Youm, 1017.

30. Adam Serwer, "Why Conservatives Invented a 'Right to Post,'" *The Atlantic*, December 9, 2022, https://www.theatlantic.com/ideas/archive/2022/12/legal-right-to-post-free-speech-social-media/672406/.

31. *Moody v. NetChoice, LLC*.

32. *Moody v. NetChoice, LLC*, 603 U.S. ___ (2024), (Barrett, J. concurring), 2–3, https://www.supremecourt.gov/opinions/23pdf/22-277_d18f.pdf.

33. *Moody v. NetChoice, LLC* (Barrett, J. concurring), 3.

34. Scholars have developed many names for the fields and subfields that relate to the study of politics and technology with an emphasis on digital platforms. See John P. Wihbey, *Digital Democracy: Accelerating a New Field of Knowledge* (Miami: John S. and James L. Knight Foundation Report, 2021), 9, https://knightfoundation.org/wp-content/uploads/2021/01/Knight-Research-Network-Assessment-Report_01_14_21.pdf; John P. Wihbey, *A Growing Community of Scholarship and Practice* (Miami: John S. and James L. Knight Foundation Report, 2022), 12–15, https://knightfoundation.org/wp-content/uploads/2022/05/KRN-_Assessment_2022_final.pdf.

35. Cass R. Sunstein, *#Republic: Divided Democracy in the Age of Social Media* (Princeton, NJ: Princeton University Press, 2017).

36. Nicholas Lemann, *Transaction Man: The Rise of the Deal and the Decline of the American Dream* (New York: Farrar, Straus and Giroux, 2019).

37. Pickard, *America's Battle for Media Democracy*, 154.

38. John Stuart Mill, *On Liberty* (January 10, 2011 [EBook #34901], Project Gutenberg), 18.

39. Derek Robertson, "How an Obscure Conservative Theory Became the Trump Era's Go-to Nerd Phrase," *Politico Magazine*, February 25, 2018, https://www.politico.com/magazine/story/2018/02/25/overton-window-explained-definition-meaning-217010/.

40. The strained analogies between the sale of physical goods and the promotion of speech have long been debated. See R. H. Coase, "The Market for Goods and the Market for Ideas," *American Economic Review* 64, no. 2 (May 1974): 384–391, https://www.jstor.org/stable/1816070.

41. This section draws on material from: Garrett Morrow and John Wihbey, "Marketplace of Ideas 3.0? A Framework for the Era of Algorithms," *Richmond Journal of Law and Technology* 29, no. 2 (2023), https://jolt.richmond.edu/files/2023/03/Morrow-Final.pdf.

42. "Abrams v. United States," Oyez, accessed May 2, 2022, https://www.oyez.org/cases/1900-1940/250us616.

43. Richard Polenberg, *Fighting Faiths: The Abrams Case, The Supreme Court, and Free Speech* (Ithaca, NY: Cornell University Press, 1999).

44. "Abrams v. United States."

45. "Abrams v. United States."

46. "Abrams v. United States."

47. "Historical Background on Free Speech Clause," *Constitution Annotated*, accessed December 21, 2023, https://constitution.congress.gov/browse/essay/amdt1-7-1/ALDE_00013537/.

48. Bernard Bailyn, *The Ideological Origins of the American Revolution* (enlarged edition) (Cambridge, MA: Belknap Press, 1992).

49. Sam Lebovic, *Free Speech and Unfree News* (Cambridge, MA: Harvard University Press, 2016); Geoffrey R. Stone, "Reflections on the First Amendment: The Evolution of the American Jurisprudence of Free Expression," *Proceedings of the American Philosophical Society* 131, no. 3 (September 1987): 251–260, https://www.jstor.org/stable/987020.

50. Jeffery A. Smith, "Freedom of Expression and the Marketplace of Ideas Concept from Milton to Jefferson," *Journal of Communication Inquiry* 7, no. 1 (June 1981): 47–63, https://doi.org/10.1177/019685998100700104; Bailyn, *The Ideological Origins of the American Revolution*; John Trenchard and Thomas Gordon, *Cato's Letters* (1720–1723), in Letter No. 15 write: "Freedom of speech is ever the symptom, as well as the effect, of good government."

51. Milton in *Areopagitica* writes: "Truth and understanding are not such wares to be monopolized and traded in by tickets and statutes and standards. We must not think to make a staple commodity of all the knowledge in the land, to mark and licence it like our broadcloth and our woolpacks." And "more than if some enemy at sea should stop up all our havens and ports and creeks, it hinders and retards the importation of our richest merchandise, truth"; "Let her and falsehood grapple; who ever knew Truth put to the worse, in a free and open encounter?"

52. Smith, "Freedom of Expression"; John Durham Peters, "The 'Marketplace of Ideas': A History of the Concept," in *Toward a Political Economy of Culture: Capitalism and Communication in the Twenty-First Century*, ed. Andrew Calabrese and Colin Sparks (Lanham, MD: Rowman & Littlefield Publishers, 2004), 65–82; Lebovic, *Free Speech and Unfree News*.

53. See the *Federalist* No. 10 (1787) for Hamilton's views of factionalism, and George Washington's 1796 Farewell Address for the first president's views. George Washington, "Farewell Address," The Avalon Project, Lillian Goldman Law Library, Yale Law School, accessed November 1, 2024, https://avalon.law.yale.edu/18th_century/washing.asp.

54. Gregg Costa, "John Marshall, The Sedition Act, and Free Speech in the Early Republic," *Texas Law Review* 77, no. 4 (March 1999): 1011–1048.

55. Smith, "Freedom of Expression."

56. Derek E. Bambauer, "Shopping Badly: Cognitive Biases, Communications, and the Fallacy of the Marketplace of Ideas," *University of Colorado Law Review* 77, no. 3 (2006): 649–770.

57. Peters, "The 'Marketplace of Ideas.'"

58. John Stuart Mill, *A System of Logic: Ratiocinative and Inductive; Being a Connected View of the Principles of Evidence and the Methods of Scientific Investigation* (Honolulu, HI: University Press of the Pacific, 2002, reprint; 1843).

59. Stanley Ingber, "The Marketplace of Ideas: A Legitimizing Myth," *Duke Law Journal* 33, no. 1 (February 1984): 1–91, https://doi.org/10.2307/1372344.

60. Vincent Blasi, "Holmes and the Marketplace of Ideas," *Supreme Court Review* (2004): 1–46, https://doi.org/10.1086/scr.2004.3536967.

61. Trevor Timm, "It's Time to Stop Using the 'Fire in a Crowded Theater' Quote," *Atlantic*, November 2, 2012, https://www.theatlantic.com/national/archive/2012/11/its-time-to-stop-using-the-fire-in-a-crowded-theater-quote/264449/.

62. W. Wat Hopkins, "The Supreme Court Defines the Marketplace of Ideas," *Journalism & Mass Communication Quarterly* 73, no. 1 (March 1996): 40–52, https://doi.org/10.1177/107769909607300105.

63. Peters, "The 'Marketplace of Ideas.'"

64. "It is the purpose of the First Amendment to preserve an uninhibited marketplace of ideas in which truth will ultimately prevail, rather than to countenance monopolization of that market, whether it be by the government itself or a private licensee," 395 U.S. 367 1969, p. 390.

65. Philip M. Napoli, "The Marketplace of Ideas Metaphor in Communications Regulation," *Journal of Communication* 49, no. 4 (February 2006), 151–169, https://doi.org/10.1111/j.1460-2466.1999.tb02822.x; Peters, "The 'Marketplace of Ideas.'"

66. Greg Kaza, "Masters of the Universe: Hayek, Friedman, and the Birth of Neoliberal Politics," *Quarterly Journal of Austrian Economics* 17, no. 4 (2014): 543–550.

67. Kate Klonick, "The New Governors: The People, Rules, and Processes Governing Online Speech," *Harvard Law Review* 131, no. 6 (April 2018): 1598–1670, https://harvardlawreview.org/print/vol-131/the-new-governors-the-people-rules-and-processes-governing-online-speech/.

68. *Packingham v. North Carolina*, 137 S. Ct. 1730, 1735, 1737 (2017).

69. For example, see Paul H. Brietzke, "How and Why the Marketplace of Ideas Fails," *Valparaiso University Law Review* 31, no. 3 (1997): 21, https://scholar.valpo.edu/vulr/vol31/iss3/4; Alvin I. Goldman, "Speech Regulation and the Marketplace of Ideas," in *Knowledge in a Social World* (Oxford: Oxford University Press, 1999); Alvin I. Goldman and James C. Cox, "Speech, Truth, and the Free Market for Ideas," *Legal Theory* 2, no. 1 (March 1996): 1–32, https://doi.org/10.1017/S1352325200000343.

70. Whitney Phillips and Ryan Milner, *You Are Here: A Field Guide for Navigating Polarized Speech, Conspiracy Theories, and Our Polluted Media Landscape* (Cambridge, MA: MIT Press, 2020).

71. The scholarship on algorithmic curation and its effects on speech, in terms of both rights and quality, is growing. For example, see Balkin, "Free Speech in the Algorithmic Society: Big Data, Private Governance, and New School Speech Regulation"; Jared Schroeder, "Toward a Discursive Marketplace of Ideas: Reimaging the Marketplace Metaphor in the Era of Social Media, Fake News, and Artificial Intelligence," *First Amendment Studies* 52, vol. 1–2 (May 2018): 38–60, https://doi.org/10.1080/21689725.2018.1460215; Soroush Vosoughi, Deb Roy, and Sinan Aral, "The Spread of True and False News Online," *Science* 359, no. 6380 (March 2018): 1146–1151, https://doi.org/10.1126/science.aap9559.

CHAPTER 2

1. Harold D. Lasswell, *Propaganda Technique in the World War* (New York: Peter Smith, 1927/1938), 222.

2. This formulation takes inspiration from Robert N. Spicer, "Lies, Damn Lies, Alternative Facts, Fake News, Propaganda, Pinocchios, Pants on Fire, Disinformation, Misinformation, Post-Truth, Data, and Statistics," in *Free Speech and False Speech* (Palgrave Macmillan: 2018), 1–31, https://doi.org/10.1007/978-3-319-69820-5_1.

3. *Oxford English Dictionary*, s.v. "disinformation (n.)," accessed September 2023, https://doi.org/10.1093/OED/7455799853.

4. John P. Wihbey, *The Social Fact: News and Knowledge in a Networked World* (Cambridge, MA: MIT Press, 2019), 179–194.

5. Dannagal Goldthwaite Young, *Wrong: How Media, Politics, and Identity Drive Our Appetite for Misinformation* (Baltimore, MD: Johns Hopkins University Press, 2023).

6. Ceren Budak, Brendan Nyhan, David M. Rothschild, Emily Thorson, and Duncan J. Watts, "Misunderstanding the Harms of Online Misinformation," *Nature* 630, no. 8015 (2024): 45–53, https://www.nature.com/articles/s41586-024-07417-w; Gregory Eady, Tom Paskhalis, Jan Zilinsky, Richard Bonneau, Jonathan Nagler, and Joshua A. Tucker, "Exposure to the Russian Internet Research Agency Foreign Influence Campaign on Twitter in the 2016 US Election and Its Relationship to Attitudes and Voting Behavior," *Nature Communications* 14, no. 1 (2023): 62, https://www.nature .com/articles/s41467-022-35576-9.

7. Marta Pérez-Escolar, Darren Lilleker, and Alejandro Tapia-Frade, "A Systematic Literature Review of the Phenomenon of Disinformation and Misinformation," *Media and Communication* 11, no. 2 (April 2023): 76–87.

8. Reed Berkowitz, "QAnon Resembles the Games I Design. But for Believers, There Is No Winning," *Washington Post*, May 11, 2021, https://www.washingtonpost.com /outlook/qanon-game-plays-believers/2021/05/10/31d8ea46-928b-11eb-a74e-1f4cf 89fd948_story.html.

9. Claire Wardle and Hossein Derakhshan, *INFORMATION DISORDER: Toward an Interdisciplinary Framework for Research and Policy Making* (London: Council of Europe, 2017), https://rm.coe.int/information-disorder-toward-an-interdisciplinary -framework-for-researc/168076277c. See also Sacha Altay, Manon Berriche, Hendrik Heuer, Johan Farkas, and Steven Rathje, "A Survey of Expert Views on Misinforma-tion: Definitions, Determinants, Solutions, and Future of the Field," *Harvard Ken-nedy School Misinformation Review* 4, no. 4 (July 27, 2023), https://doi.org/10.37016 /mr-2020-119.

10. For a comprehensive overview, see Lee McIntyre, *On Disinformation: How to Fight for Truth and Protect Democracy* (Cambridge, MA: MIT Press, 2023).

11. *Oxford English Dictionary*, s.v. "propaganda (n.)," accessed September 2023, https://doi.org/10.1093/OED/1010698303.

12. Yochai Benkler, Robert Faris, and Hal Roberts, *Network Propaganda: Manipulation, Disinformation, and Radicalization in American Politics* (Oxford: Oxford University Press, 2018), 23–38.

13. Benkler, Faris, and Roberts, *Network Propaganda*, 29.

14. Benkler, Faris, and Roberts, 32.

15. Alicia Wanless, "There Is No Getting Ahead of Disinformation Without Moving Past It," *Lawfare*, May 8, 2023, https://www.lawfaremedia.org/article/there-is-no -getting-ahead-of-disinformation-without-moving-past-it.

16. Samuel C. Woolley and Philip N. Howard, eds., *Computational Propaganda: Political Parties, Politicians, and Political Manipulation on Social Media* (Oxford: Oxford University Press, 2018), 37.

17. Thomas Rid, *Active Measures: The Secret History of Disinformation and Political Warfare* (New York: Farrar, Straus and Giroux, 2020), 10.

18. "Tactics of Disinformation: CISA," Cybersecurity & Infrastructure Security Agency, last accessed September 1, 2023, https://www.cisa.gov/resources-tools

/resources/tactics-disinformation. For academic perspectives on the varieties of disinformation, see Eleni Kapantai, Androniki Christopoulou, Christos Berberidis, and Vassilios Peristeras, "A Systematic Literature Review on Disinformation: Toward a Unified Taxonomical Framework," *New Media & Society* 23, no. 5 (September 20, 2020): 1301–1326, https://doi.org/10.1177/1461444820959296.

19. Kate Starbird, Renée DiResta, and Matt DeButts, "Influence and Improvisation: Participatory Disinformation during the 2020 US Election," *Social Media + Society* 9, no. 2 (2023), https://doi.org/10.1177/20563051231177943.

20. Some material in this chapter is also based on a forthcoming article: Daniel Kreiss, Lorcan Neill, and John P. Wihbey (in press, 2025). "Disinformation in the US: Overview and Responses," in *Disinformation: A Multidisciplinary Analysis* (Springer Nature).

21. This account comes from Creel and the primary documents he produces in his narrative: George Creel, *How We Advertised America: The First Telling of the Amazing Story of the Committee on Public Information That Carried the Gospel of Americanism to Every Corner of the Globe* (New York: Harper and Brothers, 1920), 32. For context, I also draw on: Lasswell, *Propaganda Technique in the World War*, 39; Nick Fischer, "The Committee on Public Information and the Birth of US State Propaganda," *Australasian Journal of American Studies* (2016): 51–78; Marouf A. Hasian Jr, "Freedom of Expression and Propaganda during World War I: Understanding George Creel and America's Committee on Public Information," *Free Speech YB* 36 (1998): 48.

22. Creel, *How We Advertised America*, 37. Creel's manuscript reprints in full the after-action report from Admiral Albert Gleaves, who oversaw the ships carrying the sailors.

23. Creel, 29.

24. Creel, 32.

25. "Now the Accounts Differ: Variations Between Creel's and Eyewitnesses' Stories of Sea Fight," *New York Times*, July 7, 1917.

26. "Creel as a Recurrent Storm Centre: How Government's Publicity Man Has Shown Himself an Adept at Getting into Hot Water with Congress and the Public," *New York Times*, May 19, 1918.

27. Fischer, "The Committee on Public Information and the Birth of US State Propaganda."

28. Fischer, 58.

29. Creel, *How We Advertised America*, 5.

30. "Censorship Blundering: Comment on the System Which Gives Germany News Barred Here. Sanity of American Press. Our Disorganized Censorship," *New York Times*, July 4, 1917.

31. "Censorship Blundering," *New York Times*.

32. "Creel Denies Trying to Shape Editorials: Merely Telephoned Earle Would Talk on Defective Shells; Washington Herald's Reply. Mr. Creel's Statement. The Herald's Rejoinder," *New York Times*, May 25, 1917.

33. "Press Comment on the Censorship Plan," *New York Times*, May 24, 1917.

34. Harold D. Lasswell, *Democracy Through Public Opinion* (Wisconsin: George Banta Publishing Company, 1941), 105.

35. Ronald Steel, *Walter Lippmann and the American Century* (Boston: Little, Brown, 1980), 125–126.

36. Walter Lippmann, *Liberty and the News* (New York: Harcourt, Brace and Howe, 1920), 4.

37. Walter Lippmann, *Public Opinion* (New York: Free Press Paperbacks, 1997).

38. Sue Curry Jansen, "Semantic Tyranny: How Edward L. Bernays Stole Walter Lippmann's Mojo and Got Away With It and Why It Still Matters," *International Journal of Communication* 7 (2013): 1094–1111.

39. Lippmann, *Public Opinion*, 3, 85.

40. Lippmann, 10.

41. Walter Lippmann, *The Phantom Public* (New York: Routledge), 4.

42. Lippmann, *The Phantom Public*, 122.

43. Lippmann, 125–132.

44. Dominique Trudel, "Revisiting the Origins of Communication Research: Walter Lippmann's WWII Adventure in Propaganda and Psychological Warfare," *International Journal of Communication* 11 (2017): 3721–3739.

45. Gabriel Almond, *Harold Dwight Lasswell: Biographical Memoirs* (Washington, DC: National Academies Press, 1987), 57.

46. Lasswell, *Propaganda Technique in the World War*, 24.

47. Lasswell, 181.

48. Lasswell, 184.

49. Harold D. Lasswell, "The Theory of Political Propaganda" *American Political Science Review* 21, no. 3 (August 1927): 627–631, 629, https://doi.org/10.2307/1945515.

50. Lasswell, *Democracy Through Public Opinion*, 108.

51. Lasswell, 107.

52. Lasswell, 110.

53. See Garrett Morrow, Briony Swire-Thompson, Jessica Montgomery Polny, Matthew Kopec, and John P. Wihbey, "The Emerging Science of Content Labeling: Contextualizing Social Media Content Moderation," *Journal of the Association for Information Science and Technology* 73, no. 10 (2022): 1365–1386.

54. R. C. Donnelly "The Right of Reply: An Alternative to an Action for Libel," *Virginia Law Review* 34, no. 8 (November 1948): 867–900.

55. See Richard M. Merelman, "Harold D. Lasswell's Political World: Weak Tea for Hard Times," *British Journal of Political Science* 11, no. 4: 471–497.

56. Harold D. Lasswell, "The Structure and Function of Communication in Society," in *The Communication of Ideas*, ed. Lyman Bryson (New York: Harper and Row, 1948), 37–51.

57. Lasswell, *Democracy Through Public Opinion*, 114.

58. Timothy Glander. *Origins of Mass Communications Research during the American Cold War: Educational Effects and Contemporary Implications* (Mahwah, N.J.: Lawrence Erlbaum Associates, 2000), 25–31; Frederick Elmore Lumley. *The Propaganda Menace* (London: Century/Random House UK, 1933), 25–28; Michael J. Sproule, *Propaganda and Democracy: The American Experience of Media and Mass Persuasion* (New York: Cambridge University Press, 1997), 47–52.

59. Glander, *Origins of Mass Communications Research*, 25–31; Sproule, *Propaganda and Democracy*, 47–52.

60. Daniel Kahneman, *Thinking, Fast and Slow* (New York: Macmillan, 2011).

61. Gordon Pennycook, Ziv Epstein, Mohsen Mosleh, Antonio A. Arechar, Dean Eckles and David G. Rand, "Shifting Attention to Accuracy Can Reduce Misinformation Online," *Nature* 592, no. 7855 (March 2021): 590–595, https://doi.org/10.1038/s41586-021-03344-2. Also see Gordon Pennycook and David G. Rand, "Lazy, Not Biased: Susceptibility to Partisan Fake News Is Better Explained by Lack of Reasoning than by Motivated Reasoning," *Cognition* 188 (June 2018): 39–50, https://doi.org/10.1016/j.cognition.2018.06.011; Gordon Pennycook and David G. Rand, "Accuracy Prompts Are a Replicable and Generalizable Approach for Reducing the Spread of Misinformation," *Nature Communications* 13, no. 1 (April 2022), https://doi.org/10.1038/s41467-022-30073-5.

62. Jon Roozenbeek, Rakoen Maertens, Stefan M. Herzog, Michael Geers, Ralf Kuvers, Mubashir Sultan, et al., "Susceptibility to Misinformation Is Consistent Across Question Framings and Response Modes and Better Explained by Myside Bias and Partisanship than Analytical Thinking," *Judgment and Decision Making* 17, no. 3 (May 2022): 547–573, https://doi.org/10.1017/S1930297500003570.

63. Many researchers have come to this conclusion using diverse methods. See, for example: Dimitar Nikolov, Alessandro Flammini, and Filippo Menczer, "Right and Left, Partisanship Predicts (Asymmetric) Vulnerability to Misinformation," *arXiv preprint arXiv:2010.01462* (2020); Matthew R. DeVerna, Andrew M. Guess, Adam J. Berinsky, Joshua A. Tucker, and John T. Jost, "Rumors in Retweet: Ideological Asymmetry in the Failure to Correct Misinformation," *Personality and Social Psychology Bulletin* 50, no. 1 (2024): 3–17; Ashwin Rao, Fred Morstatter, and Kristina Lerman, "Partisan Asymmetries in Exposure to Misinformation," *Scientific Reports* 12, no. 1 (2022): 15671.

64. Stephan Lewandowsky and Sander van der Linden, "Countering Misinformation and Fake News Through Inoculation and Prebunking," *European Review of Social Psychology* 32, no. 2 (2021): 348–384, https://doi.org/10.1080/10463283.2021.1876983.

65. David Ingram, "Twitter Launches 'Pre-bunks' to Get Ahead of Voting Misinformation," *NBC News*, October 26, 2020, https://www.nbcnews.com/tech/tech-news/twitter-launches-pre-bunks-get-ahead-voting-misinformation-n1244777.

66. Lewandowsky and van der Linden, "Countering Misinformation and Fake News."

67. See Anastasia Kozyreva, Philipp Lorenz-Spreen, Stefan Herzog, Ullrich Ecker, Stephan Lewandowsky, Ralph Hertwig, et al., "Toolbox of Interventions Against Online Misinformation," preprint, published December 2022, https://doi.org/10 .31234/osf.io/x8ejt; the International Panel on the Information Environment (IPIE), https://www.ipie.info/reports-and-publications, was constituted in 2023 to produce this type of synthesis work.

68. Briony Swire-Thompson, Kristen Kilgallen, Mitch Dobbs, Jacob Bodenger, John Wihbey, and Skyler Johnson, "Discrediting Health Disinformation Sources: Advantages of Highlighting Low Expertise," *Journal of Experimental Psychology: General* 153, no. 9 (2024): 2299.

69. Cameron Martel and David G. Rand, "Fact-Checker Warning Labels Are Effective Even for Those Who Distrust Fact-Checkers," *Nature Human Behaviour* (2024): 1–11.

70. John M. Carey, Elizabeth Chun, Alice Cook, Brian J. Fogarty, Leyla Jacoby, Brendan Nyhan, et al., "The Narrow Reach of Targeted Corrections: No Impact on Broader Beliefs About Election Integrity," *Political Behavior* (2024): 1–14.

71. Laura Courchesne, Julia Ilhardt, and Jacob N. Shapiro, "Review of Social Science Research on the Impact of Countermeasures Against Influence Operations," *Harvard Kennedy School Misinformation Review* (September 2021), https://doi.org/10.37016 /mr-2020-79.

72. Dancan Bwire, "Kenya President William Ruto Misses Mark in Claiming Country's Annual Food Import Bill Is Ksh500 Billion," Africa Check, October 20, 2023, https://africacheck.org/fact-checks/reports/kenya-president-william-ruto-misses -mark-claiming-countrys-annual-food-import; Africa Check, "#2019ANCManifes- toReview: Fact-Checking the Ruling Party's Claims About Progress in South Africa," September 13, 2023, https://africacheck.org/fact-checks/reports/2019ancmanifesto review-fact-checking-ruling-partys-claims-about-progress-south.

73. Laura Oliver, "The Fight for Facts in the Global South: How Four Projects Are Building a New Model," *Reuters Institute*, September 30, 2021, https://reutersinstitute .politics.ox.ac.uk/news/fight-facts-global-south-how-four-projects-are-building-new -model; Africa Check, "#2019ANCManifestoReview."

74. Author interview with Noko Makgato, December 5, 2023.

75. Daniel Funke, "Africa Check Has a New Director. Here's His Vision for Fact- Checking on the Continent," *Poynter*, March 15, 2019, https://www.poynter.org/fact -checking/2019/africa-check-has-a-new-director-heres-his-vision-for-fact-checking -on-the-continent/.

76. Meta, "Where We Have Fact-Checking: A Map of Meta's Global Third-Party Fact-Checking Partners," accessed December 18, 2023, https://www.facebook.com /formedia/mjp/programs/third-party-fact-checking/partner-map.

77. Mark Stencel, "Number of Fact-checking Outlets Surges to 188 in More than 60 countries," *Duke Reporters' Lab*, June 11, 2019, https://reporterslab.org/number-of -fact-checking-outlets-surges-to-188-in-more-than-60-countries.

78. Author interview with Noko Makgato, December 5, 2023.

79. Briony Swire-Thompson, Nicholas Miklaucic, John P. Wihbey, David Lazer, and Joseph DeGutis, "The Backfire Effect after Correcting Misinformation Is Strongly Associated with Reliability," *Journal of Experimental Psychology: General* 151, no. 7 (2022): 1655, https://doi.org/10.1037/xge0001131; Thomas Wood and Ethan Porter, "The Elusive Backfire Effect: Mass Attitudes' Steadfast Factual Adherence," *Political Behavior* 41 (2019): 135–163, https://psycnet.apa.org/doi/10.1007/s11109-018-9443-y.

80. Oliver, "The Fight for Facts in the Global South"; Africa Check, "#2019ANC ManifestoReview."

81. Author interview with Noko Makgato, December 5, 2023.

82. Funke, "Africa Check has a New Director."

83. Samitra Badrinathan and Simon Chauchard, "Researching and Countering Misinformation in the Global South," *Current Opinion in Psychology* 55 (February 2024), https://doi.org/10.1016/j.copsyc.2023.101733. For more on differences between the Global North and South, see Robert A. Blair, Jessica Gottlieb, Brendan Nyhan, Laura Paler, Pablo Argote, and Charlene J. Stainfield, "Interventions to Counter Misinformation: Lessons from the Global North and Applications to the Global South," *Current Opinion in Psychology* (2023): 101732.

84. Jason Ross Arnold, Alexandra Reckendorf, and Amanda L. Wintersieck, "Source Alerts Can Reduce the Harms of Foreign Disinformation," *Harvard Kennedy School Misinformation Review* 1 (May 2021), https://doi.org/10.37016/mr-2020-68.

85. Kenny Peng and James Grimmelmann, "Rescuing Counterspeech: A Bridging-Based Approach to Combating Misinformation," *arXiv preprint arXiv:2410.12699* (2024).

86. Philip M. Napoli, "Back from the Dead (Again): The Specter of the Fairness Doctrine and Its Lesson for Social Media Regulation," *Policy & Internet* 13, no. 2 (2021): 300–314.

87. Madison Czopek, "Why Twitter's Community Notes Feature Mostly Fails to Combat Misinformation," Poynter, June 30, 2023, https://www.poynter.org/fact-checking/2023/why-twitters-community-notes-feature-mostly-fails-to-combat-misinformation/.

88. Peng and Grimmelmann, "Rescuing Counterspeech."

CHAPTER 3

1. Maria Ressa, "Nobel Lecture," December 10, 2021, Nobel Peace Prize 2021, https://www.nobelprize.org/prizes/peace/2021/ressa/lecture/.

2. Meta, "Hate Speech," policy details, accessed January 8, 2024, https://transparency.fb.com/policies/community-standards/hate-speech/#data.

3. YouTube, "YouTube Community Guidelines Enforcement," *Google Transparency Report*, accessed January 8, 2024, https://transparencyreport.google.com/youtube-policy/removals?hl=en.

4. TikTok, *Community Guidelines Enforcement Report,* accessed January 8, 2024, https://www.tiktok.com/transparency/en/community-guidelines-enforcement-2023-3/.

5. Meta, "Hate Speech."

6. TikTok, "Safety and Civility," *Community Guidelines,* accessed January 8, 2024, https://www.tiktok.com/community-guidelines/en/safety-civility/.

7. YouTube, "Hate Speech Policy," YouTube Help, accessed January 8, 2024, https://support.google.com/youtube/answer/2801939?hl=en.

8. TikTok, *Community Guidelines Enforcement Report*; Meta, "Detecting Violations," accessed January 8, 2024, https://transparency.fb.com/enforcement/detecting-violations/; *Social Media & the January 6th Attack on the U.S. Capitol: Summary of Investigative Findings* (Washington, DC: House Select Committee to Investigate the January 6th Attack on the United States Capitol, n.d), 70.

9. Kari Paul, "Reversal of Content Policies at Alphabet, Meta and X Threaten Democracy, Warn Experts," *Guardian,* December 7, 2023, https://www.theguardian.com/media/2023/dec/07/2024-elections-social-media-content-safety-policies-moderation.

10. Nobel Prize Organisation, "2021 Nobel Peace Prize Announcement," press release, October 8, 2021, https://www.nobelprize.org/prizes/peace/2021/press-release/.

11. Julie Posetti, Diana Maynard, and Kalina Bontcheva, *Maria Ressa: Fighting an Onslaught of Online Violence* (Washington, DC: International Center for Journalists, 2021), https://www.icfj.org/our-work/maria-ressa-big-data-analysis; Julie Posetti, "Fighting Back Against Prolific Online Harassment: Maria Ressa," in *An Attack on One Is an Attack on All: Successful Initiatives to Protect Journalists and Combat Impunity* (Paris: United Nations Educational, Scientific and Cultural Organization, 2017), https://unesdoc.unesco.org/ark:/48223/pf0000259399.

12. Elahe Izadi, "The New President of the Philippines Says Many Slain Journalists Deserved It," *Washington Post,* May 31, 2016, https://www.washingtonpost.com/news/worldviews/wp/2016/05/31/the-new-president-of-the-philippines-says-many-slain-journalists-deserved-it/.

13. Human Rights Watch, "Philippines: Events of 2021," *World Report 2022,* https://www.hrw.org/world-report/2022/country-chapters/philippines.

14. Posetti, Maynard, and Bontcheva, *Maria Ressa,* 11.

15. Posetti, Maynard, and Bontcheva, 3.

16. Frederick Schauer, "The Exceptional First Amendment," in *American Exceptionalism and Human Rights,* ed. Michael Ignatieff (Princeton, NJ: Princeton University Press, 2005), 29–56.

17. David Kaye, "The Limits of Supply-Side Internet Freedom," in *The Perilous Public Square: Structural Threats to Free Expression Today,* ed. David E. Pozen (New York: Columbia University Press, 2020), 259–262; Nani Jansen Reventlow and Jonathan McCully, "Internet Freedom Without Imperialism," in *The Perilous Public Square: Structural Threats to Free Expression Today,* ed. David E. Pozen (New York: Columbia University Press, 2020), 263–267.

18. David Kaye, "David Kaye on Free Speech during a Pandemic," interview by Jack Goldsmith, *The Lawfare Podcast*, podcast audio, May 15, 2020, https://www.lawfare media.org/article/lawfare-podcast-david-kaye-free-speech-during-pandemic.

19. Jessica Maddox and Jennifer Malson, "Guidelines Without Lines, Communities Without Borders: The Marketplace of Ideas and Digital Manifest Destiny in Social Media Platform Policies," *Social Media + Society* 6, no. 2 (June 19, 2020): 1–10, https://doi.org/10.1177/2056305120926622.

20. Evelyn Douek, "New U.N. Report on Online Hate Speech," *Lawfare* (blog), October 25, 2019, https://www.lawfareblog.com/new-un-report-online-hate-speech.

21. "Brandenburg v. Ohio," 395 U.S. 444 (1969), https://www.oyez.org/cases/1968/492.

22. *State of Connecticut v. Liebenguth*, 336 Conn. 685 (Conn. 2020), https://law.justia.com/cases/connecticut/supreme-court/2021/sc20145.html#; Robert Marchant, "High Court Upholds Criminal Conviction of Greenwich Man Who Uttered Racial Slur," *Greenwich Time*, September 1, 2020, https://www.greenwichtime.com/local/article/High-court-upholds-criminal-conviction-of-15532811.php.

23. *Gersh v. Anglin*, 353 F. Supp. 3d 958 (D. Mont. 2018), https://law.justia.com/cases/federal/district-courts/montana/mtdce/9:2017cv00050/54518/259/.

24. Clay Calvert, "Troll Storms and Tort Liability for Speech Urging Action by Others: A First Amendment Analysis and an Initial Step Toward a Federal Rule," *Washington University Law Review* 97 (June 2020): 1303, 1305–1306, http://dx.doi.org/10.2139/ssrn.3625719.

25. Calvert, "Troll Storms and Tort Liability," 1306.

26. "Judge in Montana Orders Arrest of Neo-Nazi Website Founder," *Associated Press*, November 9, 2022, https://apnews.com/article/technology-religion-arrests-race-and-ethnicity-racial-injustice-712adca6c327a2ceb2a21507e1f4697f.

27. Human Rights Council, *Annual Report of the United Nations High Commissioner for Human Rights* (New York: United Nations General Assembly, 2013), https://www.ohchr.org/sites/default/files/Documents/Issues/Opinion/SeminarRabat/Rabat_draft_outcome.pdf.

28. Nadine Strossen, *Hate: Why We Should Resist It with Free Speech, Not Censorship* (Oxford: Oxford University Press, 2018), 119.

29. Strossen, *Hate*, 53.

30. David Kaye, *Report of the Special Rapporteur on the Promotion and Protection of the Right to Freedom of Opinion and Expression* (New York: United Nations General Assembly, 2019), 4, https://www.ohchr.org/sites/default/files/Documents/Issues/Opinion/A_74_486.pdf.

31. Danielle Keats Citron, *Hate Crimes in Cyberspace* (Cambridge, MA: Harvard University Press, 2014).

32. Mary Anne Franks, "Beyond the Public Square: Imagining Digital Democracy," *Yale Law Journal Forum* 131 (2021): 427.

33. Gelo Gonzales, "'Online Violence Is Real-World Violence'—Maria Ressa," Rappler, March 30, 2022, https://www.rappler.com/technology/features/woodrow-wilson -award-speech-maria-ressa-online-real-world-violence-disinformation/.

34. Anu Bradford, "The Brussels Effect," *Northwestern University School Law Review* 107, no. 1 (December 1, 2012): 25–66, https://doi.org/10.1093/oso/9780190088583 .003.0003; Anu Bradford, *The Brussels Effect: How the European Union Rules the World* (Oxford: Oxford University Press, 2020).

35. Zachary Laub, "Hate Speech on Social Media: Global Comparisons," Council on Foreign Relations, June 7, 2019, https://www.cfr.org/backgrounder/hate-speech -social-media-global-comparisons.

36. Maria Ressa, "Nobel Lecture," The Nobel Prize, December 10, 2021, https:// www.nobelprize.org/prizes/peace/2021/ressa/lecture/.

37. Ruggie, "The Social Construction of the U.N. Guiding Principles on Business and Human Rights."

38. Evelyn Aswad, "To Protect Freedom of Expression, Why Not Steal Victory from the Jaws of Defeat?," *Washington & Lee Law Review* 77, no. 2 (2020): 609, http://dx .doi.org/10.2139/ssrn.3478888.

39. Eleanor Roosevelt, *Eleanor and Harry: The Correspondence of Eleanor Roosevelt and Harry S. Truman*, ed. Steve Neal (New York: Citadel Press, 2004), 22.

40. Allida M. Black, *Casting Her Own Shadow: Eleanor Roosevelt and the Shaping of Postwar Liberalism* (New York: Columbia University Press, 1996).

41. Louis Henkin, "The Universal Declaration and the U.S. Constitution," *PS: Political Science & Politics* 31, no. 3 (September 1998): 512–516, https://doi.org/10.2307 /420609; Mary Ann Glendon, *A World Made New: Eleanor Roosevelt and the Universal Declaration of Human Rights* (New York: Random House, 2001).

42. Hans Ingvar Roth, *P. C. Chang and the Universal Declaration of Human Rights* (Philadelphia: University of Pennsylvania Press, 2016); Glenn Mitoma, "Charles H. Malik and Human Rights: Notes on a Biography," *Biography, 33,* no. 1 (2010): 222–241.

43. António Guterres, "Global Trends: Forced Displacement in 2015" (Geneva: United Nations High Commissioner of Refugees, 2015), https://www.unhcr.org/576408cd7.

44. Eleanor Roosevelt, "The Struggle for Human Rights," September 28, 1948, Eleanor Roosevelt Papers Project, George Washington University, https://erpapers .columbian.gwu.edu/struggle-human-rights-1948.

45. International Covenant on Civil and Political Rights, "U.S. Reservations, Declarations, and Understandings," 138 Cong. Rec. S4781–01 (daily ed., April 2, 1992), http://hrlibrary.umn.edu/usdocs/civilres.html.

46. "Commission on Human Rights, Sixth Session," United Nations and Economic Social Council, 174th Meeting, May 6, 1950, https://uvallsc.s3.amazonaws.com /travaux/s3fs-public/E-CN_4-SR_174.pdf (accessed November 15, 2024).

47. Susan Benesch, "But Facebook's Not a Country: How to Interpret Human Rights Law for Social Media Companies," *Yale Journal on Regulation* (2020), https://www

.yalejreg.com/bulletin/but-facebooks-not-a-country-how-to-interpret-human-rights-law-for-social-media-companies/; David Kaye, "Human Rights Standards Should Guide Company Decisions," UC Irvine School of Law Research Paper 2022-36 (2022), https://ssrn.com/abstract=4246044.

48. UN Office on Genocide Prevention in collaboration with the ESRC Human Rights, Big Data and Technology Project, University of Essex, *Countering and Addressing Online Hate Speech: A Guide for Policy Makers and Practitioners* (United Nations, July 2023), https://www.un.org/en/genocideprevention/documents/publications-and-resources/Countering_Online_Hate_Speech_Guide_policy_makers_practitioners_July_2023.pdf, 7.

49. UN Office on Genocide Prevention, *Countering and Addressing Online Hate Speech*, 11.

50. Lee C. Bollinger, "Preface: The Idea of Global Norms of Freedom of Speech and Press," in Bollinger and Callamard, *Regardless of Frontiers*, xvi.

51. Ein Prozent v. Facebook Ireland Ltd., *Global Freedom of Expression*, Columbia University, accessed January 4, 2024, https://globalfreedomofexpression.columbia.edu/cases/ein-prozent-v-facebook-ireland-ltd/.

52. For more on the complex dynamics of NetzDG, see Robert Gorwa, "Elections, Institutions, and the Regulatory Politics of Platform Governance: The Case of the German NetzDG," *Telecommunications Policy* 45, no. 6 (July 2021), https://doi.org/10.1016/j.telpol.2021.102145.

53. Ein Prozent v. Facebook Ireland Ltd., *Global Freedom of Expression*.

54. Oversight Board, "Case Decision 2020-002-FB-UA," Oversight Board, 2020, https://oversightboard.com/decision/FB-I2T6526K/.

55. Kate Klonick, "Inside the Making of Facebook's Supreme Court," *New Yorker*, February 12, 2021, https://www.newyorker.com/tech/annals-of-technology/inside-the-making-of-facebooks-supreme-court.

56. Oversight Board, "Case Decision 2020-002-FB-UA."

57. Facebook, "Community Standards," Transparency Center, accessed April 1, 2022, https://transparency.fb.com/policies/community-standards/.

58. Oversight Board, "Case Decision 2020-002-FB-UA."

59. Dunstan Allison-Hope, "Our Human Rights Impact Assessment of Facebook in Myanmar," *BSR Blog* (blog), November 5, 2018, https://www.bsr.org/en/our-insights/blog-view/facebook-in-myanmar-human-rights-impact-assessment; Human Rights Council, *Report of the Detailed Findings of the Independent International Fact-Finding, Mission on Myanmar* (New York: United Nations General Assembly, 2018), https://www.ohchr.org/sites/default/files/Documents/HRBodies/HRCouncil/FFM-Myanmar/A_HRC_39_CRP.2.pdf.

60. Victoria Milko and Barbara Ortutay, "'Kill More': Facebook Fails to Detect Hate against Rohingya," *Associated Press*, March 21, 2021, https://apnews.com/article/technology-business-bangladesh-myanmar-united-nations-f7d89e38c54f7bae464762fa23bd96b2.

61. *Social Media & the January 6th Attack on the U.S. Capitol*, 53.

62. *Social Media & the January 6th Attack on the U.S. Capitol*, 55.

63. Laura Savolainen, "The Shadow Banning Controversy: Perceived Governance and Algorithmic Folklore," *Media, Culture & Society* 44, no. 6 (2022): 1091–1109; Sarah Myers West, "Censored, Suspended, Shadowbanned: User Interpretations of Content Moderation on Social Media Platforms," *New Media & Society* 20, no. 11 (2018): 4366–4383.

64. For a range of the work being done in this field, see Stephanie Ullmann, "Workshop Report for 'Understanding and Automating Counterspeech,'" *Center for Research in the Arts, Science and Humanities* (blog), July 27, 2022, https://www.crassh.cam.ac .uk/blog/workshop-report-for-understanding-and-automating-counterspeech/.

65. Ronald E. Robertson, "Uncommon Yet Consequential Online Harms," *Journal of Online Trust and Safety* 1, no. 3 (2022), https://doi.org/10.54501/jots.v1i3.87.

66. Bertie Vidgen, Helen Margetts, and Alex Harris, *How Much Online Abuse Is There? A Systematic Review of Evidence for the UK* (London: Alan Turing Institute, 2019), https://www.turing.ac.uk/sites/default/files/2019-11/online_abuse_prevalence_full _24.11.2019_-_formatted_0.pdf.

67. Dominik Hangartner, Gloria Gennaro, Sary Alasiri and Karsten Donnay, "Empathy-Based Counterspeech Can Reduce Racist Hate Speech in a Social Media Field Experiment," *Proceedings of the National Academy of Sciences* 118, no. 50 (2021), https://doi.org/10.1073/pnas.2116310118.

68. Buerger, "#iamhere."

69. Joshua Garland, Keyan Ghazi-Zahedi, Jean-Gabriel Young, Laurent Hébert-Dufresne, and Mirta Galesic, "Impact and Dynamics of Hate and Counter Speech Online," *EPJ Data Science* 11, no. 3 (2022), https://doi.org/10.1140/epjds/s13688-021 -00314-6.

70. Joseph B. Walther, "Social Media and Online Hate," *Current Opinion in Psychology* 45, no. 101298 (June 2022), https://doi.org/10.1016/j.copsyc.2021.12.010.

71. For a sense of this type of activity as an escapade, raid, or general (deviant) adventure, see Enrico Mariconti et. al, "'You Know What to Do': Proactive Detection of YouTube Videos Targeted by Coordinated Hate Attacks," *22nd ACM Conference on Computer-Supported Cooperative Work and Social Computing (CSCW 2019)*, https://doi .org/10.48550/arXiv.1805.08168.

72. Walther, "Social Media and Online Hate," 1–2.

73. Jocelyn J. Bélanger, Daniel W. Snook, Domnica Dzitac, and Abdelhak Cheppih, "Challenging Extremism: A Randomized Control Trial Examining the Impact of Counternarratives in the Middle East and North Africa," *Current Research in Ecological and Social Psychology* 4 (2023), https://doi.org/10.1016/j.cresp.2023.100097.

74. Erin Saltman, Farshad Kooti, and Karly Vockery, "New Models for Deploying Counterspeech: Measuring Behavioral Change and Sentiment Analysis," *Studies in Conflict & Terrorism* 46, no. 9 (March 2021): 1547–1574, https://doi.org/10.1080/10 57610X.2021.1888404.

75. Rossine Fallorina, Jose Mari Hall Lanuza, Juan Gabriel Felix, Fernanda Sanchz II, Jonathan Corpus Ong, and Nicole Curato, *From Disinformation to Influence Operations: The Evolution of Disinformation in Three Electoral Cycles* (Internews, 2023), 42, https://internews.org/resource/from-disinformation-to-influence-operations-the-evolution-of-disinformation-in-three-electoral-cycles/.

76. Craig Silverman, "The Philippines Was A Test Of Facebook's New Approach To Countering Disinformation. Things Got Worse," *BuzzFeed News*, August 7, 2019, https://www.buzzfeednews.com/article/craigsilverman/2020-philippines-disinformation.

77. Julie McCarthy, "Fake Sexual Material Targets the Only Woman Running for President in the Philippines," *National Public Radio*, April 17, 2022, https://www.npr.org/2022/04/16/1093189740/philippines-presidential-race-leni-robredo; Leni Robredo, "Public Service in Pink," interview by Shriya Yarlagadda, *Harvard International Review*, February 3, 2023, https://hir.harvard.edu/interview-with-leni-robredo/.

78. Data report forthcoming at Ethics of Social Media Content Moderation Project, Ethics Institute, Northeastern University, https://cssh.northeastern.edu/ethics/the-ethics-of-content-labeling-examining-new-approaches-for-social-media-and-online-platforms/, accessed June 1, 2024. Results archived at "2023 Surveys in US and Philippines: Content Moderation and Free Speech," Digital Repository Service, Northeastern University Library, https://repository.library.northeastern.edu/collections/neu:h989t153k.

79. Paige Occeñola, "Exclusive: PH Was Cambridge Analytica's 'Petri Dish'—Whistle-Blower Christopher Wylie," Rappler, September 10, 2019, https://www.rappler.com/technology/social-media/239606-cambridge-analytica-philippines-online-propaganda-christopher-wylie/.

CHAPTER 4

1. "Whitney v. California."

2. Caroline Crystal, "Facebook, Telegram, and the Ongoing Struggle Against Online Hate Speech," Carnegie Endowment for International Peace, September 7, 2023, https://carnegieendowment.org/research/2023/09/facebook-telegram-and-the-ongoing-struggle-against-online-hate-speech?lang=en&center=middle-east.

3. Alan Z. Rozenshtein and Jed Handelsman Shugerman, "January 6, Ambiguously Inciting Speech, and the Overt-Acts Rule," *Constitutional Comment* 37 (2022): 275.

4. Donald Trump, "Transcript of Trump's Speech at Rally before US Capitol Riot," *Associated Press*, January 13, 2021, Transcript, apnews.com/article/election-2020-joe-biden-donald-trump-capitol-siege-media-e79eb5164613d6718e9f4502eb471f27.

5. Alan Feuer, Michael S. Schmidt, and Luke Broadwater, "New Focus on How a Trump Tweet Incited Far-Right Groups Ahead of Jan. 6," *New York Times*, March 29, 2022, https://www.nytimes.com/2022/03/29/us/politics/trump-tweet-jan-6.html.

6. Cat Zakrzewski, Cristiano Lima, and Drew Harwell, "What the Jan. 6 Probe Found Out About Social Media, but Didn't Report," *Washington Post*, January 17, 2023,

https://www.washingtonpost.com/technology/2023/01/17/jan6-committee-report
-social-media/. The main document analyzed in that article was made public by
the press and disclosed as *Social Media & the January 6th Attack on the U.S. Capitol:
Summary of Investigative Findings* (Washington, DC: House Select Committee to
Investigate the January 6th Attack on the United States Capitol, n.d). While that
leaked 120-page report is marked as "draft," investigators and authors have subsequently talked about the report publicly as a definitive account and factual basis
that informed the main Committee report. See Justin Hendrix, "Results of the January 6th Committee's Social Media Investigation," *Tech Policy Press*, January 6, 2023,
https://www.techpolicy.press/results-of-the-january-6th-committees-social-media
-investigation/. The author of this book also spoke with the lead researcher who
wrote relevant sections of the congressional report that are drawn on here. Author
interview with Dean Jackson, December 22, 2023.

7. Shayan Sardarizadeh and Jessica Lussenhop, "The 65 Days That Led to Chaos at
the Capitol 9th January 2021," *BBC News*, January 9, 2021, https://www.bbc.com
/news/world-us-canada-55592332.

8. Sarah D. Wire, "'How Are We Going to Defend Ourselves?' Inside the Capitol
during the Jan. 6 Insurrection," *Los Angeles Times*, January 4, 2024, https://www
.latimes.com/politics/story/2024-01-04/jan-6-third-anniversary-inside-capitol-retro
spective.

9. *Social Media & the January 6th Attack on the U.S. Capitol*, 10.

10. *Social Media & the January 6th Attack on the U.S. Capitol*, 11.

11. Jazmin Goodwin, "Gab: Everything You Need to Know About the Fast-Growing,
Controversial Social Network," *CNN Business*, January 17, 2021, https://www.cnn.com
/2021/01/17/tech/what-is-gab-explainer/index.html.

12. *Social Media & the January 6th Attack on the U.S. Capitol*, 11.

13. *Social Media & the January 6th Attack on the U.S. Capitol*, 16–17.

14. *Social Media & the January 6th Attack on the U.S. Capitol*, 17.

15. *Social Media & the January 6th Attack on the U.S. Capitol*, 18.

16. *Social Media & the January 6th Attack on the U.S. Capitol*, 18.

17. *Social Media & the January 6th Attack on the U.S. Capitol*, 19.

18. Charles Duan and James Grimmelmann, "Content Moderation on End-to-end
Encrypted Systems: A Legal Analysis," *Georgetown Law Technology Review* 8 (2024): 1.

19. Nora Benavidez, *Big Tech Backslide: How Social-Media Rollbacks Endanger Democracy Ahead of the 2024 Elections* (Washington, DC.: Free Press, December 2023),
https://www.freepress.net/big-tech-backslide-report; William T. Adler and Samir Jain,
*Seismic Shifts: How Economic, Technological, and Political Trends Are Challenging Inde-
pendent Counter-Election-Disinformation Initiatives in the United States* (Washington,
DC: Center for Democracy and Technology, September 21, 2023), https://cdt.org
/insights/seismic-shifts-how-economic-technological-and-political-trends-are-chal
lenging-independent-counter-election-disinformation-initiatives-in-the-united-states/.

20. Dean Jackson, Justin Hendrix, and Tim Bernard, "The Science of Social Media's Role in January 6," *Tech Policy Press*, October 29, 2024, https://www.techpolicy.press /the-science-of-social-medias-role-in-january-6/.

21. Cary O'Dell, "America's Town Meeting of the Air: Should Our Ships Convoy Materials to England?," *Library of Congress*, 2009, https://www.loc.gov/static/programs /national-recording-preservation-board/documents/AMERICA%27S%20TOWN%20 MEETING.pdf; *"America's Town Meeting of the Air,"* Wikipedia, last modified July 1, 2023, https://en.wikipedia.org/wiki/America%27s_Town_Meeting_of_the_Air.

22. "Speech Curb Held 'Suicide' of Nation: Foes of Democracy Should Be Allowed to Express Ideas, Jerome Frank Warns 'Instant Reply' Is Urged Professor Lasswell Suggests Enemies Here Be Forced to Pay for Own Rebuttal," *New York Times*, March 24, 1939.

23. Lasswell, *Democracy Through Public Opinion*, 107.

24. Eugene Volokh, "The Speech Integral to Criminal Conduct Exception," *Cornell Law Review* 101 (2015): 981.

25. Shannon Bond and Bobby Allyn, "How the 'Stop the Steal' Movement Outwitted Facebook Ahead of the Jan. 6 Insurrection," *National Public Radio*, October 22, 2021, https://www.npr.org/2021/10/22/1048543513/facebook-groups-jan-6-insurrec tion; Meta published a detailed defense of its actions around the election. See Guy Rosen, "Our Comprehensive Approach to Protecting the US 2020 Elections Through Inauguration Day," *Meta Newsroom*, October 22, 2021, https://about.fb.com/news /2021/10/protecting-us-2020-elections-inauguration-day/. For a full account of how this movement grew online, see Joan Donovan, Emily Dreyfuss, and Brian Friedberg, *Meme Wars: The Untold Story of the Online Battles Upending Democracy in America* (New York: Bloomsbury Publishing, 2022), 303–332.

26. *Social Media & the January 6th Attack on the U.S. Capitol*, 33.

27. Discussion here of "Break the Glass" and measures to combat dangerous organizations draws on: *Social Media & the January 6th Attack on the U.S. Capitol*, 29–68; "CTRL0000071093—Transcribed Interview of Brian Fishman (April 26, 2022)," January 6th Committee Final Report and Supporting Materials Collection (Government Publishing Office, April 25, 2022), https://www.govinfo.gov/app/details/GPO -J6-TRANSCRIPT-CTRL0000071093.

28. *Social Media & the January 6th Attack on the U.S. Capitol*, 32.

29. "CTRL0000071093—Transcribed Interview of Brian Fishman (April 26, 2022)," 36–37.

30. Ruggie, "The Social Construction of the U.N. Guiding Principles on Business and Human Rights," 63–86. These so-called Ruggie Principles will be explored in chapter 7.

31. "'Total System Collapse': Far-right Telegram Network Incites Hate & Violence after Southport Stabbings," Institute for Strategic Dialogue, n.d., https://www.isd global.org/digital_dispatches/total-system-collapse-far-right-telegram-network -incites-accelerationist-violence-after-southport-stabbings/.

32. Rozenshtein and Shugerman, "January 6, Ambiguously Inciting Speech, and the Overt-Acts Rule," 278.

33. Rozenshtein and Shugerman, 303.

34. Rozenshtein and Shugerman, 277–278.

35. Mariana Olaizola Rosenblat, Inga K. Trauthig, and Samuel C. Woolley, *Covert Campaigns: Safeguarding Encrypted Messaging Platforms from Voter Manipulation* (NYU Stern Center for Business and Human Rights, 2024), https://bhr.stern.nyu.edu /publication/safeguarding-encrypted-messaging-platforms/.

36. Alex Wickham, Jeff Stone, Daniel Zuidijk, and Eleanor Thornber, "Suspected Foreign Accounts Aid UK Extremists to Incite Riots," Bloomberg News, August 7, 2024, https://www.bloomberg.com/news/articles/2024-08-07/suspected-foreign-agi tators-boost-uk-extremists-to-inflame-riots; Wei Zhong, Catie Bailard, David Bronia- towski, and Rebekah Tromble, "Proud Boys on Telegram," *Journal of Quantitative Description: Digital Media* 4 (2024): 1–47.

37. Aurelien Breeden and Adam Satariano, "Telegram Founder Charged with Wide Range of Crimes in France," *New York Times*, August 28, 2024, https://www.nytimes .com/2024/08/28/business/telegram-ceo-pavel-durov-charged.html.

38. Cat Zakrzewski, Gerrit De Vynck, Niha Masih, and Shibani Mahtani, "How Face- book Neglected the Rest of the World, Fueling Hate Speech and Violence in India," *Washington Post*, October 24, 2021, https://www.washingtonpost.com/technology /2021/10/24/india-facebook-misinformation-hate-speech/.

39. "India Lynchings: WhatsApp Sets New Rules after Mob Killings," *BBC News*, July 20, 2018, https://www.bbc.com/news/world-asia-india-44897714.

40. Matt Burgess, "Switched to Telegram? You Need to Know This About Its Encryp- tion," *Wired*, January 27, 2021, https://www.wired.com/story/telegram-encryption -end-to-end-features/.

41. Christoph Schmon, "European Court of Human Rights Confirms: Weakening Encryption Violates Fundamental Rights," Electronic Frontier Foundation, March 5, 2024, https://www.eff.org/deeplinks/2024/03/european-court-human-rights-con firms-undermining-encryption-violates-fundamental.

42. Duan and Grimmelmann, "Content Moderation on End-to-end Encrypted Sys- tems," 1, 90.

43. Seny Kamara, Mallory Knodel, Emma Llansó, Greg Nojeim, Lucy Qin, Dhanaraj Thakur, et al., "Outside Looking In: Approaches to Content Moderation in End-to- end Encrypted Systems," preprint, submitted February 9, 2022, https://arxiv.org/abs /2202.04617.

44. Harold Abelson, Ross Anderson, Steven M. Bellovin, Josh Benaloh, Matt Blaze, Jon Callas, et al., "Bugs in Our Pockets: The Risks of Client-side Scanning," *Journal of Cybersecurity* 10, no. 1 (2024): tyad020.

45. Duan and Grimmelmann, "Content Moderation on End-to-end Encrypted Systems"; Sarah Scheffler and Jonathan Mayer, "Sok: Content Moderation for End-

to-end Encryption," preprint, submitted March 7, 2023, https://arxiv.org/abs/2303
.03979.

46. Katlyn Glover, Mirya Dila, Neeley Pate, Inga Kristina Trauthig, Samuel C. Woolley, and Kaiya Little, *Encrypted Messaging Applications and Political Messaging: How
They Work and Why Understanding Them Is Important for Combating Global Disinformation*, Center for Media Engagement (University of Texas at Austin, June 2023),
https://mediaengagement.org/research/encrypted-messaging-applications-and
-political-messaging/.

CHAPTER 5

1. A. M. Turing, "Computing Machinery and Intelligence," *Mind* 59, no. 236 (October 1950): 433–460, https://doi.org/10.1093/mind/LIX.236.433.

2. Dave Willner and Samidh Chakrabarti, "Using LLMs for Policy-Driven Content
Classification," Tech Policy Press, January 29, 2024, https://www.techpolicy.press
/using-llms-for-policy-driven-content-classification/.

3. Prithvi Iyer, "Transcript: Dave Willner on Moderating with AI at the Institute for
Rebooting Social Media," Tech Policy Press, April 3, 2024, https://www.techpolicy
.press/transcript-dave-willner-on-moderating-with-ai-at-the-institute-for-rebooting
-social-media/.

4. Roberts, *Behind the Screen*.

5. Nazanin Sabri, Bella Chen, Annabelle Teoh, Steven P. Dow, Kristen Vaccaro, and
Mai Elsherief, "Challenges of Moderating Social Virtual Reality," *Proceedings of the
2023 CHI Conference on Human Factors in Computing Systems* (2023): 1–20.

6. Joshua Rothman, "Why the Godfather of A.I. Fears What He's Built," *New Yorker*,
November 13, 2023, https://www.newyorker.com/magazine/2023/11/20/geoffrey
-hinton-profile-ai; Matt O'Brien, "Scientists Warn of AI Dangers But Don't Agree on
Solutions," *Associated Press*, May 3, 2023, https://apnews.com/article/ai-godfather
-google-geoffrey-hinton-yoshua-bengio-chatgpt-5f7dc295a576833dfc3378071b57
16f2.

7. Reed Albergotti, "How Advances in AI Can Make Content Moderation Harder—
and Easier," *Semafor*, October 27, 2023, https://www.semafor.com/article/10/27/2023
/how-advances-in-ai-can-make-content-moderation-harder-and-easier.

8. "U.S. Senate AI Insight Forum: Elections & Democracy Written Statement of Alex
Stamos Director, Stanford Internet Observatory Stanford University," November
8, 2023, https://www.schumer.senate.gov/newsroom/press-releases/statements-from
-the-fifth-bipartisan-senate-forum-on-artificial-intelligence; Josh A. Goldstein, Jason
Chao, Shelby Grossman, Alex Stamos, and Michael Tomz, "Can AI Write Persuasive
Propaganda?," *SocArXiv*, April 2023, https://osf.io/preprints/socarxiv/fp87b_v1.

9. William Marcellino, Nathan Beauchamp-Mustafaga, Amanda Kerrigan, Lev
Navarre Chao and Jackson Smith, *The Rise of Generative AI and the Coming Era of
Social Media Manipulation 3.0: Next-Generation Chinese Astroturfing and Coping with*

Ubiquitous AI (Santa Monica, CA: RAND Corporation 2023), 9–10, https://www.rand .org/pubs/perspectives/PEA2679-1.html.

10. Lluis de Nadal and Peter Jančárik, "Beyond the Deepfake Hype: AI, Democracy, and 'the Slovak Case,'" *Harvard Kennedy School Misinformation Review*, August 22, 2024, https://misinforeview.hks.harvard.edu/article/beyond-the-deepfake-hype-ai -democracy-and-the-slovak-case/.

11. Holly Ramer and Ali Swenson, "Political Consultant behind Fake Biden Robocalls Faces $6 Million Fine and Criminal Charges," *Associated Press*, May 23, 2024, https:// apnews.com/article/biden-robocalls-ai-new-hampshire-charges-fines-9e9cc63a71eb9 c78b9bb0d1ec2aa6e9c.

12. Meghan Bobrowsky and Miles Kruppa, "Mickey Mouse Smoking: How AI Image Tools Are Generating New Content-Moderation Problems," *Wall Street Journal*, September 2, 2024, https://www.wsj.com/tech/ai/mickey-mouse-smoking-how-ai-image -tools-are-generating-new-content-moderation-problems-da90148e.

13. Vittoria Elliott, "AI-Fakes Detection Is Failing Voters in the Global South," *Wired*, September 2, 2024, https://www.wired.com/story/generative-ai-detection-gap/.

14. "AI and Democracy with Jason Matheny, President & CEO of The Rand Corporation," Los Angeles World Affairs Council and Town Hall, June 15, 2023, YouTube video, https://www.youtube.com/watch?v=n_K0xQITiH8.

15. "Content Moderation in a New Era for AI and Automation," Meta Oversight Board, September 2024, https://www.oversightboard.com/news/content-moderation -in-a-new-era-for-ai-and-automation/; "Best Practices for AI and Automation in Trust & Safety," Digital Trust & Safety Partnership, September 2024, https://dtspartnership .org/best-practices-for-ai-and-automation-in-trust-and-safety/.

16. Lilian Weng, Vik Goel, and Andrea Vallone, "Using GPT-4 for Content Moderation," *OpenAI* (blog), August 15, 2023, https://openai.com/blog/using-gpt-4-for-con tent-moderation.

17. Meta, *Meta's Adversarial Threat Report Third Quarter* (Menlo Park, CA: Meta, 2023), https://transparency.fb.com/metasecurity/threat-reporting.

18. "Responding to Crises," Christchurch Call, 2023, https://www.christchurchcall .com/our-work/crisis-response#:~:text=The%20goal%20is%20to%20prevent,perpe trator%20or%20accomplice%2Dproduced%20conten.

19. Cristina Criddle, "Can Big Tech Make Livestreams Safe?," *Financial Times*, January 22, 2023, https://www.ft.com/content/5280535a-4dd5-482d-ad0d-730e47354d4a.

20. Center for Technology and Society, "Livestreaming Violence: What Platforms Should Do," *Anti-Defamation League* (blog), October 10, 2023, https://www.adl.org /resources/blog/livestreaming-violence-what-platforms-should-do.

21. Tessa Lyons, "The Three-part Recipe for Cleaning Up Your News Feed," Meta Newsroom, May 22, 2018, https://about.fb.com/news/2018/05/inside-feed-reduce -remove-inform/.

22. Parts of this chapter section come from a working conference paper this author presented: John Wihbey, "AI and Epistemic Risk for Democracy: A Coming Crisis of

Public Knowledge?," Conference on Democracy's Mega Challenges: How Climate Change, Migration, and Big Data Threaten the Future of Liberal Democratic Governance, Trinity College, Hartford, CT, April 19–20, 2024, http://dx.doi.org/10.2139/ssrn.4805026.

23. Shagun Jhaver, Iris Birman, Eric Gilbert and Amy Bruckman, "Human-Machine Collaboration for Content Regulation: The Case of Reddit Automoderator," *ACM Transactions on Computer-Human Interaction (TOCHI)* 26, no. 5 (July 2019): 1–35, https://doi.org/10.1145/3338243; Eshwar Chandrasekharan, Chaitrali Gandhi, Matthew W. Mustelier and Eric Gilbert, "Crossmod: A Cross-Community Learning-Based System to Assist Reddit Moderators," *Proceedings of the ACM on Human-Computer Interaction*, 3, no. 174 (November 2019): 1–30, https://doi.org/10.1145/3359276.

24. Weng, Goel, and Vallone, "Using GPT-4 for Content Moderation."

25. Mike Isaac and Cade Metz, "Meet the A.I. Jane Austen: Meta Weaves A.I. Throughout Its Apps," *New York Times*, September 27, 2023, https://www.nytimes.com/2023/09/27/technology/meta-ai-celebrities.html.

26. Thomas H. Costello, Gordon Pennycook, and David Rand, "Durably Reducing Conspiracy Beliefs Through Dialogues with AI," *Science* 385, no. 6714 (September 13, 2024), https://www.science.org/doi/10.1126/science.adq1814.

27. Michal Luria and Stuart Candy, "Letters from the Future: Exploring Ethical Dilemmas in the Design of Social Agents," in *Proceedings of the 2022 CHI Conference on Human Factors in Computing Systems* (April 2022): 1–13, https://doi.org/10.1145/3491102.3517536.

28. Sayash Kapoor and Arvind Narayanan, "How to Prepare for the Deluge of Generative AI on Social Media: A Grounded Analysis of the Challenges and Opportunities," Knight First Amendment Center, Columbia University (June 16, 2023), https://knightcolumbia.org/content/how-to-prepare-for-the-deluge-of-generative-ai-on-social-media.

29. Isabelle Augenstein, Timothy Baldwin, Meeyoung Cha, Tanmoy Chakraborty, Giovanni Luca Ciampaglia, David Corney, et al., "Factuality Challenges in the Era of Large Language Models and Opportunities for Fact-checking," *Nature Machine Intelligence* (2024): 1–12; Matthew R. DeVerna, Harry Youjun Yan, Kai-Cheng Yang, and Filipo Menczer, "Artificial Intelligence Is Ineffective and Potentially Harmful for Fact Checking," preprint, published September 2023, https://doi.orgx/10.48550/arXiv.2308.10800.

30. Manoel Ribeiro, Justin Cheng, and Robert West, "Automated Content Moderation Increases Adherence to Community Guidelines," preprint, published February 2023, https://doi.org/10.48550/arXiv.2210.10454; Matthew Katsaros, Jisu Kim, and Tom Tyler, "Online Content Moderation: Does Justice Need a Human Face?," *International Journal of Human–Computer Interaction* (May 2023): 1- 12, https://doi.org/10.1080/10447318.2023.2210879.

31. These findings are based on: John Wihbey and Garrett Morrow, *Social Media's New Referees?: Public Attitudes toward AI Content Moderation Bots across Three Countries* (Boston: Northeastern University Ethics Institute, December 2023).

32. Joanna Weiss, Michael Workman, Rupal Patel, John Wihbey, and Garrett Morrow, *How Americans See AI: Caution, Skepticism, and Hope*, AI Literacy Lab, Northeastern University (Boston: Northeastern University, 2023), https://bpb-us-e1.wp mucdn.com/sites.northeastern.edu/dist/f/4599/files/2023/10/report-1017-2.pdf.

33. Leticia Bode and Emily K. Vraga, "Correction Experiences on Social Media during COVID-19," *Social Media + Society* 7, no. 2 (2021): 20563051211008829.

34. Susan Benesch and Cathy Buerger, "Can AI Rescue Democracy? Nope, It's Not Funny Enough," TechPolicy Press, March 11, 2024, https://www.techpolicy.press/can -ai-rescue-democracy-nope-its-not-funny-enough/.

35. Alan Z. Rozenshtein, "Moderating the Fediverse: Content Moderation on Distributed Social Media." *Journal of Free Speech Law* 3 (2023): 217.

36. Yoel Roth and Samantha Lai, "Securing Federated Platforms: Collective Risks and Responses," *Journal of Online Trust and Safety* 2, no. 2 (2024), https://www.ts journal.org/index.php/jots/article/view/171.

37. Luciano Floridi and Josh Cowls, "A Unified Framework of Five Principles for AI in Society," *Harvard Data Science Review* 1, no. 1, https://doi.org/10.1162/99608f92 .8cd550d1.

38. Sahana Udupa, Antonis Maronikolakis, and Axel Wisiorek, "Ethical Scaling for Content Moderation: Extreme Speech and the (In) significance of Artificial Intelligence," *Big Data & Society* 10, no. 1 (2023), https://journals.sagepub.com/doi/full /10.1177/20539517231172424.

39. Chris Perry, *Perspective Agents: A Human Guide to the Autonomous Age* (New York: Fast Company Press, 2024).

40. Sarah Kreps and Doug Kriner, "How AI Threatens Democracy," *Journal of Democracy* 34, no. 4 (2023): 122–131; John Danaher, "The Threat of Algocracy: Reality, Resistance and Accommodation," *Philosophy & Technology* 29, no. 3 (2016): 245–268; Mustafa Suleyman, *The Coming Wave: Technology, Power, and the Twenty-first Century's Greatest Dilemma* (New York: Crown, 2023).

41. Chenyan Jia, Michelle S. Lam, Minh Chau Mai, Jeffrey T. Hancock, and Michael S. Bernstein, "Embedding Democratic Values into Social Media AIs via Societal Objective Functions." *Proceedings of the ACM on Human-Computer Interaction* 8, no. CSCW1 (2024): 1–36.

42. John Wihbey, Matthew Kopec, and Ronald Sandler, "Informational Quality Labeling on Social Media: In Defense of a Social Epistemology Strategy," *Yale Journal of Law & Technology: Special Issue: Social Media Governance* 23 (2021), https://yjolt .org/new-light-social-media-governance-reconsidered.

43. Phillips and Milner, *You Are Here*.

44. Don Fallis, "The Epistemic Threat of Deepfakes," *Philosophy & Technology* 34, no. 4 (2021): 623–643; Joshua Habgood-Coote, "Deepfakes and the Epistemic Apocalypse," *Synthese* 201, no. 3 (2023): 103.

45. Christopher Cyr, Tara Tobin Cataldo, Brittany Brannon, Amy Buhler, Ixchel Faniel, Lynn Silipigni Connaway, et al., "Backgrounds and Behaviors: Which

Students Successfully Identify Online Resources in the Face of Container Collapse," *First Monday* (2021), https://firstmonday.org/ojs/index.php/fm/article/view/10871/10080.

46. Zeve Sanderson, Megan A. Brown, Richard Bonneau, Jonathan Nagler, and Joshua A. Tucker, "Twitter Flagged Donald Trump's Tweets with Election Misinformation: They Continued to Spread Both on and off the Platform," *Harvard Kennedy School Misinformation Review* (August 2021), https://misinforeview.hks.harvard.edu/article/twitter-flagged-donald-trumps-tweets-with-election-misinformation-they-continued-to-spread-both-on-and-off-the-platform/; Wihbey, Kopec, and Sandler, "Informational Quality Labeling on Social Media."

47. Saadia Gabriel, Liang Lyu, James Siderius, Marzyeh Ghassemi, Jacob Andreas, and Asu Ozdaglar, "Generative AI in the Era of 'Alternative Facts,'" *arXiv:2410.09949* (2024).

48. Chloe Wittenberg, Ziv Epstein, Gabrielle Péloquin-Skulski, Adam J. Berinsky, and David G. Rand, "Labeling AI-Generated Media Online," preprint, submitted July 11, 2024, https://osf.io/preprints/psyarxiv/b238p.

49. Steven Adler, Zoë Hitzig, Shrey Jain, Catherine Brewer, Wayne Chang, Renée DiResta, et al., "Personhood Credentials: Artificial Intelligence and the Value of Privacy-preserving Tools to Distinguish Who Is Real Online," preprint, submitted August 15, 2025, https://arxiv.org/abs/2408.07892.

50. Liz Arcamona, Louisa Bartolo, Yvonne Lee, and Sarah Shirazyan, "Exploring Tradeoffs in Ranking and Recommendation Algorithms," *Lawfare*, September 29, 2023, https://www.lawfaremedia.org/article/exploring-tradeoffs-in-ranking-and-recommendation-algorithms.

51. This five-part framework is formulated in Wihbey, Kopec, and Sandler, "Informational Quality Labeling on Social Media," 188.

52. Tom Cunningham, Sana Pandey, Leif Sigerson, Jonathan Stray, Jeff Allen, Bonnie Barrilleaux, et al., "What We Know About Using Non-Engagement Signals in Content Ranking," *arXiv preprint arXiv:2402.06831* (2024).

53. Myojung Chung and John Wihbey, "The Algorithmic Knowledge Gap within and between Countries: Implications for Combatting Misinformation," *Harvard Kennedy School Misinformation Review* 5, no. 4 (August 2024), https://misinforeview.hks.harvard.edu/article/the-algorithmic-knowledge-gap-within-and-between-countries-implications-for-combatting-misinformation/.

CHAPTER 6

1. James C. Scott, *Seeing Like a State: How Certain Schemes to Improve the Human Condition Have Failed* (New Haven: Yale University Press, 2020), 11.

2. Klonick, "The New Governors: The People, Rules, and Processes Governing Online Speech."

3. Craig Silverman, "Facebook Is Turning to Fact-Checkers to Fight Fake News," *BuzzFeedNews*, December 15, 2016, https://www.buzzfeednews.com/article/craigsilverman/facebook-and-fact-checkers-fight-fake-news.

4. Morrow et al., "The Emerging Science of Content Labeling."

5. Naomi Appelman and Paddy Leerssen, "On 'Trusted' Flaggers," *Yale Journal of Law & Technology* 24 (2022): 452.

6. Meta, "Content Restrictions Based on Local Law," Transparency Center, accessed January 5, 2024, https://transparency.fb.com/reports/content-restrictions/; Meta, "How We Assess Reports of Content Violating Local Law," Transparency Center, accessed January 5, 2024, https://transparency.fb.com/reports/content-restrictions /content-violating-local-law.

7. Foundational to our understanding in this field, sometimes called critical internet studies, and the sociology of content moderation specifically are works such as Tarleton Gillespie, *Custodians of the Internet: Platforms, Content Moderation, and the Hidden Decisions that Shape Social Media* (New Haven: Yale University Press, 2018); and Roberts, *Behind the Screen*.

8. Hannah Bloch-Wehba, "Automation in Moderation," *Cornell International Law Journal* 53 (2020): 41–96.

9. "YouTube for Press," *The YouTube Blog*, accessed January 4, 2024, https://blog .youtube/press/.

10. Morrow et al., "The Emerging Science of Content Labeling."

11. Robyn Caplan, *Content or Context Moderation? Artisanal, Community-Reliant, and Industrial Approaches* (New York: Data & Society Research Institute, 2020), https:// datasociety.net/wp-content/uploads/2018/11/DS_Content_or_Context_Moderation .pdf. For a definitive overview of this field's development, see Gillespie, *Custodians of the Internet*.

12. Chenyan Jia, Alexander Boltz, Angie Zhang, Anqing Chen, and Min Kyung Lee, "Understanding Effects of Algorithmic vs. Community Label on Perceived Accuracy of Hyper-partisan Misinformation," *Proceedings of the ACM on Human-Computer Interaction* 6, no. CSCW2 (2022): 1–27.

13. Ferenc Huszár, Sofia Ira Ktena, Conor O'Brien, Luca Belli, Andrew Schlaikjer, and Moritz Hardt, "Algorithmic Amplification of Politics on Twitter," *Proceedings of the National Academy of Sciences* 119, no. 1 (2022): e2025334119; Sandra González-Bailón, Valeria d'Andrea, Deen Freelon, and Manlio De Domenico, "The Advantage of the Right in Social Media News Sharing," *PNAS Nexus* 1, no. 3 (2022): 1–8.

14. Arcamona et al., "Exploring Tradeoffs in Ranking and Recommendation Algorithms."

15. This section draws on *Social Media & the January 6th Attack on the U.S. Capitol*, 69–77.

16. *Social Media & the January 6th Attack on the U.S. Capitol*, 70.

17. The research findings are complex and not always clear-cut on this issue of YouTube "rabbit holes" and the alleged promotion of radicalization/extremist content. See Homa Hosseinmardi, Amir Ghasemian, Aaron Clauset, Markus Mobius, David M. Rothschild, and Duncan J. Watts, "Examining the Consumption of Radical

Content on YouTube," *Proceedings of the National Academy of Sciences* 118, no. 32 (2021): e2101967118; Annie Y. Chen, Brendan Nyhan, Jason Reifler, Ronald E. Robertson, and Christo Wilson, "Resentful Users to Alternative and Extremist YouTube Channels," *Science Advances* 9, no. 35 (2023), https://www.science.org/doi/10.1126 /sciadv.add8080.

18. *Social Media & the January 6th Attack on the U.S. Capitol*, 73.

19. *Social Media & the January 6th Attack on the U.S. Capitol*, 72. For comparative perspective across platforms, see Laura Edelson, "Content Moderation in Practice," *Journal of Free Speech Law* 3 (2023): 183.

20. *Social Media & the January 6th Attack on the U.S. Capitol*, 71.

21. *Social Media & the January 6th Attack on the U.S. Capitol*, 72.

22. Clare Duffy, "YouTube Will Now Allow 2020 Election Denialism Content, in Policy Reversal," CNN, June 2, 2023, https://www.cnn.com/2023/06/02/business /youtube-election-misinformation-policy/index.html.

23. For more on these debates, see Adrian Shabaz, *The Rise of Digital Authoritarianism* (Washington, DC: Freedom House, 2018), https://freedomhouse.org/report/freedom -net/2018/rise-digital-authoritarianism; James Tager, *Splintered Speech: Digital Sovereignty and the Future of the Internet* (New York: PEN America, 2021), https://pen.org /report/splintered-speech-digital-sovereignty-and-the-future-of-the-internet/; French President Emmanuel Macron, "Internet Governance Forum 2018 Speech," transcript of speech delivered at the Internet Governance Forum, November 12, 2018, https:// www.intgovforum.org/en/content/igf-2018-speech-by-french-president-emmanuel -macron.

24. Finbarr Bermingham and Catherine Wong, "China's Outgoing EU Envoy to Lead Shanghai Cooperation Organisation. Can the Group Punch Its Weight?," *South China Morning Post*, January 5, 2022, https://www.scmp.com/news/china/diplomacy /article/3162223/chinas-outgoing-eu-envoy-lead-shanghai-cooperation; Tate Ryan-Mosley, "The World Is Moving Closer to a New Cold War Fought with Authoritarian Tech," *MIT Technology Review*, September 22, 2022, https://www.technologyreview .com/2022/09/22/1059823/cold-war-authoritarian-tech-china-iran-sco/.

25. "In-Depth Interview with SCO Secretary-General Zhang Ming," interview by Tian Wei, *CGTN*, September 15, 2022, YouTube video, https://www.youtube.com /watch?v=8LfBhZKJevs.

26. Ambassador Zhang Ming, "Delivering a Better Life for the People Is China's Development Goal," Mission of the People's Republic of China to the European Union, June 10, 2021, http://eu.china-mission.gov.cn/eng/mh/202106/t20210610 _9095064.htm.

27. "IntelBrief: China's Counterterrorism Inroads in Central Asia," The Soufan Center, February 19, 2021, https://thesoufancenter.org/intelbrief-2021-february-19/.

28. Adriel Kasonta, "Opinion: How SCO's Growing Credibility Reflects the Emerging Multipolar World Order," *South China Morning Post (Hong Kong)*, October 2, 2022, https://www.scmp.com/comment/opinion/asia/article/3194269/how-scos-growing

-credibility-reflects-emerging-multipolar.; "China's Xi Says 'Color Revolutions' Must Be Prevented," *VOA News*, September 16, 2022, https://www.voanews.com/a/china-xi -says-color-revolutions-must-be-prevented/6750450.html.

29. Yuxi Wei, "China-Russia Cybersecurity Cooperation: Working Towards Cyber-Sovereignty," Jackson School of International Studies, June 21, 2016, https://jsis .washington.edu/news/china-russia-cybersecurity-cooperation-working-towards -cyber-sovereignty/.

30. U.S.-China Economic and Security Review Commission, *2022 Report to Congress*, November 15, 2022, chapter 3, section 2, "China's Cyber Capabilities: Warfare, Espionage, and Implications for the United States," 460, https://www.uscc.gov/sites /default/files/2022-11/2022_Annual_Report_to_Congress.pdf.

31. Alexander Cooley, "The Rise of Global Counter Norms," in Bollinger and Callamard, *Regardless of Frontiers*, 309–326.

32. Melissa Fleming, "Fighting Disinformation to Survive," December 9, 2022, in *Awake at Night*, United Nations podcast, 39:21, https://www.un.org/en/awake-at-night /S6-E4-irene-khan-fighting-disinformation-to-survive.

33. Irene Khan, *Disinformation and Freedom of Opinion and Expression during Armed Conflicts* (New York: United Nations General Assembly, 2021), 18, https://documents -dds-ny.un.org/doc/UNDOC/GEN/N22/459/30/PDF/N2245930.pdf?OpenElement.

34. Khan, *Disinformation and Freedom of Opinion and Expression*, 17.

35. Irene Khan, *Promotion and Protection of the Right to Freedom of Opinion and Expression* (New York: United Nations General Assembly, 2023), 4, https://documents-dds -ny.un.org/doc/UNDOC/GEN/N23/233/65/PDF/N2323365.pdf?OpenElement.

36. Khan, *Promotion and Protection of the Right to Freedom of Opinion and Expression*, 19.

37. European Commission, "Questions and Answers on the Digital Services Act," February 23, 2024, https://ec.europa.eu/commission/presscorner/detail/en/QANDA _20_2348.

38. Bradford, *The Brussels Effect*.

39. Margarethe Vestager, "Margarethe Vestager Talks Investigating Amazon, Fining Apple, Facebook Lying, and What She's Learned," interview by Noah Kulwin, *Intelligencer*, October 25, 2018, https://nymag.com/intelligencer/2018/10/e-u-competition -commissioner-margrethe-vestager-interview.html.

40. Magdaline Duncan, "Vestager: 'I Do Work with Tax and I Am a Woman,'" *Politico*, April 18, 2019, https://www.politico.eu/article/margrethe-vestager-i-do-work-with -tax-and-i-am-a-woman-donald-trump-google/.

41. European Commission, "Digital Markets Act: Commission Designates Six Gatekeepers," press release, September 6, 2023, https://ec.europa.eu/commission /presscorner/detail/en/ip_23_4328.

42. European Commission, "DSA: Very Large Online Platforms and Search Engines," Shaping Europe's Digital Future, accessed December 21, 2023, https://digital-strategy .ec.europa.eu/en/policies/dsa-vlops.

43. Margarethe Vestager, "Tearing Down Big Tech's Walls," Project Syndicate, March 9, 2023, https://www.project-syndicate.org/commentary/eu-big-tech-legisla tion-digital-services-markets-by-margrethe-vestager-2023-03.

44. Vestager, "Tearing Down Big Tech's Walls."

45. Thibault Larger, Mark Scott, Laura Kayali, and Nicholas Vinocur, "Inside the EU's Divisions on How to Go after Big Tech," *Politico Europe*, December 14, 2020, https://www.politico.eu/article/margrethe-vestager-thierry-breton-europe-big-tech -regulation-digital-services-markets-act/.

46. "The Final Text of the Digital Services Act (DSA) Article 16, Notice and Action Mechanisms—the Digital Services Act (DSA)," European Commission, (n.d.), https:// www.eu-digital-services-act.com/Digital_Services_Act_Article_16.html.

47. Clothilde Goujard, "EU Charges Elon Musk's X for Letting Disinfo Run Wild," *Politico*, July 12, 2024, https://www.politico.eu/article/eu-charges-musks-x-for-letting -disinfo-run-wild/.

48. Jacob Berntsson and Maygane Janin, "Online Regulation of Terrorist and Harm-ful Content," *Lawfare* (blog), October 14, 2021, https://www.lawfareblog.com/online -regulation-terrorist-and-harmful-content; Cecilia Kang and Adam Satariano, "Regu-lators Around the World Are Circling Facebook," *New York Times*, April 25, 2019, https://www.nytimes.com/2019/04/25/technology/facebook-regulation-ftc-fine.html; Anshu Siripurapu and Will Merrow, "How Countries Regulate Online Speech," In Brief, Council on Foreign Relations, February 9, 2021, https://www.cfr.org/in-brief /social-media-and-online-speech-how-should-countries-regulate-tech-giants.

49. David Kaye, *Speech Police: The Global Struggle to Govern the Internet* (New York: Columbia Global Reports, 2019).

50. Paul M. Barrett, *Who Moderates the Social Media Giants? A Call to End Outsourcing* (New York: NYU Stern Center for Business and Human Rights, 2020), https://bhr .stern.nyu.edu/tech-content-moderation-june-2020; Caplan, *Content or Context Mod-eration? Artisanal, Community-Reliant, and Industrial Approaches*; Robyn Caplan, "The Artisan and the Decision Factory: The Organizational Dynamics of Private Speech Governance," in *Digital Technology and Democratic Theory*, 1st ed., ed. Lucy Bernholz, Hélène Landemore, and Rob Reich (Chicago: University of Chicago Press, 2021), 167–190.

51. Tom Simonite, "Facebook Is Everywhere; Its Moderation Is Nowhere Close," *Wired*, October 25, 2021, https://www.wired.com/story/facebooks-global-reach-exceeds -linguistic-grasp/; Vittoria Elliott, "New Laws Requiring Social Media Platforms to Hire Local Staff Could Endanger Employees," *Rest of World*, May 14, 2021, https:// restofworld.org/2021/social-media-laws-twitter-facebook/.

52. Jacob Mchangama, "People Want Free Speech—For Themselves," *Foreign Policy*, June 8, 2021, https://foreignpolicy.com/2021/06/08/people-want-free-speech-for-them selves/.

53. Jack Goldsmith and Andrew Keane Woods, "Internet Speech Will Never Go Back to Normal," *Atlantic*, April 25, 2020, https://www.theatlantic.com/ideas/archive

/2020/04/what-covid-revealed-about-internet/610549/; Ian Bremmer, "The Technopolar Moment: How Digital Powers Will Reshape the Global Order," *Foreign Affairs* (November/December 2021), https://www.foreignaffairs.com/articles/world/ian-bremmer-big-tech-global-order.

54. Mathew Ingram, "The Challenges of Global Content Moderation," *Columbia Journalism Review*, June 10, 2021, https://www.cjr.org/the_media_today/the-challenges-of-global-content-moderation.php.

55. "In Some Countries, People Think They Have Too Much Freedom of Speech," *Economist*, June 7, 2021, http://www.economist.com/graphic-detail/2021/06/07/in-some-countries-people-think-they-have-too-much-freedom-of-speech.

56. Findings in this chapter section derive from: Myojung Chung and John Wihbey, "Social Media Regulation, Third-person Effect, and Public Views: A Comparative Study of the United States, the United Kingdom, South Korea, and Mexico," *New Media & Society* 26, no. 8 (2024): 4534–4553, https://doi.org/10.1177/14614448221122996; John Wihbey et. al., "Divergent Global Views on Social Media, Free Speech, and Platform Regulation: Findings from the United Kingdom, South Korea, Mexico, and the United States," Ethics Institute, Northeastern University (January 2022), https://papers.ssrn.com/abstract=3999454.

57. Martin J. Riedl, Kelsey N. Whipple, and Ryan Wallace, "Antecedents of Support for Social Media Content Moderation and Platform Regulation: The Role of Presumed Effects on Self and Others," *Information, Communication & Society* 25, no. 11 (January 2021): 1–18, https://doi.org/10.1080/1369118X.2021.1874040.

58. Monica Anderson, "Most Americans Say Social Media Companies Have Too Much Power, Influence in Politics," Pew Research Center, July 22, 2020, https://www.pewresearch.org/fact-tank/2020/07/22/most-americans-say-social-media-companies-have-too-much-power-influence-in-politics/.

59. Carole Cadwalladr, "The Great British Brexit Robbery: How Our Democracy Was Hijacked," *Guardian*, May 7, 2017, https://www.theguardian.com/technology/2017/may/07/the-great-british-brexit-robbery-hijacked-democracy; Philip N. Howard, *Lie Machines: How to Save Democracy from Troll Armies, Deceitful Robots, Junk News Operations, and Political Operatives* (New Haven, CT: Yale University Press, 2020).

60. For reference to the other countries in our study, during this period the United States ranked number 44 on the Reporters Without Borders index, the United Kingdom number 33, and Mexico number 143. Reporters Without Borders, "2021 World Press Freedom Index." Also see Choe Sang-Hun, "'Historical Distortions' Test South Korea's Commitment to Free Speech," *New York Times*, July 18, 2021, https://www.nytimes.com/2021/07/18/world/asia/korea-misinformation-youtube.html.

61. Alan Abramowitz and Jennifer McCoy, "United States: Racial Resentment, Negative Partisanship, and Polarization in Trump's America," *The ANNALS of the American Academy of Political and Social Science* 681, no. 1 (December 2018): 137–156, https://doi.org/10.1177/0002716218811309; Julie Jiang, "Political Polarization Drives Online Conversations About COVID-19 in the United States," *Human Behavior and Emerging Technologies* 2, no. 3 (June 2020), 200–211, https://doi.org/10.1002

/hbe2.202; Musadiq Bidar, "Lawmakers Vow Stricter Regulations on Social Media Platforms to Combat Misinformation," *CBS News*, March 25, 2020, https://www .cbsnews.com/news/misinformation-extremism-hearing-google-facebook-twitter -watch-live-stream-today-2021-03-25/.

62. Nina Lakhani, "Mexico World's Deadliest Country for Journalists, New Report Finds," *Guardian*, December 22, 2020, https://www.theguardian.com/world/2020 /dec/22/mexico-journalists-deadly-cpr-press-freedom.

63. Janan Ganesh, "Of Venusian Americans and Martian Europeans," *Financial Times*, December 18, 2021, https://www.ft.com/content/bd012071-0bd4-439d-8d6b -157b53c1d703.

64. Myojung Chung, "Individualism-Collectivism Revisited: Analysis of Self-Other Perceptions in Korea and the U.S.," *Asian Communication Research*, 13, no. 1 (June 2016): 58–79, 10.20879/acr.2016.13.1.58.

65. British Social Attitudes, *Political Consequences of Brexit: Has Brexit Damaged Our Politics?* (London: National Center for Social Research, 2019), https://bsa.natcen.ac.uk /latest-report/british-social-attitudes-37/consequences-of-brexit.aspx.

66. Cadwalladr, "The Great British Brexit Robbery"; Howard, *Lie Machines*.

67. Megan Brenan, "Americans' Trust in Government Remains Low," *Gallup*, September 30, 2021, https://news.gallup.com/poll/355124/americans-trust-government -remains-low.aspx; Jack Citrin, "Comment: The Political Relevance of Trust in Government," *American Political Science Review* 68, no. 3 (September 1974): 973–988, https://doi.org/10.2307/1959141.

68. Russel Hardin, "Government Without Trust," *Journal of Trust Research* 3, no. 1 (April 2013): 32–52, https://doi.org/10.1080/21515581.2013.771502.

69. John Wihbey, Garrett Morrow, Myojung Chung, and Mike Peacey, "The Bipartisan Case for Labeling as a Content Moderation Method: Findings from a National Survey," Ethics Institute, Northeastern University (September 2021), http://dx.doi .org/10.2139/ssrn.3923905.

70. Reporters Without Borders, 2021 World Press Freedom Index, https://rsf.org/en /2021-world-press-freedom-index-journalism-vaccine-against-disinformation-blocked -more-130-countries. *Reporters Without Borders*, "2021 World Press Freedom Index," https://rsf.org/en/index?year=2021.

71. Chung, "Individualism-Collectivism Revisited."

72. Scholars have focused increasingly on the conflicts among these three models of regulation. See Anu Bradford, *Digital Empires: The Global Battle to Regulate Technology* (Oxford: Oxford University Press, 2023).

73. European Commission, "Europe Fit for the Digital Age: Commission Proposes New Rules and Actions for Excellence and Trust in Artificial Intelligence," press release, April 21, 2021, https://ec.europa.eu/commission/presscorner/detail/en/IP_21 _1682.

74. European Commission, "Europe Fit for the Digital Age."

75. Adam Satariano and Cecilia Kang, "How Nations Are Losing a Global Race to Tackle A.I.'s Harms," *New York Times*, December 6, 2023, https://www.nytimes.com /2023/12/06/technology/ai-regulation-policies.html.

76. Nathaniel Fick, *One Bullet Away: The Making of a Marine Officer* (Boston: Houghton Mifflin Harcourt, 2006).

77. Nathaniel C. Fick, "US Leadership in Tech Diplomacy: A Conversation with Ambassador Nathaniel C. Fick," interview by Patrick M. Cronin, Hudson Institute, June 21, 2023, https://www.hudson.org/events/us-leadership-tech-diplomacy-con versation-ambassador-nathaniel-c-fick.

78. Fick, "US Leadership in Tech Diplomacy."

79. Joe Biden, "Republicans and Democrats, Unite Against Big Tech Abuses," *Washington Post*, January 11, 2023, https://www.wsj.com/articles/unite-against-big-tech -abuses-social-media-privacy-competition-antitrust-children-algorithm-11673439411.

80. Fick, "US Leadership in Tech Diplomacy."

81. Bremmer, "The Technopolar Moment."

82. Paul B. Stephan, *The World Crisis and International Law: The Knowledge Economy and the Battle for the Future* (New York: Cambridge University Press, 2023).

83. Dean Jackson and Berin Szóka, "The Far Right's War on Content Moderation Comes to Europe," *Tech20 Policy Press*, February 11, 2025, https://www.techpolicy .press/the-far-rights-war-on-content-moderation-comes-to-europe/.

84. Meaghan Tobin, "TikTok Is Facing Legal Backlash Around the World," *New York Times*, January 9, 2025, https://www.nytimes.com/2025/01/09/technology/tiktok-ban -global-legal-battles.html.

CHAPTER 7

1. Roosevelt, "The Struggle for Human Rights."

2. See Wihbey, *Digital Democracy*, 9; Wihbey, *A Growing Community of Scholarship and Practice*, 12–13; Jedediah S. Purdy, Jo Guildi, Jairus Grove, Robert Paarlberg, Andreas Malm, David Keith, et al., "The New Nature," *Boston Review* 41, no. 1 (2016): 10.

3. Jack Snyder, *Human Rights for Pragmatists: Social Power in Modern Times* (Princeton, NJ: Princeton University Press, 2022), 148–151.

4. Robin Mansell, Flavia Durach, Matthias Kettemann, Theophile Lenoir, Rob Procter, Gyan Tripathi, et al., "Information Ecosystems and Troubled Democracy: A Global Synthesis of the State of Knowledge on News Media, AI and Data Governance," Observatory on Information and Democracy, January 2025, https://observatory.informa tiondemocracy.org/report/information-ecosystem-and-troubled-democracy/.

5. "International Panel on the Information Environment Launches at 2023 Nobel Prize Summit," Oxford Martin School, May 22, 2023, https://www.oxfordmartin .ox.ac.uk/news/international-panel-on-the-information-environment-launches-at -2023-nobel-prize-summit. The author notes that he is a member of this panel.

6. Sarah Lynch Baldwin, "Watch: Jamal Khashoggi Criticizes Saudi Crown Prince's 'Impulsive Behavior' in 2017 Interview," *CBS News*, October 18, 2018, https://www .cbsnews.com/news/jamal-khashoggi-saudi-journalist-called-saudi-arabia-crown -prince-mohammed-bin-salmans-behavior-in-foreign-policy-impulsive-2017/.

7. Martin Chulov, "Jamal Khashoggi: Murder in the Consulate," *Guardian*, October 21, 2018, https://www.theguardian.com/world/2018/oct/21/death-of-dissident-jamal -khashoggi-mohammed-bin-salman; David D Kirkpatrick and Carlotta Gall, "Audio Offers Gruesome Details of Jamal Khashoggi Killing, Turkish Official Says," *New York Times*, October 17, 2017, https://www.nytimes.com/2018/10/17/world/europe /turkey-saudi-khashoggi-dismember.html.

8. Jennifer Dunham, *Deadly Year for Journalists as Killings Rose Sharply in 2022* (New York: Committee to Protect Journalists, 2022), https://cpj.org/reports/2023/01 /deadly-year-for-journalists-as-killings-rose-sharply-in-2022/.

9. Jamal Khashoggi, "What the Arab World Needs Most Is Free Expression," *Washington Post*, October 17, 2018, https://www.washingtonpost.com/opinions/global -opinions/jamal-khashoggi-what-the-arab-world-needs-most-is-free-expression/2018 /10/17/adfc8c44-d21d-11e8-8c22-fa2ef74bd6d6_story.html.

10. Khashoggi, "What the Arab World Needs Most Is Free Expression."

11. Noah Feldman, *Arab Winter: A Tragedy* (Princeton, NJ: Princeton University Press, 2021).

12. Jonathan Rauch, *The Constitution of Knowledge: A Defense of Truth* (Washington, DC: Brookings Institution Press, 2021).

13. Jerome A. Barron, "Access to the Press: A New First Amendment Right," *Harvard Law Review* 80, no. 8 (June 1967): 1641–1678, https://doi.org/10.2307/1339417.

14. Barron, "The Right of Reply to the Media in the United States."

15. See Napoli, *Social Media and the Public Interest*, 191–192; Sunstein, *#Republic*, 213–233; Tim Wu, "Is the First Amendment Obsolete?," in *The Perilous Public Square: Structural Threats to Free Expression Today*, ed. David E. Pozen (New York: Columbia University Press, 2019), 15–61.

16. Jack M. Balkin, "Media Access: A Question of Design," *George Washington Law Review* 78, no. 4 (June 2008): 76, 933, https://ssrn.com/abstract=1161990.

17. Anup Kaphle, "40 Companies That Are Beating the West," *Rest of World*, October 5, 2023, https://restofworld.org/2023/rest-vs-west/.

18. Former FCC chairman Tom Wheeler has been advocating for a new "expert agency." See Wheeler, *Techlash*, 184–185.

19. Konstantinos Komaitis, Katitza Rodriguez and Christoph Schmon, "Enforcement Overreach Could Turn Out to Be a Real Problem in the EU's Digital Services Act," Electronic Frontier Foundation (EFF), February 18, 2022, https://www.eff.org /deeplinks/2022/02/enforcement-overreach-could-turn-out-be-real-problem-eus -digital-services-act.

20. Chiara Drolsbach and Nicolas Pröllochs, "Content Moderation on Social Media in the EU: Insights from the DSA Transparency Database," preprint, submitted December 7, 2023, https://arxiv.org/abs/2312.04431.

21. Wheeler, "Crossing the Regulatory Rubicon."

22. "Murthy v. Missouri," Oyez, accessed November 15, 2024, https://www.oyez.org/cases/2023/23-411; Eugene Volokh, "The Future of Government Pressure on Social Media Platforms," *Daedalus* 153, no. 3 (2024): 226–243.

23. Amy Howe, "Supreme Court Strikes Down *Chevron*, Curtailing Power of Federal Agencies," *SCOTUSblog*, June 28, 2024, https://www.scotusblog.com/2024/06/supreme-court-strikes-down-chevron-curtailing-power-of-federal-agencies/.

24. Lasswell, *Democracy Through Public Opinion*, 108.

25. Friendly, *The Good Guys, the Bad Guys and the First Amendment*, 24.

26. Trahan, "Fact Sheet"; Perrino, "Platform Accountability and Transparency Act Reintroduced in Senate."

27. I have borrowed this idea and phrasing from legal scholar Jedediah Purdy, who applied it in a different context. See Jedediah Purdy, "The Long Environmental Justice Movement," *Ecology Law Quarterly* 44, no. 4 (April 2018): 809–864, https://doi.org/10.15779/Z382F7JR1V.

28. Nathaniel Persily, "A Proposal for Researcher Access to Platform Data: The Platform Transparency and Accountability Act," *Journal of Online Trust and Safety* 1, no. 1 (October 2021), https://doi.org/10.54501/jots.v1i1.22.

29. See "Global Free Expression Report 2023," Article 19, (n.d.), https://www.globalexpressionreport.org/.

30. Agnes Callamard, "Introduction: Regardless of Frontiers? Global Freedom of Expression Norms for a Troubled World," in Bollinger and Callamard, *Regardless of Frontiers*, 1–24.

31. John Gerard Ruggie, *Just Business: Multinational Corporations and Human Rights*, Norton Global Ethics Series (New York: W. W. Norton, 2013).

32. John Gerard Ruggie, "The Social Construction of the UN Guiding Principles on Business and Human Rights," *Faculty Research Working Paper Series*, no. 67 (Cambridge, MA: Harvard Kennedy School, 2017): 3.

33. James Harrison, "Establishing a Meaningful Human Rights Due Diligence Process for Corporations: Learning from Experience of Human Rights Impact Assessment," *Impact Assessment and Project Appraisal* 31, no. 2 (May 2013): 107–117, https://doi.org/10.1080/14615517.2013.774718.

34. Mark Latonero and Aaina Agarwal, *Human Rights Impact Assessments for AI: Learning from Facebook's Failure in Myanmar*, Carr Center for Human Rights Policy, Harvard Kennedy School, March 19, 2021, https://www.hks.harvard.edu/centers/carr/publications/human-rights-impact-assessments-ai-learning-facebooks-failure-myanmar.

35. Jeff Kosseff, a law professor at the United States Naval Academy, has provided a comprehensive overview of the formidable challenges to any changing of rules

in this area. See Jeff Kosseff, *Liar in a Crowded Theater* (Baltimore: Johns Hopkins University Press, 2023).

36. Jonathan Zittrain, "We Need to Control AI Agents Now," *Atlantic*, July 2, 2024, https://www.theatlantic.com/technology/archive/2024/07/ai-agents-safety-risks/678864/.

37. Richard L. Hasen, *Cheap Speech: How Disinformation Poisons Our Politics—and How to Cure It* (New Haven, CT: Yale University Press, 2022), 130–131.

38. Paul Gowder, *The Networked Leviathan: For Democratic Platforms* (Cambridge: Cambridge University Press, 2023), 99–108.

39. Goodman, "Digital Information Fidelity and Friction."

40. See, for example, Sabrina Skacan, "Neely Center Design Code Leads the Way on Social Media Reform," USC Marshall School of Business, October 20, 2023, https://www.marshall.usc.edu/posts/neely-center-continues-its-leading-ethical-voice-toward-designing-a-better-social-media-ecosystem; David A. Broniatowski et. al., "The Efficacy of Facebook's Vaccine Misinformation Policies and Architecture during the COVID-19 Pandemic," *Science Advances* 9, no. 37 (September 2023), https://doi.org/10.1126/sciadv.adh2132.

INDEX

Page numbers in italics refer to figures.

Publisher contact:
The MIT Press
Massachusetts Institute of Technology
77 Massachusetts Avenue, Cambridge, MA 02139
mitpress.mit.edu

EU Authorised Representative:
Easy Access System Europe, Mustamäe tee 50,
10621 Tallinn, Estonia
gpsr.requests@easproject.com

Printed by Integrated Books International,
United States of America